Houses

Roberta C. Bondi

Houses

A Family Memoir of Grace

ABINGDON PRESS
Nashville

HOUSES
A FAMILY MEMOIR OF GRACE

Copyright © 2000 by Abingdon Press

This book is printed on recycled, acid-free, elemental-chlorine–free paper.

Library of Congress Cataloging in Publication Data

Bondi, Roberta C.
    Houses : a family memoir of grace / Roberta C. Bondi.
      p. cm.
    ISBN 0-687-02405-6 (alk. paper)
      1. Bondi, Roberta C.—Family. 2. Christian biography—United States. I. Title.

BR 1725.B62   A3   2000
230'.044'092—dc21
[B]   00-056600

00 01 02 03 04 05 06 07 08 09—10 9 8 7 6 5 4 3 2 1

MANUFACTURED IN THE UNITED STATES OF AMERICA

For Mama

Contents

Preface

The following book is one story made up of many stories about a single family which happens to be mine. It is not an objective history, as if there could be such a thing, anyway. It is a memoir, the product of my own childhood memories, which like everyone else's are no doubt frequently unreliable because they are based in so many misunderstandings of the adult world around them. It also comes out of my adult memories which have been shaped in ways I can't fully grasp both by my own individual, particular, earlier experiences and my conscious and unconscious imagination working on those experiences.

Houses is thus a very different account of events than the ones that would be given by my brothers, my aunts and uncles, or even my mother, all of whom necessarily experienced and understand the things I have written about in the context of their own memories and imagination. I have tried to warn the reader of the slippery nature of all accounts of the ongoing lives of families by the very forms I use in the book: third person narratives, including dialogue, that I couldn't possibly have heard, or the report of feelings I can only be guessing at, alternating with letters from me to my long departed grandmother that I could not conceivably have written even while she was alive.

On the other hand, I want to stress that *Houses* is not a story I have only invented out of my own imagination and humanly faulty memory. Rather, I have taken what I really do remember of particular events, of what happened and how things were. This I have combined, in some cases, with what I was actually told or overheard as a child, and in other cases, with what I have observed for myself or been told by my mother, my aunts Suzie and Kas, and my Great-aunt Blacky. Though I have done my own sorting of it all, made my own hypotheses, and given my own interpretation to what has happened as best I can, I have rarely or never flat out made things up.

But, given the problematic nature of an attempt like this one, why would anyone even want to try to tell such a story or series of interlocking stories about the life of a family? For me, it seems important for a number of reasons. To begin, telling family stories is true to the traditions of the family itself. As far back as I can remember I have heard the women on my mother's side of the family recounting stories. When I was a child in New York, and my mother would bring us to my grandparents' house in Union County, Kentucky, during summer vacation, the stories my aunts and great-aunts, grandmother and great-grandmother told provided the music by which they shared their work. In those hot summer days of the forties and fifties, no meal that took more than one woman to cook and clean up after it was prepared without tales exchanged. There were no tomatoes put up, pies baked, grape jelly made, or chickens slaughtered and plucked for frying without these stories.

Some were dramatic, like the one about the time Aunt Nacky burned down my great-grandmother's house, or another about my great-great-great-grandmother breaking all the dishes her husband brought home to her from Pittsburgh. Some were tragic, like the tale of my grandmother's loss of Caroline, her second child, in the great influenza epidemic, or of Papa Charles's thwarted attempts to be a schoolteacher, or of my great-grandfather's attempts to steal his grandson, Uncle Bob. I could tell that many were funny, too, though I often didn't understand the joke, as was true of those involving Cousin Swear-to-God Brooks, or Great Uncle John Bundy's unsuccessful courtships, or Great-aunt Ginny's numerous beaus. Then there were the ones that hurt me to listen to, that made fun of folks who did not have the qualities deemed by my family to be necessary for civilized living, about people who were not "hardworking" enough or "smart" enough or Southern enough or tough enough. Finally there were other stories that were simply head-shakers, like those which told how it was that Papa came to acquire the land he owned.

From where I am in my life now I can see that, from the standpoint of entertainment, almost all of these were good stories. They generally had a beginning, a middle, and an end, satisfying plot twists, good characterization, and a fair amount of dramatic tension. As a child, however, I didn't like them much. I didn't even know who many of them were about since many of the aunts, grandmothers, and cousins in them were dead. Worse by far, however, all these stories seemed to be demanding something of me, a city girl, and a Yankee, which I could neither give nor understand. Their very telling, it seemed, placed me under judgment and found me condemned.

There is no doubt that I was largely wrong about this last point. As a self-conscious child and adolescent, what I was hearing as stories about my own failures were not deliberately meant to be directed at me at all. There were no sadists among my aunts and grandmothers; I am quite certain they never intended me to be made unhappy by their tales.

At the same time, the way these stories touched, shaped, and disciplined me in spite of myself was not a fluke. I believe that family stories, when they are told in contexts like those in which I heard them, are "meant" in the most subtle and unsubtle ways to form their listeners. Though their tellers may very well not be consciously aware of it, these stories are "supposed to" inculcate into family members who hear them the moral, social, and often religious values and interpretations of key events that unite that family across the generations into a single, albeit messy, living organism.

Of course, I am not suggesting that there is no such thing as an individual, or that all the members of a single family are alike. Obviously, this is not true. As they say, it is certainly the case that in the last analysis, "everyone dies alone." Even apart from this potentially depressing fact, in the most cohesive family not everyone hears their stories and are formed by them in the same way. Different people in their formative years pick up certain traits and ignore others. Frugality in one person becomes stinginess in another. The burning down of a house in one generation may produce an ability not to cling to possessions which the next generation experiences as a sense of rootlessness, and which the next generation after that may feel as a need to settle in one place and never move again.

Though all this variety is very real, it is also vitally important to notice how often the same themes, images, and values seem to run, transmuted, through the generations, and, whether for good or for ill, shape them. A grandmother's advice on marriage given to her oldest granddaughter fundamentally determines the course of the long first marriage of her great-granddaughter two generations later. A grandfather's assumptions about his rights to a grandson named for him fifty years later sets the course for the life of that grandson's son.

Let me ask you to notice here that when I speak of a family as a single organism I am not only talking about shared experiences, feelings, ideas, and convictions that run through the generations; I am also talking about memory and identity. I have pondered for a long time the meaning of the confusion I feel and have felt over the whole question of where the bounds of my own memory, and hence my own identity, lie. What is me? Where do my mother or my grandmother leave off and where do I begin? What does it mean that I have always had such a vivid and intimate knowledge of the House on the Hill my mother and grandmother were born in, in spite of never having been in it until I was over fifty years old? What does it mean when I ask a friend about something that occurred in her childhood, and she tells me about it and then concludes by saying, "But I'm not sure that this really happened to me; I often mix up what I remember of my own childhood with my mother's memories"?

I know that the struggle to understand this question of identity is mostly a modern problem and not one that would have bothered our ancestors in the periods of the early church and the Middle Ages I teach. I remember when I was in seminary and first was baffled by the notion of the solidarity of the human race, which is absolutely central to the understanding of Christian salvation in the writings of Athanasius, Anselm, and Julian of Norwich. I was certain that the concept of salvation could apply only to the individual in any rational sense. What could it possibly mean to Athanasius, practically speaking, that God the Word took on, not a particular human being named Jesus in the Incarnation, but the whole of humanity in order to defeat death? How could Anselm's theory of the substitutionary atonement rest on

12

the assumption that Christ's death took place to set right not the sins of individual human beings, but the sin of the human race as a whole? Even more, how could Julian not only think that the first Adam included all of us, but insist that the Fall came about not from malice or disobedience, but as a result of Adam's desire to rush off and do the will of his Lord? Surely all this was based in some kind of abstract and esoteric Platonism that had nothing to do with reality as I experienced it!

Having been swimming in these theological waters for so many years that my whole body looks like a prune, I am convinced now that our ancestors' talk about the solidarity of humanity and the ultimate singleness of salvation was not fanciful. It was simply descriptive of the way things really are. Whether we like it or not, the human race does stand or fall together. That we are ultimately one is the only way to make sense of the confusion of time and memory, the blurring and merging of identities, for good or for ill, that we all experience. This is well illustrated, I hope, in the following stories that come together to make up the larger story which I tell. And, of course, what is true of the way individuals exist within families is equally true with respect to how families are with each other, for no single family is a self-enclosed independent universe. Rather, it only is what it is as its makeup shifts and changes, as it merges with other families—indeed, with all the families of the earth, to whom its salvation ultimately is linked.

If this were a different kind of book I could elaborate prosaically on the observation that necessity is making us increasingly aware of our common identity once again. It is common knowledge that the survival of our marriages, families, church communities, cities, even our species depends upon our giving up the notion that there can be such a thing as total autonomy. We understand, for example, how the price we pay for a dress in a local department store is related not only to our own immediate Western economy but is also tied to the wages, hunger, ill health, and hardship of strangers of different races and cultures more than half a world away. We are properly frightened by the way human pollution, degradation and overuse of the air, earth, and water threaten to destroy the ecosystem of the entire planet. Even schoolchildren learn that if we were to use our powerful weapons we could wipe out human life entirely.

13

The amazing, painful, and wonderful thing, nevertheless, is that, in spite of everything I've said, the fleeting, individual lives of all living things, including human beings and their stories, have such absolute significance in the overall scheme of things. Whatever else the theology of the fourth century intended, God's taking on the whole of humanity as one in the Incarnation was not meant to reduce the significance of individual human lives. Indeed, just the opposite. Such a sharing in a single humanity is a visible representation of God's infinite care, love, and honoring of each one of us and our unique experiences in all our particular, excruciatingly beautiful, fleeting mortality.

Right now the fact of mortality lies heavily upon me. Most of the people in this book are dead—my grandparents Panny and Papa Charles; their parents, Ama and Robert, Ibbey and Lee; and, of course, their parents and brothers and sisters; all my great aunts and uncles except Aunt Blacky, who is ninety-two and very feeble; my uncles Bo and Bob, and Uncle Bob's son Bobby Wynn. My aunts are both alive, as is (thank God) my mother, who is the central character in this book; so are both of my brothers and my cousins. Still, the very world of my great-grandparents and grandparents, and even of my mother's youth, is gone forever, as the psalmist says, like the grass that fades and the flower that withers.

The pinky tan of my grandmother's living room rug in the house I lived in with her the year I turned twelve, the color of the dirt in the garden on the way to the cherry tree, the smell of rotting peaches in the chicken yard, the coolness of my great-grandmother's porch where John Bundy and two of my great aunts lived, the sounds of women's voices in the kitchens, the scent of men's cigars, conversation overheard, the glow of coal in a fireplace, the school where my mother learned to read and write, skating on the ice on the pond at the House on the Hill, the time Grammar's Beautiful House burned down, Panny and Papa Charles in Casey County when they were first married, the wily power of Papa on his high horse, the sadness of my mama's loss of her first house coupled with her loss of my father, the joy of the house she inherited whose picture is on the front of this book—I carry all this within me. I cannot bear to live another day, much less die, without my own attempt to honor, love, and preserve in memory the beauty, goodness, stubbornness, humor, outrageousness, difficulty, grief, bravery, and love displayed in their stories. Nor can I keep any longer to myself

my sense of the way in which God's grace repeatedly touched their lives and, through them, me.

Finally, I bring them and their stories to you, the reader, in the hope that you will find in them something of the grace in your own stories and those of the ones you have loved, that you may better live in the light of the mysterious Beauty that shines through all true human stories, even those of sorrow, grief, and loss. As my great-grandmother Grammar used to say, "Blood is thicker than water." May these stories, so particular to this one family which happens to be my own, help you feel more deeply the fundamental connection, the common blood of memory and identity which we share with the rest of humanity.

Before I begin, there are so many people I would thank. There is Allen Tullos at Emory University, a historian of southern American culture, who first urged me to make these stories into a book and lent me a tape recorder to record many interviews with family members. As usual, there is Caroline Walker Bynum, who by her enthusiasm and wisdom not only kept me bucked up throughout the process of writing, which was several years longer than any book I've written before, but often saved me from sinking so far into my own memory that I drowned altogether. There is Melissa Walker, who read and read, suggested and suggested, encouraged and encouraged from the difficult beginning and the even more difficult end of the project.

Chuck Foster, Rod Hunter, Don Saliers, and Barbara Patterson, colleagues at Emory, read bits and pieces and cheered me on in the early stages. Carol Newsom, also friend and colleague, urged me to take the project on in the first place. Tere Canzoneri, Deborah Wight-Knight, Marylou Greenwood Boice, Marion Dolan, and Maggie Kulyk read it at the later stages and kept me at it.

Bobbi Patterson, Peggy Courtwright, and Wendy Farley bore me up and sustained me. Mary Logan, Jim Rule, Henry Close, and Kate Hauk listened patiently to my wrestlings when they surely had things of their own to discuss. My many sisters at St. Benedict's Monastery in St. Joseph, Minnesota, with their constant love prayed, laughed, and dragged me through it. From where I see it now, I can hardly imagine finishing this project without a single one of these people.

I thank my aunts Kas and Suzie and great-aunt Blacky, as well as the

other family members who spent hours telling me stories, no doubt only to find them appearing in this book in forms they didn't expect or given interpretations they wouldn't necessarily agree with.

I thank my brothers, Fred and Wesley, for their support. Fred offered many suggestions for improving the manuscript in spite of his differing experience and interpretation of so many of the key events I've written about, and I have attempted to incorporate these suggestions. At the same time, I have tried hard not to speak for either of my brothers or encroach on their memories or interpretations of some of the painful happenings I've written about, but in spite of my efforts I know that I have frequently failed.

Most especially, I want to thank Richard, my husband, first, because of his wonderful criticisms and suggestions, but even more, because he lived with me and kept on loving me through my enthusiasm, sadness, frustration, bafflement, and just plain depression that went on every single day for years as I wrote or tried to write it. Though I believe he is a saint, he may actually be a masochist.

Last, of course, I thank my mother, whose story this really is. Thank you, Mama, for being who you are, for making me one with your memories and your mother's memories, for encouraging me even when what I was asking and writing about was so painful to you that you could hardly stand it. Thank you for your sudden long distance phone calls when you remembered something you hadn't told me before, and thank you for making me laugh so much oftener and harder than you ever made me cry. Thank you for your permission at the end to publish *Houses*, even though it didn't come out the way you had anticipated.

Every memory, every phrase, the whole of the story, I dedicate to you.

CHAPTER ONE

Houses

You know, Panny, when I was a small child I always liked the Twenty-third Psalm. I'm not entirely sure how I learned this particular piece of scripture. I know Mama didn't teach it to me along with my "now-I-lay-me's"; most probably it was Aunt Ginny who taught it to me. As you will surely remember, every summer until the time I turned eleven, when Mama and Fred and I would come to visit you and Papa Charles on your farm in Union County, I would attend her vacation Bible school class at Pond Fork Baptist Church.

I liked vacation Bible school in those days, out at the little church in the middle of a field close to the Big Ditch, and I liked having your sister Aunt Ginny for my teacher. I recall Aunt Ginny put a lot of stock in having us memorize Bible verses, though I couldn't say now whether this was more the result of her religious convictions or whether it simply followed from her total inability to understand children.

Not that it really matters how I learned it: the fact is that I liked it. It comforted me during those long summer weeks when I would stay with you in faraway Kentucky. Separated then as I was both from my father and from my familiar home in New York, I needed to believe that the Lord really was my own personal shepherd. Though I never saw a shepherd or a sheep in all my visits to Kentucky, I needed to think that in that place of alien farm buildings, strange houses, and hard-working relatives among whom I felt myself to be a self-conscious, unhappy intruder, God was able to make me lie down in green pastures and provide for me well enough that I might not die.

17

So I would recite the words of the familiar psalm to myself over and over every night, falling asleep as best I could in the high, too soft bed in your rickety back bedroom that overlooked the low Dyer Hills in the distance and the sweet pea-and-blackberry-covered fence of the chicken yard below my window. Did you know the disgust and despair with which your chicken yard would fill me? I wondered, why wouldn't you have a bathroom like the one I had at home? I hated walking barefoot in the dew-covered grass through the chicken yard to the outhouse at its back, and I hated the peach trees that grew in that chicken yard and dropped their bruised, black-spotted peaches among the slops and mess the chickens made. How clean and beautiful were the green pastures I prayed for in my bed at night!

The words were a comfort in those days, and not just in bed, either. I remember reciting them often almost as a magical charm as I wandered, sick with longing for New York and my father, out of your ramshacklety house and down the gravel road that passed through the strong-smelling summer fields of hay and corn, grazing cows, and rooting pigs to my great-grandmother and your mother Grammar's house, where she lived with Papa and your grown sisters, Aunt Ginny and Aunt Nacky, and your brother, John Bundy. I remember how the very sight of that big squat house across the fields could make me forget my gloom and homesickness. Though it was as dark and quiet as your own, I loved that house where my great aunts thrived and played.

Still, it is not the two houses, yours or Grammar's, that the words of the psalm evoke for me now so much as the road between them and the actual complexity of my feelings as I walked it. Comfort, anxiety, pleasure—I felt them all. The soothing images of ponds and grass, of oil and overflowing cup, the fearful image of a table set in the presence of my enemies are all entwined now with images of the wildflowers I loved in spite of myself as I passed them on the way—orange cowslips that grew all tangled over the barbed-wire fences that marked the fields, yellow black-eyed susans, blue cornflowers, and white strong-stemmed Queen Anne's lace that blossomed in the tall grass beside the flat road.

Comfort, pleasure, and a general anxiety were not the only things I felt on that white gravel road between your two houses; there was fear, too. Indeed, as often as not, when I caught myself reciting the words of

verse 3—"he leads me in the paths of righteousness for his name's sake"— real terror would come upon me. I was reciting that psalm, after all, as a prayer in which I understood I was making a bargain with God. God would give me what I wanted from God—to be kept safe to return to my home—in return for my promise to give to God what God demanded from me—to walk in those paths of righteousness by becoming God's namesake. Surely God would send me to hell forever for promising such an impossible thing!

For the fact of the matter was this: by promising to be God's namesake, I was perjuring myself. I was lying to God. I didn't want to be lying to God, but I was. I could never be God's namesake no matter how hard I tried, and I knew it before I ever promised it. It was too late. I was spoken for. I was Roberta, the eldest daughter of your eldest daughter, and that was all there was to it. I was already your namesake.

All the fine details of what it meant to be anybody's namesake, and your namesake in particular, I didn't know. About broad outlines, however, I think I was always quite certain. To be your namesake meant that as my name was not my own, neither was my person. I am not talking about "Panny," of course, which was the name your grandchildren who couldn't originally say "Granny" called you by ever after. It was as "Roberta" you claimed me for yourself to make me one with you in ways I might not understand but could never reject.

Panny, did you know when I was a child how painful it was to be your namesake? How mysterious you were to me; how powerful in your deep sighing sadness and your silence! Though I was terrified of hell, it terrified me even more to know that, out of all those myriads of people inhabiting the universe, it was to you my soul belonged. It was horrible to think that because I had been named for all eternity with your name, I must inexorably grow up so sad and silent myself that no one, not even God, could rescue me.

Sadness and silence were my duty, my inherited lot in life that came with my name. Laid out like this in the bare light of day, I can see now how odd it was that as a child I should have thought that this is what it meant to be your namesake. It is odder to me now that I not only continued to believe it through so many of my adult years, but that I thought that I could escape it simply by keeping myself as far away from you as possible right through all those years of my first unhappy marriage, my schooling, the birth of my two children, and my own divorce. As your namesake, I should have known all along that distance could no more save me than the happy promises of my second marriage. And yet, I bear witness to you now, I have been saved.

Sometime during the year I turned forty, two years or so before you died, I dreamed of all this namesaking. It was the only dream of you and me together I have ever had. I knew it was a significant dream from the moment I woke up, and not one of those ordinary ones we have all the time that are really no more than a relived jumble of pictures, words, and feelings from the day before. This was a real dream, a dream from God, nearly inexplicable at first, yet at the same time full of light and power. It was the kind of dream that claims the whole of a person, heart and head and stomach, too, a dream that says, "If life is what you want, then wake up in your sleep and pay attention. I am full of goodness; I am beautiful, and what I speak to you is truth." Not that there was anything at the beginning of my dream that suggested all this to me.

The dream started as I was being chased by an angry crowd through the streets of some unfamiliar medieval city of gray stone and mortar and mud where you were living. I was coming to pay you a visit, and you had asked me to shop for bread and milk before I arrived. I had done this, and the populace was furious. I did not even try to imagine why my shopping had angered them enough to want to kill me.

I remember, however, that I ran and ran until I came to the steps of a narrow old building of blackened stone where I knew you lived. Bursting through the front door, I found myself racing in the dark with pounding feet behind me, up several flights of stairs until at last I found your low, secret door on one of the landings. Shopping bag under my arm and still pursued by murderous strangers, I frantically banged on the door until you opened it and pulled me in to safety. As you shut the door behind me, the sound of following feet was blotted out and I found myself in silence.

At first, my heart was racing so hard and my breathing was so fast that I hardly noticed where I was. As I became calmer, I began to look around me with interest. It struck me that the place where you lived and into which you had drawn me did not seem to belong to the building I had entered. According to the outside shape of the structure, I had expected no more than a small, closet-like apartment. I wondered now to see that we were standing not in an apartment at all, but in a tall and spacious round tower. Though I had never been there before, I knew that we were in the middle room of this tower. Without asking or being told, I also somehow knew that there was a room below us and another above us.

Then I noticed that there were several things odd about the light in the room in which we found ourselves. The light was whiter than that to which I was accustomed, but it was also reflected in strange directions and it threw up unexpected patterns of brightness and shadow upon the ceilings and floor. Puzzled, I walked over to look out of one of the high windows that surrounded the round room; then I understood the reason for the quality of the light. Nothing was visible from any of the windows all around except flat water: the tower was surrounded by a tidal river. Hanging in the white sky like an enormous disk of glowing iron, the low red sun winked and flashed against the smooth black surface of the water and filled our room with shifting light. Though you never told me so, I knew when I saw it. Twice a day, every day forever, this river would slowly rise to lap the bottom of your tower with brackish water, not quite sweet and not quite salty. Twice a day the water would draw away again, leaving behind at the base of the tower the stench and stickiness of marsh, red beetles and small water birds, wet black reeds and dark water grasses bent down with the weight of silt and salt.

Fear filled me as I stood there wondering at the desolation and the silence of what you'd set before my eyes. You reached up to touch my shoulder. "This is yours," you said, "I am giving it to you for you to do your work in. It will be your house forever."

Quickly, before I could think or look around the room in which I found myself you led me back toward the door and down a wide flight of stone steps out to the room that comprised the floor below us. What was in that room, I could hardly tell you now, though, having passed the whole of your life there, I'm sure that you remember well. I do recall, however, my wonder that such a room could be set so high above the level of the water, and my astonishment at the gracefulness of its shape and the beautiful proportions of its windows.

I also remember how as I stood there pondering it all, you touched my shoulder once again. "Come," you said, "I must show you the top room." Then, puffing and sighing on your short heavy legs, you led the way back up two flights of stone steps that wound around the walls to open into the single chamber that made up the top floor of your tower. This room, too, like the two rooms below it, was full of windows. I could see at once what it contained. On a raised platform, in a bed covered with worn white sheets and ragged quilts lay your husband, my grandfather, Papa Charles, dying and unconscious like a wounded king in some medieval legend.

I turned to you in astonishment, to ask you to explain the meaning of what you were showing me, but you only shook your head and would not answer. Then you touched my arm a third time and spoke again. "Come," you said, "it is time to go. I must show you your place, the place where you will work."

I followed you once more down the stairs to that middle room which I had first entered, and now for the first time I began to understand what you were showing me. Oh Panny, how dreary was this place you were bequeathing me! How old and worn and full of musty smells! Save for a small single bed jutting into the center of the room, a little oil-cloth-covered table with a gooseneck lamp and a straight-backed wooden chair, it was hardly furnished at all.

Across the windows, badly measured curtains, in a faded, old-fashioned print, sagged on curtain rods made of bent wire coat hangers. Green linoleum, cracked and worn with grit, peeled up around the edges of the floor. And this was the house which was the inheritance I could not refuse, the place in which I was to be locked alone for the rest of my life!

Still, in spite of all its poverty and bleakness, in spite of all my self-pity and my fear and my internal posturing, I knew that this was truly my place, received from your hands against my will, yet freely chosen by me to be my house. Here, once enclosed, as all alone as the solitary river that surrounded the tower, I would write and pass my days.

You called to me once more, saying, "This is yours." You smiled at me the mysterious, close-lipped smile I remember from my childhood.

Then you opened the door and went out. I heard your key locking me in from the outside. I had become your namesake; I was alone, and there was only silence.

Oh, Panny, do you know how very many hours, how many nights and days I have spent puzzling over this dream of mine, trying to make sense of it, trying first to live out of it and then to live into it? And, do you know, the more I pore over it, the more I discover that the dream itself is exactly like the tower I received from you. From the street, it appears to be so small that it is almost invisible; from the inside, it is a three-storied universe, a continent of dry land upon the primeval waters.

It is a single house spacious enough to hold within its ancient walls all the houses over which the women in our family have suffered throughout our generations. Under its high roof are to be found the metaphorical houses of silence and pain in which we, every one, have suffered—the mythical houses at the beginning of this last century whose losses shaped everything, all memories, that were to come: the House on the Hill and Grammar's Beautiful House, the One That Burned; the houses of grief that followed out of those earlier losses; the hired hand's house in which my mother, your daughter, found herself first entrapped and then abandoned; houses that, in spite of everything she should have known, she taught me to seek out and live in. There is the house of vindication: my mother's House on Willow Avenue that began to set right, not just for her but for you and for me even, so great a loss as the loss of the House on the Hill.

Last, there is my own house, the house that I, your namesake, have both inherited from your hands and built for myself, out of the stories of all these other houses. It is rarely a fully comfortable house; the pastures surrounding it are not always green, nor the waters beside it that I drink from sweet. Still, it has strong walls and it is full of light. It is my house and I love it.

CHAPTER TWO

Education

*P*apa Charles, Mary Virginia's father, was not the sort of man Grammar thought her oldest granddaughter ought to marry. As they say in Union County, Papa Charles just wasn't a worker. The physical end of his farm work was bad enough, but his management was even worse. Even under the best of conditions Papa Charles could hardly manage the business end of farming—not that he ever should have had to do it.

Charles Wesley hated farming from the time he was a child growing up on his parents' farm on the ridge in Casey County. For one thing, he didn't like to be by himself, and he never could understand the boys he knew who thought you couldn't be a man unless you talked to women and children in grunts or shouts. Charles hated the kind of silence that wasn't inhabited by human beings, and he loved the cramming together of children and teacher at school, the laughter of parties and family reunions, the sobs and testimony of camp meetings.

Charles was irredeemably sociable. Partly, it was because he had been born twelfth in a family of thirteen children living together in a very small house. Partly it was because of the unusual nature of the Wesleys themselves there in the harsh Calvinistic climate of the Kentucky mountains, where even among Methodists, who should have known better, the law was valued above love, and labor valued even above law. In those mountains where all farming was subsistence farming, men, and women, too, prided themselves on the hardness of their unbending moral and social judgments and the bluntness of their ridicule of the weak. The members of this Wesley family, by contrast, were noted for what made them different. They were gentle with each other, they enjoyed each other's company, and, in keeping with their Methodist heritage, they knew that trying to follow God's will did not exempt them from being wrong.

Charles's desire for company was not the only reason he hated farming. From the time Charles Wesley was tiny, in an unmanly sort of way, he was allergic to practically everything, leafed or feathered, furred or bladed. If it could be found on a farm, it would make him sneeze, and his sneezes were not of the occasional, discrete kind, easily hidden from the ladies in a gentlemanly white handkerchief. They were a series of violent upheavals that filled the house and the outhouses, the barn and the fields around it with noise, shaking his body and turning his chest inside out with pain.

It was August of the year he turned ten when he first fainted in the fields from the sun. Fortunately, he wasn't alone. All the men and boys were out there together trying as hard as they could to bring in the hay under a brain-frying four o'clock summer sun. Charles's father was the first to see him wipe his face with his bandanna, gasp in the heavy air, stagger in the stubble, and drop. Before either of them even knew what happened, he picked up his son like a baby and carried him out of the field and over the split-rail fence, past the old gray barn, the chicken yard, the outhouse, and the pump and onto the saggy back porch.

By the time they reached the back porch, Charles started coming around. Keeping a good grip on his son, Lee set him down by the door. "Ma," Charles gasped out as he stumbled out of his father's arms and into the dark kitchen from the bright August afternoon. His head hurt. He was sweating and nauseated and hanging onto his father's waist, and the ground under his feet was still swinging from side to side like a carnival ride.

As they entered, Ibby was bending over the square kitchen table crimping the edges of the pies for supper. Charles could see the dark circles of sweat under her arms and around her neck. She straightened up and turned around when Lee called her name.

"Oh, son," she said as she saw her youngest, his head hanging and his tan skin pale. Wiping her floury hands on her apron, she led him to the other side of the table from the pies and sat him down in her cane-bottom chair.

Charles was not ashamed to be led. He could hardly think, and the light hurt his eyes. He crossed his arms on the worn white oilcloth on the table and laid his head on his arms, face down. His damp arms stuck to the oilcloth, but it felt cool and comforting.

"Charles." Touching his shoulder, his mother called him back. He raised his head for the dipper of water and guided it to his mouth. He coughed as the cold water went up his nostrils and ran down his chest onto the top of his overalls.

His mother fetched a blue and white dish towel to wipe his face and neck. She wet it and wrung it out over the slop bucket, her back to her husband. She glanced at Lee, then looked away, out the kitchen window to where she could see three red chickens scrabbling in the dry dirt along the wire fence of the chicken yard.

The blood rushed to her face and down her neck as she turned back to him. She was shaking with anger and frustration, and she pushed away a loose strand of gray hair impatiently.

"Just what do you think you're doing, Lee?" she said. "You know he gets sick when the sun's on him too long. What on earth were you thinking about?"

Her husband took off his hat and began turning it over and over in his hands. He was covered with a panicky sweat that made the little yellow pieces of broken straw around the brim of the hat prickle the tough skin of his palms.

"Ibby, you know the boy won't work unless I make him. You say yourself not a boy we have will use his back if he can use his brain instead. Charles'll never be worth a hill of beans if he can't work on a farm. You know I didn't mean for him to pass out."

Ibby was in no mood to back down. "Well," she said, "using your head instead of your back doesn't mean you're lazy. Besides, you surely didn't need him to help with the hay; just about every boy you've got is out there in those fields today." She turned away again and stood there, silently.

By this time Charles was beginning to feel better. He raised his head off the table to enter into the unusual weather of his parents' conversation. He took a deep breath.

"Ma, Pa," he said. He was as scared now as he had been sick a few minutes earlier. His parents were so caught up in their talk that both were taken off guard when he spoke.

"Yes, son," said Lee. Ibby just stood there.

Charles cleared his throat and twisted his hands on the table in front of him. "I've decided I ain't going to farm when I grow up," he said in a self-conscious voice. He didn't know what his pa would think once he said the rest of his piece. He thought about his friend Tom Smith from down the ridge. Tom's family was Baptist and they talked a lot about sin. Tom's daddy always said that, except for the preachers, a man who wouldn't farm wasn't a man at all. Charles suspected his pa saw things pretty much the same way.

Charles didn't look at his father standing next to him or his mother across the table facing him. His eyes filled with tears.

"I reckon I'm going to get me a job in the schoolhouse when I grow up," he said.

Lee sighed. He was tired of fighting his boys to get them to work, and he was worn out worrying about what any of them would amount to. He laid his hand on his son's shoulder. "As lazy as you are, school-teaching'll suit you just fine," he said.

Lee was out the door and off the porch. Ibby dumped the dishpan of apple peelings she had just filled into the slop bucket of eggshells and green bean strings and ham rinds by the door. She kissed the top of Charles's head. "Get yourself up and take this bucket and go slop the hogs," she said to him, "and while you're out, bring me some more coal for the stove. Now, let me get this pie in the oven."

Charles felt confused and a little let down. Was that all there was going to be to it? It was. He was going to be a teacher.

From that point on until he was eighteen, life was good, relatively speaking. Charles had what he needed. He went to school in the winter, sneezed on the farm in the summer, and, when Lee and Ibby could bully him into it, did odd jobs for the few neighbors who could pay him. He tried to save a little money for college at Bowling Green. When he could get away with it, he sneaked away to the races in Lexington to spend his money betting on the horses with the boys from the next farm over. Other than that, he had a good time, and he pretty much stayed out of trouble.

27

It was not actually until the spring of the year following his first fall in Bowling Green, where he had finally gone to live in a boardinghouse and study at Teachers' College, that his life began to take a different kind of turn. This was when he fell in love with Bert and, not so long afterward, into the hands of his father-in-law, Papa.

Not that he knew anything of what was coming in his first months in Bowling Green. From the time Charles stepped off the train with his steamer trunk to move into Mrs. Jameson's wide-porched boarding-house, he had been delighted to be where he was. Unlike many of the boys and girls who had not come half so far across the state of Kentucky, he was not threatened by the new ideas, partly because he never took them very seriously. He liked his classes and he admired his teachers, whom he believed lived a fine life of ease.

He missed his parents and the teasing of his brothers and sisters, but his disposition was too cheerful to let him imagine a time when he would permanently have to live his life without anything or anybody he really wanted. For the first time he could remember, he felt like a man. He made a point of getting up late. He enjoyed having not only a bed to sleep in that he didn't have to share, but his own room with a wardrobe, a dresser, and a washstand all to himself.

For someone who had been more or less with the same people every day of his life, he got to know a variety of people very quickly. Charles had always been popular, even in Casey County High after he had declared his intentions to be a teacher. The young men and women he met in his classes now liked him for his Wesley nonjudgmentalism and his silly sense of humor. Soon he had made friends with other more or less aspiring teachers from places all over Kentucky. In those first months, Charles spent many evenings at innocent parties, and a few at some that were less innocent.

During his first semester, Charles was not the only one enjoying himself in the Teachers' College. That year the fall was a good time for everybody. During the cool days of September and October a yellow sun shone every day in a sky so blue that it appeared to be opaque. The air was filled with late black butterflies that hovered over the chrysan-themums bordering the thick green grass of the campus and the board-inghouses. Dark spruce and cedar trees cast deep shadows on the red brick walks. Fall picnics were everywhere.

Then the weather changed, and with it the spirits of the students. The warm and sunny autumn turned all at once into a bitterly cold and dreary winter. At the beginning of November, the wind blew without letup, and a biting rain fell. At the end of the rain the leaves dropped straight down from the trees without having turned their usual bright colors. Through the following months the same leaves lay on the ground around Charles's white frame boardinghouse and the brick buildings of the college, slowly turning from tan to bronze to frayed black.

The ground froze before Thanksgiving, and its lumpy surfaces bruised the feet and turned the ankles of the girls from the city as they wandered off the sidewalks in their thin-soled boots. The birds disappeared from sight and hearing and the squirrels went wherever it was squirrels go in winter. Though there was little snow, for four months the sun rarely came out, and even when it did shine, it hung so low in the sky and its light was so faint that it cast only the palest of shadows across the frozen ground.

It was the lack of light that made the winter particularly hard to bear. In the cold and darkness the whole student body was depressed. They didn't hibernate, exactly, but their social lives, even the life of Charles, ran slow. The young men and women spent more time studying by themselves than they had in September and October, and by the first of December they began to brood over their futures. Demoralized and homesick, everyone went home to their families for Christmas. After the start of the new year, they returned to Bowling Green to two more months of the same dreariness they left.

Then, as suddenly as it had come, winter was over. The first week of March the sun came out again, a yolky yellow, and the temperature rose in the afternoons to sixty degrees. A week later, a window-rattling, warm wind blew in and it began to rain. For four days and four nights, heavy rain alternated with short periods of blinding sun, during which Charles and the other students walked to class through clouds of rising mist. The sharp new leaves of daffodils began to push aside their rotting predecessors. In the rain, the forsythia bloomed. In the sun, huge drops of water hung from the thick branches of the maples and the feathery branches of the cedars. Four days later, the rain was over and skinny robins went to work. After their long winter, the students were

29

disoriented with joy, and even the ones who had come to school with no intention of marrying prepared to fall in love.

On the morning of the first full day of sun, Charles Wesley rolled out of his tall boardinghouse bed and stretched. He splashed cold water onto his face from the pitcher on his dresser, then he unbuttoned his scratchy gray long johns and threw them in a heap in the corner by his wardrobe. He dug out clean summer underwear from his steamer trunk and his favorite striped shirt, and jammed his summer hat on his head. His book bag under his arm and his hands in his pockets, he ran down the wide stairs from the second floor through the fading scent of coffee, toward what should have been his second class of the day.

He came to the edge of campus shortly before nine o'clock. Classes were changing and students were out swinging their books and swaggering everywhere. It was hardly a miracle that Charles's leisurely descent down the hill from the street coincided with Bert's purposeful ascent up the same hill.

Bert was on her way to the library. Even so, she was no more inclined to resist the spring than any of the rest of her classmates. That morning she, too, had ripped off her long johns and winter petticoat and left them in the corner of her room. She had then dressed herself in a thin pink dress she had ordered at the end of the summer from a drummer in Sturgis. The dress had tiny buttons up the front, a sky-blue belt, and a pointed blue satin collar to match.

As Charles was stepping onto the campus, Bert was leaving the dripping red brick classroom building where she had uncharacteristically had to struggle to remain awake through her eight o'clock class. Now on her way to the library, she was shivering a little in her flimsy dress.

By that spring day Charles and Bert should have known each other. They had been in school together all year, and the teachers' college was small. They belonged to the same class, and they even had many of the same friends.

Still, there were reasons why they hadn't met. Bert was in Bowling Green to learn how to teach children; Charles was there so he wouldn't have to farm. With a father like hers, and having seen the birth of her sisters and her brother, Bert had decided a long time ago not to marry. However true all this might be, in that moment of Charles's going down the hill and Bert's going up, when each saw the other for the first time, the reasons they had not known each other before became irrelevant.

Charles was struck witless by the sight of Bert, a small, shivering, wispy-haired girl in a summer dress, expensive blue boots, and no coat. Her body was short and inclined toward the plump. Her face was wide and round, with a broad forehead and a thin mouth that, even resting, appeared to be smiling. In that first instant, Charles was overcome by the intelligence of her brown eyes, her self-contained manner, and her unfamiliar intensity.

Bert for her part was equally struck by the sight of Charles, a tall, well-built country boy in a frayed striped shirt open at the neck, and a straw hat pushed back on his head far enough that she could see his curly black hair. He was muscular and loose-jointed at the same time. Without seeming to look at him directly she took in the blueness of his eyes, the humor of his mouth, and what she imagined to be an entirely alien sort of carefree haphazardness.

All this falling in love had actually taken place on the hill before they had even come abreast of each other, and neither had the faintest idea what was going on in the mind of the other. Not knowing what else to do, they had come face-to-face and pretended not to notice each other. Then, both going past, each had turned back around for one more look. Embarrassed and confused, they stood there staring at each other in the road. Charles was the first to speak.

"It's a mighty fine day," he said familiarly, pushing his summer hat back even farther on his head.

"It surely is," she answered, shifting from one cold foot to the other. Both cleared their throats a time or two. He had that itchy feeling in the back of his nose.

"I don't know you, do I?" she asked after a while. Just looking at him was making her stomach turn.

He laughed and tried hard not to sneeze. She had a high voice that sounded to him as though she was singing when she talked. Though her voice wasn't loud, it was sweet and nasal like Sacred Harp singing. He had never heard a woman who actually talked like that.

"Well, I guess not," he answered. "I'm Charles Wesley, but people back home call me Charles. You can call me Charles, too, if you like. What's your name?"

"My name is Roberta Wynns, but my family calls me Bert," she said. "I'm from Union County. That's in Western Kentucky up the river from Paducah. Where are you from, Charles?" Charles seemed like a fine name to her.

"Casey County," he answered. "I'm from Casey County."

"Casey County!" she said scornfully, as they would have said it at home. She liked his voice; it didn't remind her one bit of Papa's. In fact, there was nothing about him that reminded her of Papa. "Where on earth is Casey County?"

"Oh, no place important," he answered. At last he pulled himself together. "Bert, would you care for a walk?" he asked politely.

Bert heard two robins singing overhead, and a gray squirrel poking through the leaves at her feet. What did she care about the library? "Why yes, Charles, I would," she answered, equally polite.

A month later, Charles wrote to his mother.

Dear Mother,

I'm writing you to tell you I know the girl I want to marry. Her name is Bert and she is from Union County. She is studying to be a teacher like me, but not for the same reasons. She really likes the little ones. She's real nice and pretty, too, and her daddy is a farmer like Daddy, but I think he is somebody important. I haven't really asked her yet, but I hope she'll say yes when I do. She likes me, but I guess she don't know how she likes the idea of leaving everybody she knows back home. Say hello to Daddy for me.

Love,
Charles

She had written right back:

My dear Charles,

I am so glad you have found such a smart and pretty girl to marry. I'm sure you deserve her. Since she wants to be a teacher, too, she will not mind the life and you can be happy together. I'm sure she is worrying about missing her family, but she will have all of us here in Casey County. I know I will love her like my own daughters. Is she a

Methodist, too? Your daddy and your baby sister Beulah and your aunts send their love. Come home soon. We all miss you.

Love,

your Ma

By the time Charles's mother was reading her letter in Casey County, Bert's mother in Union County was reading a letter of her own from Bert:

Dear Mama,

I'm glad to hear the new house is coming along so well and that everything will be about finished by the time I get home. What color are you going to paint the front parlor? Have you ordered any new furniture for it? It will look mighty empty if you don't put anything more in it than what is in the House on the Hill. You told me you ordered beds already for every single room, including Grampa Sam's room. I sure hope nobody gets lonesome, sleeping all by themselves like that!

In your letter last week you told me old Mrs. Daniels didn't want to teach at the Pond Fork School anymore. Could you and Papa see about me teaching there in September? It wouldn't be too far. I already know most of the children. Sarah Jane went to school there. She told me it has a good, stout stove for the winter.

Tell everybody I miss them. What are Subie and Blacky up to? What's Papa making John Bundy do, now? Has Ginny got a new beau? I've made a new friend here in Bowling Green, but I'll be glad to be getting home. This last week I've been having another one of my spells. Well, I guess I'll get through it, I always do.

Love,

Bert

By the end of the school year Bert still hadn't told her mother or her father about Charles Wesley. Charles had asked her to marry him, finally, but she still didn't quite know what to do about it. She knew very well what her mama and daddy would think of him, all the contrary things they'd say about his mountain family and his wanting to be a schoolteacher and his no-money.

On the other hand, Charles made her laugh. Next to her complicated, powerful parents, she knew Charles as an easy man. Around Charles she thought she could rest in a way she never could at home. There was something about the way Charles loved her that wasn't always asking two opposite things at once. In fact, it seemed that he hardly asked anything of her at all.

What was Bert to do? She wanted to marry Charles, and she didn't mind bucking Papa and Mama, but she could hardly bear the thought of moving so far away from them all by doing it. She had liked her year in Bowling Green, and she had met a lot of girls her age whose company she enjoyed, but they just weren't her kin. With those girls she knew where she left off and they began, but this often wasn't true with her own mother or her sisters or her aunts. It was as though together they made up a single human being in whom all of them lived. How could she continue to be herself if she were in one end of Kentucky and they in the other? Just thinking about it made her feel down and helpless.

During the last month of school, keeping her secret and wrestling with her decision had so worn her out that she had hardly known what to do. Leaning out the window in her straw hat and blue scarf when the train from Bowling Green at last rolled into the Sturgis Depot at the end of May, Bert felt like an old woman.

Papa saw Bert on the train before she spotted him on the platform. At the sight of her he clapped his hands together and gave a shout. "Bert," he called while the train was still rolling, "get down off that train, and come home where you belong."

The brakes hissed, and the train lurched two or three times before it finally stopped. Even from the window Bert could see that the Papa who had come to meet her was on his high horse, the opposite of how he had been during her visit at Christmas. Then, even on Christmas Day itself, he wouldn't get out of bed for longer than he could help. Though some years were worse than others, this was the way he always was in winter, groveling in the ashes and moaning and groaning about how they'd never pay off their debts, then hopping up and buying farms and bossing everyone around as soon as the light began to change in the spring. This was how he was now, as he ran alongside her car, waving his hat and shouting in his work boots and overalls.

"I'm coming as fast as I can come," she called back to him. "Just wait till I get off."

The train gave a final hiss and stopped, and the conductor handed her off the high steps of her car to her father. He piled all her trunks and suitcases, her hatboxes and her books on the platform beside them. "Hello, Papa," she said, reaching up to give him a kiss on his dark cheek. "I missed you."

Her short greeting took too long for Papa. He hugged her once fast and hard and whistled for the porter.

Bert looked around. "Where is everybody?" she asked. "Where's Mama?" She was glad to see her father, but it was her mother she longed for. "Where are Ginny and Nacky and Blacky and Subie? Did they forget me already?"

"Well, your mama and them were fixing to come," he said, "and they got up right early to do it, too, but I wasn't about to let them." Her father took her arm. "I said I'd fetch you and tell you all about the new house, myself. I wanted to take you right to it, but your mama said I'd have to bring you home first, so I guess I have to. The minute we're done with supper, though, I'm driving you over in the buggy. They can see you later."

Papa's high-handedness made Bert mad, but she kept her mouth shut. She knew from experience that he wouldn't even hear her.

Bert picked up the hatboxes and Papa got the rest of her things except for the footlocker and loaded them into the back of the wagon. He went back for the footlocker and threw an old quilt over the whole lot of it to keep it down. Then he helped his daughter up onto the seat.

"Your mother's right anxious to see you," Papa conceded, hopping up beside her. "I reckon they're all excited to hear what you've been up to, and see what kind of strange ideas you picked up over at that school-house in Bowling Green."

Bert sighed and didn't answer that, nor did she answer anything else on that long drive back home, either. It would have been a waste of time if she had. Papa was too busy telling her about his difficulties with the new house and his aggravations with the help to notice her silence.

"Trash," he was saying of Johnny Ray Gordon as they jounced out of town along the rutted roads to the House on the Hill. "Never would

35

work on the house after dark, no matter what I said. Says he has to take care of his cows after supper. What's a man like him want with cows, anyway?" Papa slapped his leg and laughed.

It irritated Bert to hear her father talk. Johnny Ray, and his sons, too, were good men. They had driven Papa's mules and plowed and built Papa's chicken houses and done anything else he had asked them to for thirty years.

"None of them Gordons ever could work. None of 'em will ever amount to a hill of beans, I don't care how far he wants to send that yellow-haired grandchild of his to school. Katie Jean ain't no better. She was a Smith before she got married, you know. Not a one of 'em would get up before six o'clock, no matter what."

Summers, this was the kind of thing Bert had heard in one form or another all her life. She was used to it, but it ground her down and took the joy out of life. Being in her father's presence and listening to him long enough brought on such spells of misery and despair that she sometimes couldn't get out of bed. Her mother and sisters noticed without comment; her father and brother didn't notice at all.

Jolting beside her father on the long drive home, she let her mind wander back to Charles in Casey County and forward to her mother in the House on the Hill. Bert's heart began to pound as they came in sight of home. She stood up in the wagon, Papa grabbing at her arm, as they drove up the hill to the ragged old house.

"Hello, hello, Mama, are you here?" she called through her cupped hands.

As soon as they heard her voice Bert's little sisters ran out to meet her, the older ones coming after the younger.

"Bert! Bert!" Blacky screamed, throwing her dark arms around her sister's legs and pressing her face against Bert's stomach as soon as Bert jumped down. Blacky was the baby. Except for Subie, Bert was her favorite sister. Bert hugged the little girl hard.

"You're home!" screeched the lighter skinned Subie, her brown curls and ribbons flopping as she jumped up and down for her turn. "Papa wouldn't let us come, and Mama made us clean the house all day. We always have to do everything, and Nacky and Ginny don't have to do nothing! Isn't that mean? Don't everything look nice? Do you want to see where we swept the chicken yard? Are you going to sleep with me and Blacky in the dining room or are you going to sleep in the parlor with Nacky and Ginny?" Subie pulled at Bert's arm, earnestly. Bert laughed.

Blacky let go of Bert's legs, and made a place for Subie. "Nacky says teachers don't have to work," she said; "they just read books. That's why she wants to be a teacher. Are you going to sit in a tree all day and read just like Nacky?" she finished.

Bewildered by this assault, Bert smiled at her little sisters. She had missed them all. She had missed their intensity, their good humor, and her mother's seriousness. At the same time, in the months away she had become accustomed to quiet.

"Now, you leave Bert alone till she gets in the house," said her mother, Ama, coming out the door and off the porch at last. The tall woman pushed the little girls aside and gave her oldest daughter an awkward, dignified hug. Tears came to Bert's eyes. Physical contact always made her mother uncomfortable, but her time away had left her starved for her mother's body. Bert leaned against Ama for the few minutes her mother would permit, then followed her onto the porch and into the house.

Ama and the girls put the food on the table while John Bundy came in from the barn and washed up outside. After that, they sat down in the hot little kitchen off the back, the blue walls closing in on the eight of them around the table like a collapsing sky.

Papa said the blessing, thanking God for the food and asking God, as he had at every meal since Bert could remember, to give them strength to set aside their own wills in order to follow God's will instead. As they all said "amen," Bert wondered irreverently how she could possibly hope to follow God's will if she couldn't even figure out what her own was to give it up.

They ate the good food and began all talking at once. Ginny teased her about her city clothes. Nacky asked for the titles and precis of the most interesting books she had read while she was gone. Then, before the plates had even been cleared away, Papa pushed himself back from the table and carried her off to see the new house.

By then, Bert was glad for a little quiet. Though Papa drove like a madman over the rutted roads, the early summer countryside was calm and beautiful. The low sun threw long shadows on the new green fields of corn, and it lit up the delicate white faces of the wild blackberry blossoms along the barbed-wire fences. Red cows grazed in grasses full of little daisies, and drank from ponds around which the bullfrogs sang. On the seat of the buggy the feel of the cooling air against Bert's face and hands rested her.

When they came to the new house with its high roof and its wrap-around porch Bert could only look at it in amazement. In spite of what they had told her, she wasn't prepared for it. The white frame house was at least five or six times the size of the battered old House on the Hill, where she had lived since she'd been born. Stunned, she went through the first floor with its two parlors, its enormous kitchen, its pantries, and its dining room. In silence she climbed the as yet uncarpeted stairs past the wide landing with its gigantic stained-glass window to the second floor. Upstairs, she looked out each window of the seven enormous bedrooms. From the front windows she saw the flat green fields with the gray road running through them, tall clumps of trees, a new barn, and the old tenant farm's house down the lane.

Outside, without speaking she followed her father around the sides and back of the big house. She dragged the hem of her dress over huge piles of raw stone, great clods of black dirt, and enormous tree stumps entwined with withering Virginia creeper. He took her around the two-hole brick privy, the shed for the farm equipment, the smokehouse, the chicken yard, and the grape arbor and vegetable garden.

They sat down at last on the front steps to the porch. Papa was well satisfied. He stripped off the band from a Cuban cigar, dropped the wrapper in the black dirt at his feet, bit off the end of it, and lit it with a match. The time he spent sucking in the air was the only time he had stopped talking since they had left home.

"Well, Bertie," Papa had said after the first puff. He squinted into the setting sun, out over the rows of low corn in front of him, sprouting from the ground in endless bouquets of blue leaves.

"Here it is, the best house in the county, the best house you'll ever live in. Pick yourself out a room, Bertie." He leaned back, stomach out and knees spread wide. "Pick yourself out a room, and I'll finish it up for you."

For a moment or two more Bert continued to sit in silence. As much as she loved Papa, as much as she loved them all, she had decided in that moment that she would not live a minute more than she had to with the periods of darkness, the exhaustion, and the mental confusion being around him brought about in her, not even in this splendid house. How she would manage the loss of the rest of them she would figure out later.

"Don't make a room for me," she said at last. "Don't make a room for me; I'm getting married."

"Married!" He leaped up off the step, shouting. "Is this some sweet-faced little boy you met in Bowling Green?" Beside himself with rage, he gritted his teeth around the cigar.

She didn't even try to answer him. "Papa," she just repeated again, "whatever you say, I'm getting married."

None of them was happy at her news. Just as she had expected, they liked nothing she had to say about Charles Wesley, anymore than they had liked the other young men who had courted Bert through the years. In general, Ama wasn't so keen on the idea of marriage for any woman. More specifically, however, as Ama's oldest daughter, Bert had special family responsibilities she simply wasn't going to be able to fulfill by going off with some man who lived halfway across the world in Casey County.

Papa was enraged at the thought that Bert would make a decision without asking his permission. Even more, however, Papa had social pretensions, and Ama was a little bit of a snob, herself. Both were sure Charles wasn't good enough for her, or at any rate, good enough for the family. He was a nobody, from a family of nobodies. How did they know this Methodist hillbilly was even saved? And certainly there had to be something wrong with a grown man who had been raised on a farm wanting to be a teacher of children.

Bert had decided. They could make fun of Charles all they wanted to. Bert was determined to marry Charles Wesley. She could be as stubborn as Papa. She was going to move to Casey County and that was that. There was nothing any of them could do to stop her. They loved her, and for the moment even Papa accepted it.

It was a short summer that followed Bert's decision and an even shorter winter. In July the family moved out of the saggy old House on the Hill and into Grammar's Beautiful New House. In September Bert began her one and only year of teaching in Pond Fork School, the one-room schoolhouse by the Great Ditch that her sister Nacky would take over from her the next year.

For Bert, it was a happier year than usual. Over that winter, camping out in the new house in which her sisters were now permanent residents, she stitched her trousseau and quilted quilts on the great frame that cranked up and down from the ceiling in Grammar's room. She was never alone. Grandma Nack and aunts, great-aunts, and cousins flooded the kitchens and the bedrooms with their female presence. In addition to Papa in his full strength, John Bundy, Grandpa Sam, and other visiting Baptist revival preachers brought a slightly debilitated male presence.

At Christmas, Charles came to stay for ten days. During his trip the previous July the family had begun to like him. They appreciated his size and his muscles. They enjoyed his humor and his easygoing spirits. Besides his schoolteaching, his sneezes gave them something to poke fun at. Between Christmas and the New Year, Ama threw an enormous Rook party, which Papa dragged himself out of bed for. It gave the Wynns a chance to show off their new house, as well as to introduce Charles to their new neighbors who lived in their own fine houses up and down the road around Pond Fork Church.

On a rainy day at the end of the following spring Bert and Charles were married in the parlor of the Beautiful New House. Immediately after the wedding dinner that followed, Bert began the trip with Charles to their little two-room house in Casey County.

Their house was a mile or two from the school and not much farther to the farm of Ibby and Lee. It was not much to look at compared to the Beautiful New House Bert had just left, but it wasn't all that much different, really, from the House on the Hill she'd grown up in. The Casey County house was drafty and old, its faded yellow wallpaper scuffed and peeling. Still, in the daytime its long, old-fashioned windows made the rooms of their new home bright with sun, and on hot days the high ceiling of the kitchen made it almost as cool as the front room. The outside of the house was weathered gray boards. There was a low porch with a swing and a rocker where Bert could sit and listen to the creek in the woods while she peeled potatoes or snapped beans, and every afternoon after that she could read.

Apart from her spells, Bert liked her life very much that first summer and fall. She expected being a wife to be hard work, however beautiful a house she might find herself living in. Laundry was still, after all, laundry, and cooking, cooking. Here, unlike home, there were only the two of them to do for. At least she had a stove and not an open fire to cook on like Charles's mother had had when her children were growing up on the ridge.

Bert also had her chickens and a cow for milk and butter, and she had her garden. Her father-in-law had dug the enormous plot and begun to plant it for her for a wedding present before she had ever come to Casey County. All summer she tended her potatoes, beans, and limas, squash, cabbage, and greens with pleasure, while Charles temporarily helped out on Ma and Pa Wesley's farm.

Most Sundays Bert and Charles went to Ibby and Lee's for dinner with the rest of Charles's family. On their best evenings, holding hands and Charles whistling, the two of them would walk through the woods to the rough square school where Charles was going to teach. They would sit next to each other in its battered desks and look at the low hooks on the wall of the cloakroom and imagine it full of children's coats. They would walk back home in the dusk while Charles told her some of the silly stories he remembered from Bowling Green. She liked to laugh at his silly stories, though she would never let him tell her the ones about farmer's daughters or hapless preachers.

The only thing that got in the way of their happiness was the spells that she had expected to escape by marrying Charles. Sometimes it seemed to Bert that it was the memories of school that brought on the spells that could render her silent for as much as four or five days; sometimes it was the memories of her sisters and her parents in their fine house so far away. During these periods of restless sadness and homesickness, Bert would be bothered by what then would seem to her to be the no-accountness of their lives. She couldn't understand why the Wesleys didn't care whether they made anything of themselves. She wasn't sure exactly what she meant by "making something of themselves," but she knew it didn't include Charles becoming a schoolteacher. In the darkness of her mind, she suspected her happiness and Charles's was founded in a culpable laziness for which she would have to answer in some future life, not only to her father and her mother, but also to God.

In her spells Bert would miss her mother and her sisters so much that her entire chest cavity and abdomen would feel hollow. During these times Charles's sneezing fits would cause her actual physical pain. Until a spell was over a day or two later, Bert would shut herself up in the house so in need of silence that she could hardly bear even the sound of the leaves rustling outside the window beside their bed.

Though they never talked about it, Charles knew his mother didn't know what to make of Bert's spells. It pleased him that Bert and his family seemed to be so well content with each other. He hated to think about his mother worrying about his wife.

As for Charles, he wasn't worried, himself. It just wasn't his nature to worry. He knew she was homesick. At some unarticulated level he was aware that she was alternately relieved and frightened to be living in the midst of what he figured she regarded as the Wesley family laziness. He was sure she'd get over it if they didn't talk about it. Her spells were her business, not his. If she were having a spell when a patch of his sneezes came on, he went outside and did his sneezing in the pasture.

This is the way things were that first half year of their marriage. It was not until sometime in the middle of winter of that year that things took a turn for the worse. Bert woke up in the middle of a long night in December, covered with a cold sweat and her insides heaving so hard she was propelled out of bed. Once on her feet she could hardly stand up. Though she had washed the dishes carefully and had taken out the scraps to the chickens afterwards, the bitter smell of the fried ham from the night before forced itself down her throat and made her gag. She somehow pulled herself past the banked coal fire in the fireplace to the front door and out into the ice-cold air of the porch. Leaning over the railing, she threw up her ham and biscuits and greens, retching repeatedly before she dragged herself back to bed.

She never went back to sleep. At dawn two hours later she finally shook her husband awake. Once awake, he had not known what was wrong or what to do for her. He dressed quickly and ran to fetch his mother. That morning when he left for school, Ibby was wringing out rags in a basin by the bed and wiping his wife's limp arms and slack face.

In the evening when Charles came home, Ibby was gone and Bert was lying asleep on top of the bed dressed in her work clothes, a quilt pulled up over her to the armpits. Her skin looked blue. He had stood

42

beside her sleeping body for a minute, then walked on through to the kitchen. The far end of the white enamel top of the table in the kitchen was set for one. Some food on blue and white dishes he recognized as his mother's was at the other end of the table. A pitcher of buttermilk covered with a cloth stood beside the food.

When he came back through to the front room, Bert was awake. Though he was afraid to talk to her, he pulled up a chair beside her and took her hand. She had turned her head to smile at him. She asked him whether he had eaten the food his mother had brought. He asked her how she felt. When she told him what his mother had said about the reason for her sickness he had slapped both knees and shouted with happiness.

Charles's delight in his coming baby did not make Bert's stomach settle or the dizzy, continuous exhaustion go away. After a day or two of lying around on the bed, Bert understood that for the next few months this was what her life was going to be like. There was no way she could stay in bed. All that winter, she dragged herself upright, fetched the eggs, milked the cow, made the fire and cooked; she lay down and she got up again. Some days she boiled her laundry behind the house in the cold; some days she leaned over her flatirons or churned the butter in the kitchen, but she never felt good.

She lived continually now in a spell of depression. She longed for the baby, but the pleasure of her life with Charles was gone. Charles was at school every day, fooling around and playing games with the children. Sometimes she was glad he was at school; most of the time she resented it. She felt, rightly, that she had become too complicated for him. Though he came home to her every night, he was somehow never really there. Though once a day Ibby came over to bring her something she might crave and a little encouragement, she thought of herself as abandoned.

When she wasn't too sick to feel it, it was the first time Bert could remember truly being afraid. She became convinced that she was going to die. She wondered whether she would go to hell if she did, or whether this sickness itself was her punishment for following her own will to marry Charles. She was confused about the will of God and confused about hell.

She had terrible dreams. Lying in the dark beside her unconscious husband, she dreamed she was a child running out of a burning house only to realize in her first moment of safety that she had left her parents, her sisters, and her brother to go up in flames. In another dream she was tangled helplessly in a blackberry bush that rose above her head as far as she could see, wreathing the sun with thorns. In a third dream, she was standing in a boat drifting down a shadowy river. She was calling out desperately to Charles, but he had his back to her. He was talking to some children and wouldn't listen to her.

By this time, Charles himself was in a bad way. Bert was right in thinking she had become too much for him. On the rare occasions when Charles woke up in the night, he would lie beside her pretending to be asleep as he listened to her moaning, "Mama, Mama, Mama, Mama." Charles was stumped. He had heard before of women getting sick when a baby was on the way, but never anything like this. This sickness never let up. It cut off his wife from him entirely, slamming the front door in his face and throwing him off the porch. She wouldn't talk to him about it, and if she had tried he wouldn't have known how to let her. The whole thing made him want to run away, and that made him feel helpless and ashamed.

At the beginning of March, Ama and Papa arrived. Under normal circumstances Papa would never have left the work of the farm at such a time of year. He had had a particularly nasty winter of groveling in the ashes, however, and Ama was thoroughly sick of him and his whining by the time it began to let up.

Though there was nothing she could point her finger at, all winter there had been something odd in Bert's letters home. No woman felt good in her early months, but Ama suspected something might be really wrong with Bert beyond the obvious, and she had no intention of humoring her husband any further. Now that the days were lengthening and his energy was beginning to surge again, she decided to put his energy to work in driving her to Casey County.

The trip itself had been pleasant enough. In spite of herself Ama had enjoyed riding in Papa's new black Chevrolet with its electric starter. Ama and Papa arrived at the little house in Casey County at suppertime. They left the car on the flat ground in a thicket a little distance from the front porch.

Their mood had shifted at once at the sight of the battered house. Though Bert had warned them clearly enough in her letters, neither of them had had any idea of the house's smallness or its shabbiness.

They were up the steps and through the door fast enough to take Bert by surprise. They found her in a cold kitchen, leaning over the old enamel table, her face beaded with sweat. Though her apron was clean and ironed, it was tied high under her arms like a child's. Her hair was hanging in her face and she had huge blue circles under her eyes. She was trying to slice the hard country ham without smelling it, and tears were running through her sweat down her face.

Charles was nowhere in sight, and that accidental absence was probably his undoing. In the few minutes it took him to return from his mother's house with the layer cake she had baked for his in-laws, Papa had thought the situation over.

Before they sat down for that evening's meal, Papa took Charles by the elbow, out the door, and into the car for a talk. Papa was angry and he was big and he was blunt. Bert was expecting a baby and she was clearly not doing well, and it was somebody's fault. This somebody couldn't be anyone other than Charles. Charles had married her; Charles had taken her away, and Charles had gotten her like this. Bert needed her mother, and Bert needed a real husband—a husband who knew how to work, a farmer, not some silly schoolteacher.

Charles was certainly not that husband, but, Papa said, he had a proposition. If Charles, at that moment, of his own free will, without consulting Bert, would give up his degrading idea of being a schoolteacher and living like a hired hand, Papa would give Charles a chance to be a man. Charles was to bring Bert back to Union County. Papa would let them live in the House on the Hill for free, asking only that Charles farm the farm that went with the house.

Charles was to make up his mind. He could leave off his foolishness in Casey County and bring his wife home where she belonged, or he could stay right there, be as stubborn as he wanted, and kill her. Papa would give him five minutes to think about it.

Charles didn't want to farm—he hated farming and it made him sick. He wanted to teach school. He resented his father-in-law's bullying interference in his and Bert's lives. He had seen enough of the man by now to know for certain that any deal by Papa, no matter how that deal was described, always ended up with Papa on top. Even if the land were of any value, which Charles was quite certain it wasn't, Papa would never leave him and Bert to take care of things in peace.

Also, how was he going to make such a decision without hearing what Bert had to say? It wasn't Charles's way to make decisions for the two of them, and it certainly wasn't Bert's way to let him do it. What would she want him to do? Would she see it as a betrayal if he said yes, or a decision against her if he said no?

Charles didn't understand what was happening to his wife. He couldn't talk to her about it, but he loved her—he loved her with his whole innocent, straightforward, sneezing self. If things went on here in Casey County as they were, he was afraid of losing her. She could die, or she could go into a spell and never come out. He couldn't bear the thought of either of those things happening through what might be no more than his own selfishness.

In the end he accepted. What else could he have done? It wasn't for nothing that the whole family called Papa "Papa" without any accompanying use of his personal name. There wasn't a person in Union County who would call God by God's personal name, either. But God, at least, could be resisted, which is more than anyone would say for Papa.

Two weeks after her parents' visit to Casey County, Bert lost the baby she was pregnant with, and once she recovered, Charles and Bert went back to Union County to the House on the Hill.

Nobody knew how Papa had originally acquired the House on the Hill, the house in Union County into which Bert and Charles moved. The house having been built in 1850, Papa wasn't old enough to have built it himself, and with a father and a father-in-law who were both preachers, he certainly hadn't won it in a poker game. A consensus arose in the family that he had probably bought it in one of his recurrent fits of megalomania. Each year, as the light lengthened into spring, he awakened from his gloomy winter slumbers to buy up farms and houses indiscriminately from neighbors and even relatives who the year before had been weakened by debts.

There is no question that when the House on the Hill was first built it had been a good house. Originally a low, one-story, white frame building set high on a hill with a good view of the farms and fields that were to grow up around it, it had two porches—one along the front for company and evening sitting, and a separate porch on one side for day-time food preparation and sewing. Inside, it had two enormous high-ceilinged, cherry-paneled rooms. These rooms were joined together by a spacious hall that ran from the front door to the back for ventilation in the summer and insulation in the winter. In the early days of the House on the Hill, the kitchen was not attached to the two big rooms. Instead, as was the case with many houses of the period, it stood behind the house in a separate building.

Without doubt, the House on the Hill was far larger than Charles and Bert's Casey County cabin had been—larger, in fact, than when it had first been built. At some point along the way, the House on the Hill had been expanded to four rooms. The two big original rooms still stood as they had been, opening onto a wide hall that went from the front of the house to the back, but now the hall dead-ended onto a kitchen porch, which was partially enclosed by the outside wall of the little added-on kitchen, the dining room, and another rough little place, more like a shed than a room, that stuck off behind the parlor.

The spring of the year Bert and Charles moved into the House on the Hill, there wasn't much of its original splendor left. Though nobody knew how long Papa had it, everybody knew he and Ama had lived in it long enough for all six of their children to be born in it, and for Bert, the oldest, to be raised in it. After he and Ama moved into their Beautiful House that later burned, Papa had passed it on to a tenant farmer for a while.

By the time Bert and Charles moved in, the paneling in the two front rooms was long gone, and the remaining plaster cracked and chipped. The porches were in obvious need of repair, and everywhere they looked, inside and out, there was work to be done if the house were not simply to collapse around their shoulders. For the most part, the work would never get done.

From her first moments back in Union County, Bert was confused by being back with her husband in the very house she had been born in. It is true that she was happy to be home in Union County, close to the authority of her mother and the comfort of her sisters and her aunts.

Still, when she had decided to marry Charles, Bert had believed that she would escape her father's arbitrary moods and power. Now she could not forget the way her father had intervened in her marriage. Papa had single-handedly made a decision about their life that she and Charles should have made together. From her first moment in the House on the Hill, in a far, back corner of herself, Bert despised Charles for letting himself be manipulated by her father.

Later on, when she was middle-aged, and her ongoing spells of depression began to alternate, like Papa's, with periods on her high horse, she would sometimes give herself airs. During these times, she would deny her birthplace altogether.

"I was never born in a little old house like that, " she would say. "I was born in a better place than that." Her sisters, who had been born in the same high bed in the same front room as she, would tease her. "Well, then, Bert," they would say, "tell us where you were born?" But Bert would only make the corners of her mouth go down until the bristly hair on her chin stuck out, and she would shake her head, stubbornly.

"I don't care what you say," she would reply. "Mama would never have had me in that dinky old place."

As for Charles, he never said anything to anybody about how he felt about the move to the House on the Hill, but he wasn't about to do a lick of work on that house. From the beginning of their life in Union County, Charles made a terrible farmer; he fainted in the fields and sneezed from morning till night. Even if he hadn't been, the farm itself was terrible. It was all clay, and nothing would grow. It was no life for a gregarious man who didn't much like to work. It wasn't long before he left the Methodist church in Sturgis and found the racetrack in Henderson.

Papa blamed Charles, and Bert blamed them both.

CHAPTER THREE

Memory

*P*anny, can you recall your feelings during those years when you were away at school, with half of you determined to get away from all the things back in Union County that bound you and hurt you, while the other half of you was so homesick you could hardly bear it? Do you remember what it felt like to know that, however fed up you might get with your aunts and your sisters, your grandmothers and, most of all, your mother, they were so much a part of you and you of them that you didn't know where they left off and you began? Were you always aware that there was as much of you outside your skin and inside them as there was inside your own, or did you not find this out until you went away?

As for myself, during most of my childhood and even the years of my early adolescence, my awareness of the urge to escape the family and being your namesake and everything else all of you represented was so strong that it blotted out my consciousness of our single, ongoing life. No, I haven't put that exactly right. Rather, I should say that nothing in me in those years was quite so strong as my desperation to get away from what seemed to me a rock-hard fact: if I were to be one of you, then I would have no choice but to live by imitation the same kind of life the women in the family lived.

When I think about it now, I can see that I didn't know as much about that life as I thought I did. Indeed, the actual flesh and bone of it, the complexity of the strength and weakness of muscle, the subtlety of nerve from spine to brain, the diversity of impulse and organ—all were invisible to me. All that was visible was the outer layer of skin of the life of my mother, but even this I mistakenly took to be no more than a simple, perfect copy of what I imagined your own to be. Of Mama's life, which she lived within the secret, inner house of her spirit which was visible only to God, I knew almost nothing—apart from the sentimentalized and fatalistic things she said to me about her marriage to my father, and my own distant, mopey marriage to some man unknown.

I hated what I could see of marriage. For as long as I can remember, the very idea of it as she held it up before me filled me with such panic that I could hardly see around it. I loathed the idea that I, like my mother—and I assumed like you, my grandmother, and Grammar, my great-grandmother—must be a slave, so utterly smitten with my husband that my greatest pleasure in life would be to work so hard all day that I could barely stand up at the end of it. It made my stomach hurt and goose pimples come out on my arms to think that I, too, would actually want to be lovesick over some husband whose right it was, merely by virtue of being my husband, to order me around in my own house, to permit my comings and to forbid my goings, my lying down and my standing up, like the law of God regulated the life of Israel in the book of Deuteronomy.

Not until I was almost forty years old and I was divorced and about to be remarried did it occur to me that, whatever problems you and Grammar had with Papa Charles and Papa, they weren't these, and they didn't have to be mine, either. Though you and Grammar were both as vulnerable to sentimentality in the telling of stories as Mama was—you relied on sentiment and platitude, I am sure, to temper the harshness and sometimes helplessness of your lives—neither of you would ever have bowed down meekly before any man. You may have lost some major battles in those long years with your husbands, but you were not women to tangle with. Indeed, I am certain now, without any doubt, that I really am bone of your bone, flesh of your flesh, and most of all, memory of your memory, and I am glad of it. My sure sense that I live in our common house is a great gift of God's grace.

I only began to know any of this consciously, however, twenty years ago. It was under the shock of the final October separation from my first husband. The event wasn't a horrible surprise, of course, even to you, good Southern Baptist that you were. From the beginning having utterly different temperaments, as well as holding to very different convictions about how women and men should be together in a marriage, my husband and I had thrashed around together in the center of a deep pool of misery from the beginning. I had been working up to asking for a separation gradually and unhappily over a very long time.

Once he accepted the inevitability of it, we made the arrangements. Mama would come and get the two children, Anna Grace and Benjamin, to take them with her to Louisville for a week. I would drive to Evanston, above Chicago, for the weekend to stay with a gay friend who was a former student. My husband, meanwhile, would remove his clothes from the house as well as the things we had agreed on to take them to his new apartment.

The weekend, which from start to finish would have been impossible for a member of the family in your day, was exactly what I needed. I left South Bend early enough on that sunny afternoon to avoid the Friday afternoon traffic on the Chicago expressways, and this was fortunate, for I arrived at my friend's little basement apartment in Evanston in such a distraught state that I hardly knew what I was doing. Battered by the continually changing tides of a salt river of pain and fear, throughout the trip I had been alternately swamped by an agitated anxiety so acute that I could barely sit still, and then by a grief that rendered me so passive I could hardly bring myself to breathe.

Philip welcomed me with generosity and sweet kindness. That first night he made me a salad and cooked me a chicken, roasted golden and covered in rosemary. (Panny, can you even begin to imagine what it is like to have a man, an actual man, do such a thing for you, and do it gladly? I'm sure you no more experienced such a thing than I did during those long years of my first marriage.) Throughout the evening, while I fluctuated between incoherent talking and tongue-tied silence, my friend's soft voice soothed me. At the end of the night, he put me to bed with infinite gentleness, tucking me in under his grandmother's quilt on the daybed in his tiny living room. I fell asleep as he sat beside me holding my hand.

I remember little of the next day besides Philip's healing food and quiet talk of his life as a graduate student and his worries over his sister. It was unseasonably warm. In the clean autumn sunlight we took a morning walk in his gray granite neighborhood, shuffling through the yellow and red maple leaves that floated down around the tall old houses. In the afternoon we walked again, this time in the wind along the pebbly beach that edges Chicago, up and down the shore of Lake Michigan. I was strangely happy. The sky was full of fat clouds and the lake dark blue. It was warm enough that late October day that there were sailboats in their white and red and yellow sails far out on the water. We watched them as they slowly dipped toward shore, then back again toward the open water.

Though fear and grief were still pulling on me with all their strength, I left the next morning, refreshed by Philip's care of me. On the two-and-a-half-hour drive back, there was little in my mind beyond my immediate awareness of the ruined steel cities I was driving past, the colors of the trees beside the road, and the mesmerizing highway.

I returned to South Bend shortly after noon to find that in my absence my home had suddenly acquired the look of a house in which no one lived. Drapes and shades were closed against the world. Grass was growing up in the flower beds and had sprouted through the sidewalk's cracks. Brown leaves clogged and overflowed every gutter, and paint sadly curled and peeled around each door and window.

Oh, Panny, how hard it was that bright day just to find my key, put it in the lock, then turn the handle on my own front door! How dreadful the darkness and the stillness once inside! My homes were gone—the exterior one in which I had lived with the children, but also the interior, spiritual one I had inhabited in lonely but familiar solitude. For a long time I simply stood there in the front hall outside what had been our bedroom, unable to move a single finger. Finally, avoiding this physical and emotional space I dreaded to enter, I began slowly to walk through the other rooms in confusion, opening drapes, and peering out each familiar window. How was it possible, I wondered, looking through those ordinary plates of glass, that, with my own interior house in rubble, the neighbors' houses and lawns should be exactly what they had always been?

I was, however, fortified by my wandering in the knowledge that the literal floor under my feet would not collapse. In the end I entered our bedroom, raised the shades, then turned around to view the devastation. It was as bad as I had feared. The closet door stood open with my clothes shoved together hard against the righthand side of the wall. The other three quarters of the closet were empty, occupied by nothing more than dust motes slowly moving in the sunlight. Naked, sharp-handled black coat hangers were scattered on the bed and strewn forlornly around the floor. Worst of all, each dresser drawer had been pulled out and left to hang down before me, empty of everything but their torn paper liners.

Panny, do you know, it was the sight of these empty drawers that utterly undid me at last, dislocating me in such a way that I hardly knew who or where or when I was. I backed out of the room in shock. Slowly, I began to walk once more through the dusty and beloved rooms that should have been as familiar to me as my own hands and found that in these rooms I had become a stranger.

As I walked I wrung my hands and talked.

"What will happen to me now?" I asked myself aloud, and then, again and again, "However will I support my three children?"

Oh Panny, can you hear what it was I said? One boy and one girl only, this is the number of my children. It was my mother, your daughter Mary Virginia, for whom there were three to support after my father divorced her in Delaware and sent her back to you in Kentucky—three children and no skills that would earn her enough of a living to put clothes on our backs and a decent roof over our heads. Do you see how, in that moment of extreme stress, pain and fear carried me straight back through the thin floor of my own immediate home into the common house of our single memory where my mother's experience of twenty-five years earlier still resided?

How odd is this common memory, this family self, this dwelling place so made with words! "However will I support my three children?" Though I don't remember it, my mother must have spoken this lament in my hearing that it should come out my mouth so naturally as my own under the impetus of my immediate fear and pain.

It makes me wonder now what shaping, grieving words of yours, indistinguishable in experience from her own, rose up in my mother under the shock of the loss of my father so many years ago and then were passed on to me. What sentences were spoken when you were displaced by Papa from your little house in Casey County, betrayed, as it seemed to you, by Papa Charles, and forced to the clayey, barren ground on which sat the House on the Hill?

The power of men in the person of Papa, the weakness of husbands and the soul-weariness of wives, the crushing darkness of Papa's manic depression and your own depression which followed upon it, poverty, mortal sickness in pregnancy, the silence of despair and the self-protective silence, the laughter of sisters and aunts, the sweet cooking of mothers, the old stove in Pond Fork Baptist Church, the happy craft of children, cabbage roses on a great-grandmother's carpet—all these for me are the furniture of one particular house, the House on the Hill where you were born and which you hated. This is the same house in which my mother, Mary Virginia, was born and which she loved and lost, the house that stands for every house, interior and exterior, demonic and spiritual that has let the rain in and sheltered us. Panny, my grandmother, the Roberta whose namesake I am, today as I begin to write these stories down, I live in the House on the Hill as mine from the beginning, as of course, in the mysterious house of God which is our common memory, it truly is.

CHAPTER FOUR

Shelling Peas

"Is that you, Mary Virginia?" Grammar called to the child as she came past the landing, down the back stairs.

"Yes'm, it is," Mary Virginia answered, her bare feet padding on the striped treads of the carpet. Over the acrid early morning odors of the chicken yard, the rhubarb plants, and gooseberry bushes on the path to the privy, Mary Virginia smelled her grandmother's coffee boiling in the blue enameled pot on the stove in the kitchen. At the foot of the dark stairs, Mary Virginia sleepily headed toward the smell.

Gruffly, her grandmother called again. "Come out here, Mary Virginia, and help me shell these peas."

Her eyes half shut, Mary Virginia changed direction and walked through the long hall past the downstairs bedroom to the outside door of the dining room. She stood there a moment rubbing her eyes before she went out on to the high porch that ran around the front and side of Grammar's two-story, white-frame farm house.

At four o'clock the afternoon before, Papa, her grandfather, had been riding his white horse up the steep hill past the House on the Hill where Bert lived, when he took a notion to carry his first grandchild home to spend the night as a present to his wife.

He had turned the horse off the rutted road and trotted up the steep lane past the broken-down picket fence that once had been pretty, before his son-in-law Charles Wesley had started in at the horse races in Henderson. He drew the horse up by the low peeling porch that ran along the front of the battered house.

"Mary Virginia!" he had hollered from the white horse's back. Papa was a shouter. It would never have occurred to him to get off May and go in the house to look for her.

Mary Virginia had heard his shout from the kitchen. She set down the plate she was washing, ran out the front door, and jumped off the porch beside her grandfather's big horse. Little wisps of dust puffed over her toes as she hit the dry dirt of the front yard. She hooked her toes over the root of the big maple that paralleled the porch, and gave her grandfather the once-over.

She could see that Papa had been some place important. He was in his clean church clothes, a white starched shirt and gray trousers in place of his usual overalls. His slicked-down black hair was covered by a fancy straw hat tipped back on his face unlike the way his straw work hat normally sat. For a moment she wondered how the top of his face could be so smooth and white while the back of his neck stayed so crisscrossed and red. The sight of her powerful grandfather filled her with satisfaction.

Papa looked down off his horse at her. "Mary Virginia," he ordered, "go and get your things. I'm taking you to your Grammar's."

It wouldn't have occurred to Papa to ask the child if she wanted to go with him, nor would he have considered asking Bert's permission. He didn't know any other way to speak to women or children or animals except in orders. As far as Papa was concerned, his grandchildren, and his children, too, were his own property. Like the centurion with the sick servant in the Gospels, Papa told them all when to come and when to go, and this included his son, John Bundy.

This suited Mary Virginia fine. Though she didn't let herself say it, it was a relief to get away from the House on the Hill to stay a night or two with her grandmother and her aunts. Still, the older she got the more she knew what it cost her mother when she wasn't there. Papa's peremptory ways kept her from feeling guilty about going.

As for Papa himself, once she got to Grammar's house she knew her grandfather would hardly speak to her. There, he would mostly talk to his daughters and his own wife in grunts. As friendly as he was with men, her father was the same; that was pretty much the way men were with women.

Mary Virginia jumped back up onto the porch and ran into the house to get her clean clothes from the pile of laundry on the dining room table. Ripping off the tea towel tied around her waist, she called out, "Mother, I'm going to Grammar's!"

Bert came out onto the porch wiping her hands on an old yellow kitchen towel of her own. She was fed up with her father. She threw the towel over her shoulder and put her hands on her hips, which had spread out considerably from her pregnancies.

"No, you're not," she yelled back into the house to her daughter. "You're not going, so put your things right back on the table where you found them, and get on into the kitchen and finish those dishes." Bert was furious; she almost never yelled, no matter how badly she was provoked.

She turned back to Papa, still on his horse. Bert was a short woman, deceptively soft-looking. Even when she was standing on the porch, the top of her head was only even with the middle of old May's neck. Bert lowered her voice.

"What do you think you're doing? She's not going with you," she stated. Bert was the only child Papa had who would actually cross him once he made his mind up about something. Ever since he had bullied Charles into their move from Casey County to the House on the Hill, Bert had been angry, at her father and at her husband, too—not that any of them would dare to mention her anger or the reason for it, either.

Mary Virginia slammed back out the porch door and stood next to her mother on the porch, her spending-the-night things folded into a pillow slip. She had sense enough to keep her mouth shut, though she was just as capable of arguing with her mother as Bert was of arguing with Papa.

"How am I going to get supper on the table without Mary Virginia?" Bert demanded. "Do you think Kas and me can do all the laundry in the morning by ourselves?"

Bert's questions were not rhetorical. Bert was not such a great manager under even the best conditions, but even if she had been, there was just too much for one grown woman around that house to do. As if that weren't enough, Bert was sick all the time, and she still had her spells.

Mary Virginia was ten and Kas eight. Charles Ray and Bob were six and four. Though Quentin and Suzie hadn't yet come along, Bert was pregnant as usual, and as was the case through the whole of every one of her pregnancies, the hard physical labor of her daily chores was punctuated by continual throwing up. Gall bladder attacks were frequent, leaving her writhing on the floor, one terrified daughter wiping her sweat-covered face with a rag, while the other rubbed her legs.

Charles was a man made for fun, not for hard times; it was what Bert had liked about him back at the teachers' college in Bowling Green, but Charles had never been any help to her. Even before they moved back to Union County, he had been afraid to be around her suffering. Now, he could hardly stand to stay on his father-in-law's terrible farm where nothing would grow and the ground cracked open in the heat. Today he was off in Henderson at the races.

Not that any of this concerned Papa. Papa didn't want to know that Bert was sick, or how hard Bert worked, especially if it got in the way of what he wanted himself, and he certainly didn't want to consider what his contribution had been to his daughter's life.

"Bert, you'll manage fine with just Kas," Papa had said. Bert had set her mouth and stomped through the torn screen door, slamming it behind her.

Though she didn't want to know any of it, Mary Virginia had understood a lot more of what had just gone on between the grown-ups than they thought, and a lot less than she supposed. She did not like to see her mother treated in so high-handed a way or her father silently sneered at. She was mad at both her parents for the injuries being done to them, and fed up with the farm.

All she had wanted was to climb up onto Old May's neck and get away to play with Aunt Subie and Aunt Blacky's magical doll furniture, then spend the night in the big, square, second-floor room over Grammar's fancy parlor. She was sick of feeling Bo's pee creep up her nightgown as she lay in the dining room in the bed that she shared with him and Kas, and she longed to sleep all by herself in Grammar's tall clean bed.

So, hardening her heart against the memory of her mother, she had gone to her grandmother's. She had sat for hours on the landing between the first and second floor arranging the tiny cut-glass punch-bowl with its matching cups on the child-sized buffet and putting her doll to bed under the quilt her grandmother had made for the little brass bed.

She fell asleep that night in the room where her great-grandfather—Grandpa Sam, the Baptist preacher—used to stay. The sight of its fire-place surrounded by blue and white tiles from Holland comforted her, and the white trellises and sweet peas on the wallpaper, and the big roses on the thick pink carpet, soothed her anger and her guilt. The bed was high, with spindles at its head and foot, a real featherbed from Grammar's geese on top of it, and under it a white porcelain pee-pot with a white porcelain lid.

Mary Virginia wasn't allowed to use the pee-pot when Aunt Ginny had young men visiting her in the parlor below for fear that the sound would carry downstairs. She didn't really mind. She liked the idea of having some part in Aunt Ginny and the young men.

Aunt Ginny's love life was endlessly fascinating. What did they do down there, she wondered, shut up in the parlor by themselves? As much as she liked having the room to herself, it was more fun when Kas was there, too. Then they would giggle and turn the rose rug back to try to listen through the floor to what was going on below. They couldn't ever hear much besides occasional guffaws from the men or Aunt Ginny playing "Throw Out the Life-Line" or "The Little Brown Church in the Vale."

This time Aunt Ginny hadn't had company and there had been nothing to listen to, so Mary Virginia had gone to sleep early. Now it was morning, hardly even dawn, and apart from Grammar, nobody else was up, not even the aunts.

Standing behind the screen door to the porch, Mary Virginia could see a skinny moon the shape of a chair rocker just visible in the whitening sky above the July corn fields. A mist was rising up from Grammar's lawn in front of the house and hanging like an apron over the two mis-shapen catalpa trees and the green glider that sat on the grass between them. A bantam hen and rooster jerked and pecked in the gravel along the side of the road, their bright feathers dark in the morning light.

"Come on, Mary Virginia, what are you waiting for?" Grammar called again. "Get on out here and help me, before we have to go in and start the ham!"

Grammar sat in the porch swing, dressed in her old brown calico dress and her lace-up shoes for the day's work. Grammar was always careful of her white skin; though the sun was not yet up, the starched ties of her sunbonnet hung down straight below her chin.

Mary Virginia stepped onto the blue boards of the porch. Shivering a little, she curled up her toes away from the early morning chill and the slippery dew that slicked the floor. Holding her nightgown up out of the wet with both hands, she walked on her heels and sat down in the slatted swing next to Grammar.

The hem of Grammar's dress was dark and wet, and Mary Virginia could see the flattened trail in the grass where Grammar had already been to the garden behind the barn. She had picked enough peas to fill the square basket that sat on the green kitchen chair by the swing. Now she was holding the fat pods in one hand, and ripping off the strings with the other. She was working so fast that the peas hit the sides of the dented washbasin between her knees like rain coming down on a tin roof. Once the peas were in the washbasin, she threw the empty pods into the slop bucket at her feet.

"Good morning, Grammar," Mary Virginia said, smiling. She didn't hug her grandmother because Grammar wouldn't like it. Instead, she scooted as close to Grammar as she could without touching her and stretched her arm across Grammar's lap to take a handful of her own peas to shell. She liked the way the pods looked. On some of them she could see papery bits of brown dried petals, and the ends of others still curled round and round like pigs' tails. Mary Virginia liked peas, and she liked to make the pods pop open between her fingers. The full-grown peas in the middle were hard, a pale, milky green, almost blue. Her favorites were the babies at the ends. They were a green just the color she imagined emeralds would be, still juicy and clinging to the mother pods.

Mary Virginia leaned across Grammar's knee and started shelling peas into the pan in her grandmother's lap. Her peas made a different sound from those of the woman, but she was fast, too, almost as fast as Grammar herself.

"One, two, buckle my shoe," Mary Virginia recited to herself as she popped open the pods. "Three, four, shut the door," she said under her breath as they fell into the pan.

As the two of them sat and worked, the air began to get lighter. Mary Virginia could hear stomping and grunting sounds in the house as Papa and Uncle John Bundy got ready to go out to feed the animals and milk. She heard a cup clatter in a saucer in the kitchen, then the sound of the back door slamming as they went out to the barn.

After a while in the early morning light, from where they were sitting on the porch they could see the hired hands start to come to work on the farm. Most of them wore mud-caked brogans, work shirts, and blue jeans. One old man was walking down the dirt track from the frame house that Aunt Ginny would live in later with her alcoholic husband, Cantrell, but most of them were walking in the road that went past Pond Fork Baptist Church.

In daydreams of her own, Mary Virginia paid the hired hands no mind, but the sight of all these men who were not yet working made Grammar restless. Soon the swing Mary Virginia and Grammar were sitting in began to go back and forth faster and faster.

"Mary Virginia, look at that man, there," her grandmother said at last, as she dropped five empty pods into the slop bucket at her feet. "Just look at that man!" Grammar took the girl roughly by the shoulder and pointed her with a jerk in the right direction.

Mary Virginia looked up. The man she saw was broad-shouldered and freckle-faced. Slowly, with his hands in his pockets, he was shuffling his feet down the road. He wasn't thinking about the need to make something of himself or of the day's work. He was turning his head to find the mockingbird they could hear singing in the Rose of Sharon bushes outside the barbed-wire fence where the road turned. He was whistling to the bird and glancing occasionally into the big red centers of the coarse flowers as he hoped for the bird to whistle back.

In spite of her grandmother, Mary Virginia liked the way the man looked. There was something about him that reminded her of her father, Papa Charles.

The man in the road also reminded her of her friend Johnny Dare. He had curly hair like Johnny's, though Johnny's was dark and the man's was light. Johnny went to school with her at the Templeton School, her one-room schoohouse not too far from the House on the Hill. Her grandmother didn't like the Dares. Johnny's father was a tenant farmer, and his family had a dog they let come right into the house and lick off the plates.

Johnny had tried to kiss her one day in the fall when Miss Ida, their teacher, led them all up the hill behind the school to see the acorn tree. Looking at the man in the road reminded her of the acorn tree and the dark green moss under it. The moss had been like fur when she looked at it standing up, but when she lay down on top of it and put her face close, it was feathery in some places and spikey in others, just like seaweed. She hadn't actually seen seaweed, herself, but she had seen pictures of it in one of Aunt Nacky's encyclopedias.

Sometimes Mary Virginia felt funny when she was around Johnny. She had wanted him to kiss her that day under the tree, but she knew Grammar would be really angry if she found out. It made her uncomfortable to think what they always did to her uncle John Bundy when he went out with girls he seemed to like. Her aunts and grandmother, too, would taunt him—"I hear she don't keep clean sheets on the bed," one of them had said. "Kisses every man who comes along," said another. "I bet you didn't know her brother sells things in a store in town," said a third.

"You see that man, Mary Virginia?" Grammar asked again.

"Yes'm," the little girl answered.

"Just look at that man! Just look how slow he's walking," her grandmother said. Mary Virginia saw him very well; he was walking so slowly it looked as if lice were falling off him.

"You watch who you marry, child," she said again. "Don't you ever marry a man like him! He'll never make you a living."

Mary Virginia jerked to attention at last.

"No, ma'am," she said. "I won't."

The peas were done. Mary Virginia stood up on the wet porch. She took the basin of peas out of Grammar's lap, and held it close to her chest. Grammar stood up, too, and ran her hands down her apron, then the two of them walked through the brightening house to the open kitchen in the back.

Mary Virginia set the peas on the back of the table under the window and covered the pan with a dish towel to keep off the flies. Grammar got out the lard and the long wooden trough of flour for the biscuits, and began working the shortening with her fingers. Mary Virginia took the pieces of gray-pink salty ham Grammar had already sliced and laid them out flat in the cast-iron skillet on top of the black stove.

While they worked, Aunt Subie came down the stairs in her black-and-white-checked ruffled robe, Aunt Blacky following behind her. Subie and Blacky were the two youngest daughters of Grammar and Papa, and in spite of being down late this morning they were the ones who usually did most of the indoor chores around the house.

Aunt Subie was the prettiest of the aunts after Aunt Ginny, and she had the sweetest disposition. Aunt Blacky was not so sweet and not so pretty. She had Papa's copper skin and black hair, and she had the almost supernatural energy Papa had in the summer, only she had it all year around.

Aunt Subie came into the kitchen and stood beside her niece, who was turning the pieces of hard meat with a long, wooden-handled fork. "Why, look at Mary Virginia frying that ham as good as her mother," she said.

Mary Virginia pretended not to hear her aunt, though the praise pleased her.

Aunt Blacky took a cup and matching saucer off the shelf on the wall. Unlike Bert's dishes, neither piece had a chip on it; none of Grammar's dishes did.

"What's Bert doing this morning?" Blacky asked Mary Virginia as she set her cup and saucer on the square kitchen table. She poured herself a cup of coffee from the blue and white pot on the back of the hot stove.

The other aunts glanced at each other and looked away.

Mary Virginia didn't answer for a moment. Her mother was going to do the laundry. Papa had told them all about his conversation with her mother at supper the night before. For the first time since she woke up Mary Virginia let herself feel the difference between her mother's life and the lives of her mother's well-tended sisters. Her cheerful aunts were lolling around as they waited for breakfast in their comfortable kitchen. Her mother, on the other hand, was surely wearing the same old layers of pinned together clothes, limp apron, and run-down slippers she always wore as she cut off slices of the hard ham Papa Charles cured in the smokehouse. She hated their kitchen and the way the children played behind the stove.

Her momentary anger turned against herself. How could she have left her mother to do all that hard work without her? She saw in her mind her little brothers, already, perhaps, shrieking and running in circles in the morning dew, her mother's face red from the heat of the open fire as she bent over the heavy tubs of laundry in the dirt of the yard behind the house. Compassion for her mother and guilt ran through her hand out into the grease in the skillet. The grease popped.

Then, deliberately, Mary Virginia hardened her heart. She made herself remember the clean laundry piled forever in its ever-present heap halfway to the ceiling on the knobby table under the window in the dining room where she slept with Kas and Charles Ray. Summer and winter, every morning when she opened her eyes that pile was the first thing she saw. She wondered occasionally what was on the bottom of the pile. She liked to imagine it was the stays and petticoats of great-great aunts whose pictures she had seen on Grammar's bedroom walls, and the stockings and knickers of their curly-haired children, but she knew that it was mostly only worn-out, gray, hand-me-down clothing none of them had been able to wear in years. She hated that laundry. Why did her mother make them live like that in the House on the Hill?

Mary Virginia began to feel better about being where she was. She gave herself a moment to finish righting herself.

"I guess she's cooking breakfast, same as we are," she said at last, her back bent to her aunts. No one answered that.

Blacky and Subie started carrying the food from the kitchen to the dining room, loading the white tablecloth with pitchers of sweet milk and buttermilk, covered glass compotes of grape jelly, cherry jam, pear honey, sour butter on its own special plate, and a silver pitcher of sorghum.

Soon, Aunt Nacky came downstairs, buttoning up her smock with one hand and waving a book of dramatic poetry with the other. Aunt Nacky tried to appear eccentric, but she didn't have to try very hard. She liked everything theatrical and had won a number of declaiming contests throughout the county. If it had been the 1950s, she would have run away to the theater in New York. As it was, she later settled on becoming the most famous second-grade teacher in the history of

Sturgis. Not much taller than Mary Virginia was then, Aunt Nacky was the shortest of the aunts.

As she came in the kitchen and saw her niece, Aunt Nacky stopped and smiled. Aunt Nacky always smiled with her mouth closed tight over her teeth, and the corners of her mouth really did seem to go from ear to ear.

"Well, Mary Virginia," she said, "look at you working, just like your mother!"

Mary Virginia smiled back while Aunt Nacky got out a blue enameled pan that matched the coffeepot, measured in some water with a dipper from the pitcher, and began making herself some oatmeal. However much home-cured ham and fried eggs the rest of the family ate, Aunt Nacky had oatmeal for breakfast every day of her life without fail.

Last down the stairs came Aunt Ginny, at not much after five o'clock in the morning already dressed in a pale green dress that made her look as if she were going to a party. Aunt Ginny couldn't cook, she wasn't very smart, and she hated to work, but she loved her big sister Bert's oldest child, and she, too, smiled at her.

Mary Virginia finished setting the table with the fancy silverplate and the dogwood dishes, while Aunt Ginny pretended to help. Then they both sat down at the kitchen table while Grammar fried the eggs and made the salty-bitter red-eye gravy.

In the yard Mary Virginia could hear Papa and John Bundy cleaning up at the pump before they came in the house, the chickens squawking out of the way while the men shook the water over the grass from their faces and hands. The heavy voices of her grandfather and uncle pulled like rough sacks against the sound of humming insects as they talked their endlessly boring talk about the crops and which field they were going to work in that day and whether it might rain in the afternoon.

Finally, the eggs and gravy were ready. "Mary Virginia, call your grandpa and John Bundy," said Grammar.

"Your breakfast is ready." Mary Virginia got up from the table to call the men through the backdoor, then walked through the kitchen to the dining room and sat back down next to Grammar, and the grown-up aunts sat down in their chairs, too.

John Bundy and Papa clumped through the house in their work

clothes and took their seats in the dining room. Everyone bowed their heads while Papa said a long grace about forgiveness for sins, and gratitude for the food, and asked God to bless them all to his service. After the blessing Grammar and Aunt Subie got back up and went to the kitchen to take the biscuits from the oven and bring them to the table.

Grammar and Aunt Subie sat down again, tucking their napkins into their laps. "I do declare, Mary Virginia," Grammar said as she sat, "I don't know how we would do without you." All the aunts turned to look at Mary Virginia, who smiled back.

She knew it was going to be a fine day. The early morning sun streamed through the long windows of the room and lit up the particles of dust that hung in the July air above the table like little tiny lights. The jams and jellies shone in their glass dishes beside the silver pitcher of sorghum. For a moment the sawing sounds of insects grew louder, as they sometimes do in summer for no apparent reason.

The grown-ups began to talk. Mary Virginia straightened her napkin in her lap, took a piece of ham and an egg from the platter in front of her, and passed them on to Aunt Nacky beside her. She took two hot biscuits that Grammar had just brought in and loaded them both with butter and pear honey, and sighed with pleasure.

She had long since forgotten the sound of the mockingbird, and the man ambling in the road by the Rose of Sharon was far away.

It was two years later when Grammar's Beautiful House burned, the morning of the last day of Pond Fork Baptist Church's summer Protracted Meeting; the event of the burning forever after was linked in Mary Virginia's mind with preachers.

Brother Johnson was staying in Grammar's house. There was nothing unusual in that. All the preachers who came to Pond Fork stayed with Grammar, both the special preachers like Brother Johnson and the regular preachers who came every other week when they weren't preaching someplace else. Grandpa Sam, Grammar's father, had been a Baptist preacher. In fact, Pond Fork Baptist Church had been founded by Grandpa Sam. He hadn't ridden around the country from church to church and from county to county like the men they had now, though W. W. Wynns, Papa's father, who had been a Presbyterian preacher, had. Grandpa Sam had been a somebody.

Not that this had always been so. Grandma Ginny, Mary Virginia's great-grandmother, had been from a wealthy family before she married Grandpa Sam. Bert told Mary Virginia frequently that Grandma Ginny had "married down," and that Grandpa Sam hadn't made Grandma Ginny a good living, but Mary Virginia hadn't seen any evidence of it. Every night she'd slept at Grammar's she'd seen the photograph of Grandma Ginny and her house in Sturgis. In the picture Grandma Ginny was standing rigidly in a striped taffeta dress with big sleeves before a white fence of closely spaced and intricate pickets. Behind the fence stood her and Grandpa Sam's one-storied house with its high, lace-covered windows, a long porch, and carved white trim around the large eaves.

Whatever Bert might have thought of the merits of Grandpa Sam when it came to making money, the rest of Grammar's daughters always joked behind her back that, after God himself, Grammar loved preachers, no matter how full of themselves or how stupid they were.

The preachers, themselves, were never so sure. They wondered whether Grammar missed their preaching to cook for them because she really thought that serving them was the same as serving God. They brooded that their preaching wasn't good enough for her. What they suspected was that she didn't actually pay attention to anything they said, no matter how polite she was to them. Did she think they didn't hear her correcting everybody's grammar but theirs? They knew they were uneducated men who couldn't tell the difference between "he don't want to" and "he ain't a-goin' to." Every last one of them was afraid of Grammar and her secret judgments.

Brother Johnson, here to preach for the Protracted Meeting, had never felt comfortable in her house, ever since the first time he had come to stay the winter before. They had eaten early that night, and he had apologized for keeping them all up later than their accustomed bedtime with an enthusiastic account of his plans for the meeting. When he felt it time to retire, Grammar had—uncharacteristically—not taken him up to his room, but had given him instructions from the foot of the stairs, saying that she herself needed to set the rolls rising before she came up.

"Go up the stairs and turn in to the first door on your right," she had said to him. "That's the room my father, the preacher who founded Pond Fork, always stayed in."

"I thank you kindly, Ma'am," Brother Johnson had replied, his stomach now nearly empty of the ham, mashed potatoes, hot rolls, greens, and pie he had eaten for supper. He added piously, "God will reward you for all you've done."

"Sleep well," Grammar only answered.

The next morning when he came down to breakfast, everyone was already at the table, their breakfast nearly finished.

"How did you rest?" asked Grammar. The aunts looked at each other and snickered.

"Oh," he said. He looked disconcerted. "I've never slept on eight feather beds, before."

"Eight feather beds?" Grammar exclaimed. "You turned the wrong way when I sent you up last night. You spent the night in the spare room where we store the bedding. Those feather beds practically touch the ceiling. Didn't you notice there weren't any sheets on the bed?"

"Why, yes," he replied, pompously. He knew he sounded like a fool. "Of course I noticed, but it's not for the Lord's servant to complain about where the Lord leads him."

Grammar passed him the biscuits, clamped her lips together without looking at him and didn't answer. The aunts glanced at each other out of the corners of their eyes and laughed behind their napkins. Brother Johnson could hardly eat. He always felt off balance in that household. He had been called by God from farming late in life, and he was used to being treated with respect in the other places he stayed. Here, he kept finding himself caught in powerful undercurrents of family feeling he never understood.

The last day of the Protracted Meeting, Grammar was expecting thirty people from the church for the noon meal. She and Papa and the rest of them had been eating with the other families before the afternoon preaching all week. Now it was her turn to feed the lot. She had asked Bert to let Mary Virginia come home with her after the evening meeting the night before to help cook, set the table, and clean up after dinner, and Bert had let her go.

The morning began uneventfully, considering the amount of work there was to do. Fortunately, it was to be a sunny day and they could get an early start even for the Beautiful House. Blacky and Subie had killed and plucked the chickens soon after dawn. The vegetables had been picked and brought in before breakfast. The white layer cakes were baked and iced with their caramel sugar icing by the middle of the morning, and the rolls were rising for the last time. The rest of the household chores had long been done. Blacky and Subie wandered back upstairs to change clothes while Mary Virginia made the pitchers of iced tea, put on the linen tablecloths, got out the best china, and set the tables. The potatoes to be mashed were boiling gently on the back of the stove, and the summer light was coming in restfully on the oil-cloth of the kitchen table.

Mary Virginia was sitting down at the table sneaking a rest as Grammar was rolling the chicken pieces with flour. The lard was near sizzling in the cast iron skillets when a crazy, grinning Nacky came down the stairs for the first time that day in her red wrapper to have a bath.

"Morning, Mary Virginia." Nacky bent over a little to kiss her niece. She turned to her mother. "I'm sorry to get in your way," she said, "but we can't be nasty for the preacher, can we?"

"My," she said, "you all have been working hard this morning!" Nacky kept on grinning as she moved her mother and the skillets aside to set the water kettles to heat on the stove.

Grammar stood there, flabbergasted. Nobody crossed Grammar any more than they did Papa.

"Nancy Wynns, what on earth are you doing?" she said at last. "You've been upstairs all morning, your nose in a book without doing a lick of work, and you want to have a bath now?"

Aunt Nacky began to rip up pieces of that morning's *Courier Journal* she had carried in with her, wadding them into loose balls and stuffing them in the stove to make the coal burn hotter.

"Ginny down yet?" she asked as she slammed the stove door shut. Grammar glared at her. Mary Virginia stood there stock still. She couldn't have said anything herself if she had tried.

Nacky dumped the cold water from the pump on the sink into the tin bathtub on the floor. The fire in the stove crackled and popped fiendishly, and the chimney was full of a roaring sound. Mary Virginia could see little flames licking out of the edges of the oven door and around the burner covers on the top.

Mary Virginia couldn't stand the tension any longer. It was a good time to pay a visit to the spiderwebs in Grammar's grape arbor. She wasn't afraid of spiders, but she was afraid of her grandmother when Grammar was upset. Though she could argue with her mother if she had to, Mary Virginia didn't like to be around any adult who was seriously upset, or angry or sick, for that matter. Bad things scared her. She didn't want to see them, she didn't want to feel them, and she didn't want to be told about them. What was going on in the kitchen was a bad thing.

Mary Virginia took a deep breath and started out to the arbor back by the vegetable gardens, determined not to think of Grammar and Nacky in the kitchen. She quickly found, however, that anxiety was not going to be so easy to escape, for she was immediately assaulted by the peaceful and everyday images of her mother and Kas doing laundry behind the House on the Hill by the chicken yard. She didn't know why these images were coming to her so strongly. Nobody was doing laundry that day. Every last one of them was going to the meeting after lunch, even Papa Charles and baby Quentin.

Still, the image was there. In her mind she watched as Bert and Kas built the fire under the black, three-legged pot that stood on the charred bricks someone had salvaged from under the porch of an abandoned house. She saw her mother pump the hard water from the deep well in the middle of the bare yard, and her sister help carry it to the wash kettle. She heard them murmur and laugh together, and then her mother singing "Bringing in the Sheaves" in her nasal church voice. She kept on watching as they heated the water to fill the two tubs, one for soapy water, one for rinsing. The white clothes and the diapers boiled, flames leaping up the sides of the kettle, as they scrubbed more laundry on the washboard, rinsed it, wrung out what they had finished and draped it on the fence and bushes. The crackling of the laundry fire under the white clothes filled her ears. She could almost smell it.

Then, suddenly, Mary Virginia knew that the fire she heard and smelled was not under the washtub at home but right where she was standing. She whirled around. Wads of blackened, burning paper from the stove were falling on the wooden shingles of the flat roof of the kitchen. Streaks of sparks were falling on the shingles like sparks from Fourth of July sparklers.

This time, she found her voice. "Grammar, Grammar," she screamed as she ran into the kitchen. "The roof's on fire!"

Grammar hadn't even gone out to look. She snatched an empty green pitcher off the kitchen table and dipped it into Nacky's still unused bath water.

"Come here, Mary Virginia," she had shouted to her granddaughter as she banged out the screened door and onto the porch. "I'll hold you up and you pour water on the roof. Nacky, you fill that other pitcher."

Again and again, Aunt Nacky filled the pitcher and handed it to Mary Virginia, who somehow—she never knew exactly how—found herself sitting on her grandmother's shoulders, Grammar's arms around her legs. Over and over Mary Virginia took the heavy pitchers from Nacky, struggling to throw the water up onto the flaming roof. It was no use. The flaming paper had carried sparks everywhere. The whole roof was on fire.

Nacky went out the backdoor, climbed her favorite tree in the front of the house, and watched it burn. Ginny in hysterics at last stopped throwing canning jars out the upstairs pantry window and ran down the front stairs and out the door to the lane. Blacky and Subie were already there. Mary Virginia and Grammar, covered in sweat and soot and burns, followed them as the thick black smoke rising from the roof summoned the men from the fields.

For, of course, there had been no men at home. Neither Papa nor John Bundy were there for the fire, nor were there any hired hands loitering in the lane to look for birds. Even Brother Johnson had left the house after breakfast to go to Pond Fork "to study the Word of God." Grammar would never have stood for able-bodied men in the house during daylight hours, unless they were there to eat and leave again. Whether the men could have saved the house even if they had been around was doubtful. There was just too much fire.

At any rate, the house burned. Grandpa Sam's room that Mary Virginia loved; Grandma Nack's mother's dishes she had sent her husband back up the river for after she had slammed to the ground every last ugly one in the barrel he had first brought on the steamboat down the river from Pittsburgh; the beautiful hand-printed wallpaper in the front hall; the room Bert never lived in; Grandma Ginny's perfect old quilts with the tiny stitches she had sewn on the quilting frame that raised and lowered from her bedroom ceiling; the brocade settees and sofas in the front room, and the glass lamps and the rose carpets; the dining room that let in the morning light; the little cut-glass punch bowl on the landing with its tiny matching cups; the stained-glass window on the stair; the wide porch on which Mary Virginia sat with Grammar to shell her peas—all of it burned until there was nothing left of any of it but dust and ashes and the family myth of Grammar's Beautiful House, the One That Burned.

There was a big crowd at the little white church beside the Great Ditch that night, much bigger than average. Earlier in the week Brother Johnson had won a few folk to the love of Christ, and a few more to the fear of hell, but what people came for this time didn't have much to do with sin, hell, or Jesus. They came to give Ama and Robert hard comfort, not soft sympathy—sympathy in that crowd was humiliating to anyone over the age of six. Everybody but the victims came to congratulate themselves a little that the house that burned wasn't theirs. The relatively well-off men and women who owned their own farms worried a little over whether their self-congratulation meant that they themselves weren't willing to "abide by the will of God for their lives" if their own houses were to burn. The tired tenant farmers and their families struggled with their self-satisfaction at the same time they told themselves that "pride goeth before a fall." Every single adult, however, whether rich or poor, came to see "how Robert and Ama were bearing up" under their disaster, for there was no doubt in anybody's mind that neither Grammar nor Papa would have been willing to make a public show of weakness by missing that service.

Grammar and Papa had no intention, however, of standing around in the gravel and dust before the service to receive condolences from the curious. The two of them and John Bundy had timed their arrival from Aunt Lucy's, where they had gone to stay, in such a way that they could walk in the double door in back only after everybody was already sitting down, right before the preacher's opening prayer.

Still, the moment they crossed the threshold, every man, woman and child in the church knew they had arrived. The scuffling, whispering teenagers in the gallery nearly fell over the rail as they leaned forward in their black straight-backed chairs to look down below. The pictures of the Lord's Supper on the Wittsel Brothers Funeral Home fans blurred in the air as the sweating ladies in their pastel dresses turned their heads toward the aisle and fanned themselves faster in the soft summer twilight. The wives and their heavy-shoed, non-fanning husbands nodded and murmured to Grammar and Papa as they walked up the aisle, their feet loud on the bare planks of the floor, to the wooden bench on the right in which they always sat. Though the little church was packed, their pew and the pew right behind it where Bert sat had been left empty for them. At the back, the children stood up openly and craned their necks to see.

Even more than Grammar and Papa, Bert had found the idea of discussing the family fire with anybody outside the family utterly shaming. She hadn't been able to trust Charles Ray and Bob not to talk, and so she left the big boys with baby Quentin back home in the House on the Hill with Blacky and Subie. Blacky and Subie would be sleeping on the Murphy bed in the parlor while Papa figured out where they would live over the next few weeks.

Bert and Charles walked in late with Mary Virginia and Kas, right after Brother Johnson finished praying for "a great outpouring of the Spirit this evening," just as everybody was getting ready to stand up for the first verse of "Revive Us Again."

Mary Virginia was dazed and exhausted as she filed in to take her place behind her grandmother. Mercifully, Grammar turned around to give her granddaughter a smile and an unusual quick pat before she stood up to sing. As she picked up the song book from her seat, it seemed to Mary Virginia that though Grammar and Papa had found other clothes to wear and had washed the soot off their arms and faces, they still seemed to smell like smoke.

For Mary Virginia, the service was endless. When it was time for Brother Johnson to read the Gospel, sure enough, it was the Parable of the Man Who Built Barns. It was evident to everybody that, as much as he loved preaching damnation, the preacher simply couldn't pass up such an opportunity to get his own back at Grammar.

In his message that followed, he never referred directly to the fire, but the gist of what he said had to do with the folly of trusting in the building of barns for the storing up of earthly treasures, with rich men and the eyes of needles, and with God's righteous wrath in the face of fine houses. All of this was set in the context of a Christian's need to accept whatever disasters came in life as the Righteous Will of God.

Papa, at least, took what he heard in stride. There was not much there he hadn't heard from his own preacher father. As for Grammar, Grammar didn't hear a thing. Just as the preachers who had slept in her bed and eaten her meals had always suspected, she never did listen to a word they had to say.

Mary Virginia, however, hunched down in her seat behind Grammar and Papa, and between Bert and Charles, heard everything. For the first time in her life she understood that the House on the Hill, her own house, was vulnerable. In her pew in Pond Fork Baptist Church, the image of the old house surrounded by its maples rose up clearly before her eyes, and she saw herself with Kas making houses of their own under the huge sickle pear tree in its front yard. She saw them hammering stobs into the hard summer ground, and stringing up rough brown baling wire between the stobs to mark the rooms. She watched herself and Kas root in the chicken yard for broken crockery to be their dishes. At the same time, images of herself, Grammar's house, and Grammar in her house jumbled together with the images, feel, and smells of the life of her mother and sister and brothers in the House on the Hill.

Mary Virginia loved all her houses, the House on the Hill, Grammar's Beautiful House That Burned, the houses she and Kas made but never played in, and they all became one for her. There was no doubt in her mind that God loved houses, too. God didn't burn down houses, even over the heads of sinners. Didn't Jesus himself say to his disciples as he was going away to die, "In my father's house are many mansions"? She had always thought of those mansions as empty houses just like Grammar's, plunked down in a great big house resting on big fluffy clouds. Now, she could see that the houses must be different from each other, some big and some little, but all of them lived in by people who loved them.

Brother Johnson was a fool. She couldn't stand the sight of him. Let them sing "Just as I am, without one plea" forever. No matter if every last man, woman, and child went forward to the communion table to confess Jesus as their personal Lord and Savior, Mary Virginia wouldn't ever again believe a word of what Brother Johnson said. Grammar could think that preachers were as wonderful as she wanted to. Mary Virginia didn't know what God thought, but she knew she hated the whole stupid lot of them.

She would certainly never marry a preacher.

CHAPTER FIVE

Getting Baptized

You know, Panny, the day I was baptized still stands out in my mind as one of the oddest, happiest, and most painful days of my life. Partly, this was because after all the revivals I had been to at Pond Fork Baptist Church, after all the fiery exhortations to believe God, to accept the gospel of Jesus Christ, and to be baptized in his name, I expected so much of baptism itself. Partly, it was because as a twelve-year-old, I still more or less assumed that grown-ups really did believe the things they said in church. Partly, I thought that my baptism would actually please my mother, since, Grammar, you and your sisters—my great-aunts—put so much stock in it.

What should have been the big event took place in the fall, as I recall, toward the end of that first year we came to live with you in Kentucky just after Daddy and Mama were divorced. I had had a painfully bitter year, the worst year of my life. Because of my grieving for my father, and because I was convinced that he had left us all only because of my own failures as a daughter and a human being, despair and shame had left me all alone, irritatingly in the way of the adults around me.

Throughout the course of those long months, in the whole of Union County, there had been only one place in which I found relief. This was in the Methodist church in Sturgis. During her high school years, as I'm sure you remember only too well, Mama had turned her rebellious face against the Baptists, among whom she had grown up, to become a Methodist. I suspect this surprising act of rebellion (Mama was such a good girl!) had its roots in a combination of friendship with another girl who lived in town, a not particularly obscure loyalty toward Papa Charles, who was certainly, from Grammar's point of view, her unsuccessful Methodist father, and a hateful memory of that Baptist preacher who had preached about the Man Who Built Barns when Grammar's Beautiful House had burned. Whatever the reasons for her original defection, however, twenty years later her denominational move provided me with just what I needed when we took up residence in a small duplex in the town of Sturgis, for the Methodist church is where she took us.

Oh, how I loved the Methodist church that year! For one thing, it provided me with a friend who was in youth group and the adult choir with me. Jane Cokely took me home with her to spend the night. She listened sympathetically to my doubts about whether God could actually love me, then she gave me snacks her mother made. Jane Cokely taught me how to roll up my hair on metal curlers, to use Noxema on my face, and to pop my chewing gum in my teeth and stick it on the bedboard before we went to sleep on the twin beds in her yellow cinder-block basement.

But there was something at the Sturgis Methodist Church even more important to me than Jane Cokely's friendship that year. There were grown-ups there, real grown-ups in that church—my bulky, badly educated Sunday school teacher, Miss Sarah Jane, and other softhearted women and men as well—who let me sing alto with them in the choir Sunday morning, Sunday night, and Wednesday night, too. These strange grown-ups, who did not even have to love me because they were not my family, took me seriously. They asked me questions about myself and my life in New York and Delaware, then listened for the answers. Even more, they knew about my parents' divorce and they expected that it hurt me; they never treated me as my Pond Fork uncles seemed to, as though I were contaminated or undeserving of their holy company.

Panny, this adult attention was everything to me that year when Mama's own pain rendered her too raw and angry to give me any attention herself which was not absentminded or designed to keep me from talking about "it." Truly, their interested gaze upon me was the balm of

Gilead to me. It is hardly surprising, then, that the love of God and the attentiveness of those adults came to be so thoroughly mixed together in my mind that soon I couldn't tell which was God and which was Mrs. Dunn, singing in the choir beside me. This is why it was inevitable that one Sunday morning during the altar call after the sermon I should go forward "to take Jesus as my personal Lord and Savior and dedicate my life to him." Being baptized, joining the church, and becoming one of these people among whom I had a place was exactly what I wanted to do.

Whether I had some sort of special instruction for baptism and church membership, or whether it simply occurred, as was the Methodist custom in those days, without fuss the very next Sunday, I can't at the moment recall. What I do remember is how the skinny, anxious girl I was waited in feverish excitement in the choir loft to be claimed by God and the body of Christ during my turn on the program. I recall, too, how I stumbled up to the front over the high-heeled shoes of the ladies and the big dark brown brogans of the men. I was almost crying with happiness as the adults I passed patted me on the back and blessed me with their hands.

What a moment that was for me, shy, lost child that I was, all alone on the platform above the assembled congregation as I said my vows to the preacher and he sprinkled me with water in the name of the Father, the Son, and the Holy Ghost! How holy I felt, then; how close God was, there in the belly of the body of Christ! For the length of the service, at least, I could truly believe that my grief might be permanently lightened by the one I had been told would bear my sorrows. I was, even then, being stripped of my shame; I was being made new.

I continued to be full of this amazing joy after the service as I stood in front of the communion table while the adults flocked around me to shake my hands and kiss me. I felt this way, too, as I left the church and got in the car with my mother and my younger brothers to ride to your house for Sunday dinner with my aunts and uncles, my great aunts and uncles, and my cousins. My joy and certainty came to an end, however, in less time than it took to hit the highway.

So far, I had volunteered nothing of how I felt about my baptism. Mama had been too busy organizing baby Wesley in the car and pulling away from the curb outside the church to speak to me before then. Now, taking off her hat and settling her purse on the seat beside her, she addressed me. "You're awfully quiet," she said.

"Oh, Mama," I answered, my chest aching with eagerness to talk about what I felt and, since I'd finally done something I expected the family to value, to hear her praises: "Wasn't it wonderful? Wasn't it just wonderful? Weren't you proud of me?" At once, without a word from her, the atmosphere in the car changed, and I understood that I had said something wrong, or at least said it, as I so often did, in the wrong way.

A few minutes of tense silence followed my outburst during which we drove past the Dairy Queen and the dreary Sturgis Motel on the edge of town. Then, one hand still on the wheel of the car, she turned around to jerk the straps on Wesley's car seat a time or two, and answered.

"Huh!" she said, "huh!" She made a grimace with her mouth and turned her eyes back to the road straight ahead as though she were warding off a headache. There was another pause and she answered. "When we get to your grandmother's," she said, "I do not want you to take in your book to read. I do want you to go in and help out your aunts and grandmother in the kitchen like your cousins Suzanne and Laura. Do you understand me? What kind of child do you want them to think I'm raising, anyway? Can't you see that everything you do reflects on me?"

What was it I had done now that was reflecting on her? Was it my baptism? I was sure that religion meant something real to Mama. It was she who had taught me to fold my hands and kneel down beside my bed to say my bedtime prayers as soon as I could talk. Even now, "now I lay me down to sleep" is all tangled up for me with the smell of clean seersucker pajamas and an earnest list of "God bless everybodies." It was Mama's passionate Baptist convictions about the evils of infant baptism and the necessity of children making their own religious decisions that led to my baptism at such a late age. What she actually thought about God and Jesus, I couldn't have said, but I did know that for her, life was about working hard and being a good person, and this was the very essence of religion.

To say that I was disappointed and shamed anew by her anger over my baptism would hardly describe my feelings, but I'm afraid that is the best I can do for you here. There was no further discussion of it. At any rate, Mama didn't mention it again, and nobody else did that day—not even you, Panny, nor did my Baptist great aunts, who presumably put a lot of stock in it, mention it, either. As far as what my mother really thought, I'd guess that what went on between a person and God was supposed to be private, and here I was, as usual, insisting on breaking the taboos and talking about it.

Even at twelve I was aware that Mama didn't like me to ask her questions about God or religion. She didn't want me to "go on and on about things like your Grandmother Cowan"—that is, she didn't want me to take religion too seriously, or talk about it in her presence, either. Maybe you and my aunts and uncles didn't think that a non-Baptist baptism was valid and that embarrassed and angered her.

I also suspect that Mama hated the idea that I should be befriended by adults at church whom the rest of the family looked down on because they weren't relatives. If I were a little cynical, I would suspect that most of you took your ties to God or to your fellow Christians with nothing like the passionate seriousness with which you took family loyalty. In fact, with a little effort I might even come to believe that when you all so easily tossed off the adage "blood is thicker than water," the blood you were referring to was that of the family, and the water, the very water in which I had been baptized.

At any rate, on my baptismal day all those years ago, nobody—not even great-aunt Ginny—who worried about us going to hell unless we were saved—acknowledged that anything out of the way had happened to me. The uncles joked and taunted as usual; the aunts told stories; the children played and fought in the grass the same way they always had, and thus, by such baffling, painful indifference my experience of my baptism (though not my baptism itself) was reduced to rubble.

It all still puzzles me, Panny. Whatever the truth of my childhood speculations, I imagine now that the ignoring of my baptism was really more about preachers than it was about me, the Sturgis Methodist Church, or the grown-ups in it. There was surely enough natural enmity between the family and preachers (even great-great-grandpa Sam, who founded Pond Fork itself, and my Presbyterian preacher great-great-grandfather, W. W. Wynns). I know for a fact that, for all her talk,

Grammar never went to church but rather stayed home every Sunday morning to fry chicken and bake cakes for Pond Fork's Brother Smith. Great aunts Nacky, Ginny, Subie, and Blacky, as well as your brother, John Bundy, all took being Baptist very seriously, but they could hardly keep themselves from making fun of ministers right to their faces.

In this respect, at least, the family hasn't changed much over the years. Your children, my aunts and uncles, and most of their children, my cousins, are there in church today every time the doors are open. Still, hardly anybody in the family would be caught dead having a conversation about God or Jesus or salvation or grace or any of those other life-and-death things that have always gripped me in the gut. Such talk embarrasses them; I imagine they find such people as might want to talk about such topics silly.

It's hard now on Mama that I teach church history and talk about God to women and men studying for the ministry. I don't think I more than half realized how hard it was until I took her to class with me one day a few years ago. Afterward, I wondered to Susan, the student who had been ushering her around, how it had gone.

"Oh," said Susan, embarrassed. "I asked her after your lecture whether she wasn't proud of you. 'Proud, of her, ha!' she exclaimed. 'When I found out she was going to seminary, I went to bed for a week and didn't get up!'"

Yet, Panny, as far as I can tell, religion was neither ridiculous nor taboo to you. You may not have spoken to me of my baptism that day, but, on the other hand, never do I remember you making fun of a preacher, no matter how ridiculous even I could see he was, nor do I ever recall having that anxious feeling around you that I felt around my mother when someone mentioned God. You didn't seem to mind when I attended seminary, in fact, it was quite the reverse. When I went off to do graduate work in England, you gave me a hundred dollars you could certainly not afford, but you looked up earnestly into my eyes and said to me, "You are my missionary, you know."

Now, Panny, when I, Roberta, who am your namesake, remember and ponder your death, I wonder if, for good or for ill, in the communion of the saints, it might be so.

Your death wasn't unexpected. Having been born in 1893, you were eighty-nine years old when you died, and you were in the hospital

81

nearly a week before it happened. Even before Papa Charles went, two years before, you had been failing. You moved slowly, and you depended emotionally on all three of your daughters in a way you never had before. You wouldn't eat much more than cake, I recall, no matter what good food Aunt Kas and Aunt Suzie would cook for you. It seemed to me from what Mama told me that you spent most of your time on your long front porch or in your shabby old living room nodding and silent-ly smiling your Mona Lisa smile.

Most of your time you spent there; still, in those last years, you also used to go through spells when you would be in such deep depressions that you wouldn't get out of bed. At other times, you had spells that the family euphemistically called being on your "high horse," and when this happened you couldn't be kept at home no matter what anybody did.

No, there is no getting around the fact that life with you during those last years wasn't easy. Once, from the back of this same high horse, you decided you needed a new car. It baffles me, still, to think how you got some gullible grandchild to take you into the Buick deal-ership in town. Poor as you were, you cleaned out your savings and bought yourself a silver Buick you couldn't even drive.

Your daughters hired a woman to come and clean and cook for you, but it certainly didn't make you happy. Do you recall how you used to accuse that poor woman of stealing sugar from the sugar bowl and Crisco from the can? I know it was hard on Mama. She would come down to stay with you for two or three weeks at a time, and before she was halfway home, you would be calling to complain to her of her neg-lect.

Did you know how your high horses would drive my loving mother and my good-natured, cheerful aunts half out of their minds with anxi-ety for you? A Methodist, a member of the Christian Church, and a Presbyterian, none of them was really conservative in matters of reli-gion. Still, the stress of the kinds of things you would say and do when you were like this would sometimes send them right back to the old revival theology that had formed them as children in Pond Fork Baptist Church. I remember how shocked I was one time to hear Presbyterian Aunt Suzie, who really does know better than this, say, "Oh, how I hope Mother isn't on one of her high horses when she dies; she'll go straight to hell for sure!"

Mercifully, in those last days in Union County Hospital you were neither depressed nor on your high horse, though nearly the whole of that time you lay there talking to yourself without recognizing anybody around you. In spite of the grief they were suffering, it was a good week, an experience of the grace of God's love, for your three daughters, and I would like to think—I need to think—that, down in the dark places of yourself, it was a good week for you, too.

Though you often confused them with Grammar or your aunts and sisters, during the long days of that week, I am sure at some level that you knew it was Mama, Aunt Kas, and Aunt Suzie who were with you putting woolen booties on your cold feet and trying to make sense of your incoherent talk. At night, too, I'm certain you felt their presence when they dragged their sleeping bags to the little lounge outside your door. There in the dark, though they didn't talk about God or the men they had married, they told each other the familiar stories of your life, of the House on the Hill and Grammar's Beautiful House, the One That Burned, and they joked about the preachers. So your daughters laughed and mourned and eased themselves and you to the very edge of your death.

Your last day was a quiet one. It had been a long time since you had eaten, and you were no longer talking much. Mostly, you were unconscious. Your family who had loved you all their lives came one by one or in little groups to dab their eyes and say good-bye. Your children remembered your desire to die in the spring with apple blossoms on your casket, and they recalled your favorite hymn, "When They Ring Those Golden Bells," and your favorite text, "in my Father's house are many mansions."

The last day did come in the spring as you wished, and even in your small hospital room the air was full of it, but you didn't seem to notice. You sighed once or twice, but mostly, you lay there still and silent while Mama, Aunt Kas, and Aunt Suzie stood around you.

At the end, while your daughters looked on in astonishment, something like a shadow came upon you. You opened your eyes and before they could even help you, somehow pulled yourself up into a sitting position. Expectantly, you searched the room with yours eyes until at last you found the invisible face you were looking for. Leaning forward, you smiled, and yearning, delighted, nothing of yourself held back, you stretched out your arms to the one who came for you.

"Jesus," you whispered in your vision, "sweet Jesus." Then, still smiling, you lay back down on your bed, took a single breath, and, as you would have said, went home.

CHAPTER SIX

Stealing Bob

Bert knew it wasn't as early as it seemed. It was dark and cold in the House on the Hill, as only early March could make it. Outside, the sky was black, and wind blew in hard gusts, rattling the windows and wrenching the doors. Between the gusts the wind wailed and sighed, never quite settling on the earth or the trees.

Bert had been dreaming before she woke up; it was a dream she recalled having in the night already. It was important that she remember it, but what the dream had been she could not recall, nor what anxiety the wind was multiplying in her.

Under the heavy layer of wool and cotton quilts Bert tried a moment longer to hold her body quiet and think. She could not lay hold of a single sight or sound from her dream. In her restless frustration, her anxiety turned to irritation. She could hardly stand it that Charles slept so blankly, so inertly as he lay facing the wall beside her. She tried not to listen to the sound of his long, even snores.

For most of her life fits of sleeplessness had accompanied her dreaming. As a child there had been long stretches of despairing midnight wakefulness in this very house. As a wakeful woman, her sleeplessness seemed worse, and the despair and darkness left over from her dreams was deeper than it had been in childhood. Now, the deep night's absence of purposeful human sounds and the awareness of the unconsciousness of her family filled her with a physical dread she associated with the presence in the house of death.

Last night had been worse than it generally was. She had been all right at bedtime. She and Charles had gone to bed early enough in the high bed by the fire in the front bedroom. The babies had gone to sleep easily an hour before, and even Bo and Bob had folded themselves into the covers and stayed quiet after she had banked the fire in the front bedroom fireplace and turned down the wick in their lamp in the dining room.

As usual, Bert had been asleep almost before she got flat; falling asleep had never been her trouble. She could barely remember Charles's climbing in beside her, cold all over from his last trip to the privy in the chicken yard. Whether it was from some sound outside the house or a spoken voice in her dream, Bert had startled awake sometime afterward. Immediately, she had heard the wind moaning and sighing in the pear tree, and she had been aware of a familiar plot and images, though she couldn't say what it was that had covered her in sweat and made her muscles and bones feel as though she had a fever.

Tuned to her mother's unease, baby Suzie had cried fretfully in Nacky's spindled cradle off and on all night. Two-year-old Quentin had been only lightly asleep on his bed on the other side of the room, and each time Suzie had cried, he had heard his mother take his new sister into bed with her and he had fussed to come, too. Charles, characteristically, had slumbered under the canopy of Bert's anxiety as though he slept alone.

Though her last night's nightmares still escaped her, all of a sudden an awareness of what it was that was anguishing her days rose up inside Bert like bubbles. It was worry over Bob. Bert closed her eyes and shuddered. She couldn't face it before she was even out of bed. She wouldn't, she mustn't think about it now. It was time to get up and work, to start breakfast for Charles and the older children. After the dinner was pitched, she would think about it. She must force herself to talk about it with Charles.

Aching and heavy, Bert slid from under the warm blankets. On the straight-backed chair by the bed her pile of clothes was waiting from the night before. The room was dark, but she did not need to see to dress. She only wanted to escape to the kitchen to find some equilibrium before everybody else woke up. Fortunately, she had already nursed the baby and put her back in her cradle, and Quentin, too, at last lay still. Bert would not risk bringing the fire in the bedroom back to life until later.

Stealthily, Bert stepped into her underwear, her stockings, and her work shoes. Shuddering and shivering in the chill of the front bedroom, she began to drape herself in layers of shapeless and colorless dresses, blouses, and old sweaters of Charles's. She would wait until the children left to heat the water to wash her face and to brush out her braid and pin it up for the day.

The long floorboards creaked and popped as she tiptoed across the bedroom through the dining room where Bo and Bob still slept, mouths open and head to toe in the fold-out bed by the door to the hall. The dining room was even colder than the front room. The cold air of the big room made her skin ache, and she stopped to light the Early Morning heater. It wouldn't make it warm enough for the boys to dress in there when they woke up, but at least it would take enough of the chill out of the air so that they could grab their clothes and run for the kitchen.

Refusing to think of Bob, Bert, in the dining room with the sleeping children, was unexpectedly oppressed by the round mahogany table pushed up against the wall. Suddenly, the familiar layered mountain of clean laundry that had covered its surface since Mary Virginia was a baby felt dangerous to her. In the faint light the kerosene heater made in the big room, the underwear and aprons, the white diapers and brown shirts reminded Bert of the great slippery mound of black slag that sat not too far from the entrance to the Number Nine Mine.

Deliberately, she put aside the images of being buried under piles of sliding laundry, trying instead to imagine herself sprinkling the sheets and shirts and dresses, rolling them up, and placing them compactly next to each other in the laundry basket. She pictured herself heating the two big flatirons on the back of the stove till the lick of spit she tested them with sizzled. This morning, if she could get up the energy for it, she would definitely iron.

Looking away from the laundry-covered table, her eyes lighted on the long brown buffet that made up a set with the dining table. She smiled to remember how Bo and Bob used to stand next to it, reaching up to milk its tear drop shaped dangling handles. She loved them so much it made her chest hurt. Now they were both big enough to do real work around the farm, too big to play milking with anything but a real cow. She sighed and wondered if Quentin and Suzie would play the same game.

Once in the brightening kitchen, Bert tied an apron around her thick waist. Her breath smoked in the cold as she bent over to light the coal oil lamp on the oilcloth-covered table. As the wide flame leaped up in the lamp, the chimney caught the intensity of the light. She turned down the wick, then rubbed her arms for a moment, musing. Mary Virginia had cleaned the lamps when she had been home from Sturgis with Kas on Saturday. Mary Virginia, and Kas, too, were almost grown. Home from high school only on the weekends during the school year, they were nearly gone.

Enough of that. Bert knelt down to start the fire in the big black stove, kindling it with the corncobs Bob and Bo had brought in the night before. As the dry cobs began to blaze and pop she tossed in some big chunks of soft coal from the coal bucket that stood on the rag rug beside the stove. The oily smells of the coal and the odor of the burning kerosene made her nauseated, as they always had, even between her pregnancies.

Bert got up off the floor and broke the ice on the water in the coffee pot to begin boiling it. Then she snatched up her coat and went out into the darkness, catching the door with her heel to keep it from slamming. This morning the big wooden box the salt pork was stored in reminded her of a coffin, even more than usual. Back in the kitchen she quietly laid the heavy piece of ham on the table and began to cut thin slices, laying them in the cold cast-iron skillet that was even blacker than her stove. After she set the skillet on the front burner, she cut up some of the last of the green apples to fry in the ham fat after she took up the meat. As the dark red meat edged in yellow fat began to fry, the house began to fill with its musky, salty smell.

Charles, awakened at last by the smells of cooking, dressed quietly in the front room. He nodded to Bert as he drifted through the kitchen on his way to feed and water the animals. This morning Bert wasn't up to even nodding back. A momentary spurt of something made the blood rush to her face as she watched him go.

Charles Ray, whom they called Bo, came into the kitchen not long after Charles. She smiled at her oldest son. In his night shirt and bare feet, he was clutching his school clothes to his chest as though they were about to get away from him.

She interrupted her work to watch him as he came over to the table for a kiss. She held her cheek up to him. Charles Ray, at eleven, was already taller than she.

"Morning, mother," he said before he ran back to the side of the warm stove, his clothes flapping over his arms.

"Morning, Bo," she answered. "Did you have a good night?"

"Terrible wind, wasn't it?" he answered. "Screamin' like a preacher!"

Bo always made her laugh. "Shame on you! Don't you let Grammar hear you say a thing like that!"

Bo's thick black hair was stuck up every which way as he poked his head through his faded school shirt. He looked like a pecking hen as he hopped on one foot and then on the other as he tried to dress without burning himself on the stove. With his copper skin and black hair, it never failed to surprise her with how little he looked like Charles and how much he looked like Papa.

Seeing him now in the gray early morning light, Bert was swamped by the peculiar combination of gratitude and dread she so often felt with this child. How close she had come to losing him! In the worst parts of the nights she often saw him still, not as he was now, but as he had been that terrible early morning when he was barely two.

That winter morning had followed another one of her bad nights. She had also gotten up that day before dawn, quickly dressing in the dark to go out to gather eggs before the children and Charles woke up. She had known it was early for the chickens, but she had been too restless to stay inside. Neither Mary Virginia nor Kas had been stirring as she dressed, and twice before she left the house Bert had checked to be sure Charles Ray was as soundly asleep as his older sisters.

Bert nearly always felt better outdoors than in the house, and that morning, too, the fluttering in her stomach had begun to subside almost as soon as she had stepped out onto the high porch outside the kitchen. The sky was just beginning to lighten, and she had known that it was still snowing even before she lit the lantern. In the light of the lantern she had seen the dark blue drifts of snow lapping the bottom of the porch and embracing the base of the black maples in the yard.

Her feet in their old rubber boots had made soft dents in the snow on the porch steps. Shuffling with the egg basket past the barn to the chicken yard, she had wondered at the purple shadows the light of her lantern made on the smooth snow around her. Deliberately, Bert had breathed in the cold air through her nose. How good the silence of the dawn and the sharp cold had felt to her!

Crossing the wooden threshold of the gray chicken house, she noticed how the cold had muffled the usual chicken house smells of feathers, old straw, and chicken manure. Some of the black and white hens were already up and about, pecking in the straw, while others fluffed themselves and preened, stirring and clucking on their nests around the wall.

She left the lantern on the packed dirt just inside the door. Then, just as she had reached under the first hen, she heard a sound that wasn't chickens. She turned around to see, and her heart nearly stopped.

There was Charles Ray, little Bo, standing right outside the door in the snow in his thin white nightgown, the snow halfway up his baby legs. He was looking up at her, his eyes huge and black, and tears were running down his round face. He didn't say a word or cry out as he held up his arms to her. She dropped the egg basket and snatched him up. He was so hot with fever that his face almost burned her face as she carried him into the house, holding both of his little cold feet in one of her hands.

She called out for Charles to go and get Uncle John. This time, Charles leapt out of bed, saddled the horse, and went. She wrapped the baby in quilts and rocked him while she waited for the doctor. Uncle John was kind, but he was worried by what the fever might do to the child if he lived. After he had finished, he left to fetch his sister, Bert's mother. Charles went out to grieve and do the chores. In the chair by the fire in the front room, Bert rocked her son and cried over him. She cried over him for many days after that, rocking him on her big belly where Bob was growing inside her.

Remembering all that as she started her biscuits, Bert glanced again at her son. Ever since the fever Charles Ray had had trouble holding still or paying attention to anything more than a little while at a time. For the first six months after the day he appeared in the chicken yard it had been much worse; he had been dull and uncharacteristically quiet.

Then, one hot, still afternoon she had come into the kitchen to find

Bo carefully climbing down off the big kitchen chair, his whole being concentrated on a single chicken egg in his cupped hands. Looking to see what he was doing, she had found every egg but one lined up on the floor against the wall by the door. Her egg basket was empty on the top of the kitchen cabinet. Methodically, the two-year-old had climbed the chair onto the counter fourteen times, stepped up onto the shelf, stretched his arms over his head to the basket and climbed down again with an egg without breaking it. She knew he would be all right.

Bert glanced up, smiling even now, at the top shelf of the kitchen cupboard. Taking the eggs down so gently was the last delicate thing Bo ever did in his life. The accident with the cabinet a year and a half later had been truer to Bo as he was now. She had known at the time that from the perspective of the climbing four-year-old Bo and his two-year-old brother Bob, the temptations of that piece of furniture would be irresistible. With its pull-out countertop; its flour sifter; drawers and bins for sugar, salt, and spices, its shelves for dishes and glasses; its drawers for knives and forks; and spaces for food and pots and pans and lids and towels, it was there to be climbed. It was a wonder they both weren't killed the morning they pulled it over. As it was, every dish was smashed, and cold, wet greens were scattered everywhere, mingled with broken eggs.

Bert sighed and reached for the buttermilk on the table at her elbow. A moment later Bob came through behind his brother from the dining room, tiptoeing with his bare feet on the ice-cold floor.

This morning, he was afraid to look at her. "Morning, Mother," he mumbled. His mumbling shiftiness angered her, and tuned as he was to his mother's disapproval, Bob knew she was angry. Deciding not to risk the kiss his brother had taken for granted, he turned back to the stove to drop his clothes on the floor and dress, his face a familiar mix of sheepishness and sullenness.

She glanced at Bob in spite of herself; he was putting on the new shirt and overalls Papa had bought him Saturday. Bob's fancy brown shoes shone next to his brother's worn-out boots. She hated that her children's clothes were worn out; she hated Bob's new clothes even more.

Once more Bert could feel the blood rush to her face. She was sick of being caught this way between the helpless rage and despair she had felt since she and Charles had moved back to Union County.

However the thing was going to get better, it wasn't about to happen now. She sighed again; she must try harder not to make Bob bear the brunt of her anger. Though she was as angry with her son as she was with her father, she knew it wasn't reasonable to hold the nine-year-old as responsible as the grown man.

Half dressed and sensing her change in mood, the little boy approached her again for a kiss. This time she turned her cheek to him and gave him a quick hug before she set the long, trough-like bread bowl on the table, the flour inside it parted and piled up at each end like the Red Sea. Bob stood beside her awkwardly as she scooped up out of the lard can a ball of the white lard she had rendered herself. Only partly reassured, he turned back to the stove to finish dressing, watching her anxiously as she warmed the lard with her fingers.

Bert could feel his black eyes on her as she worked the flour into the lard with her fingers, pulling in the flour from the edges of the bowl little by little until the crumb was just right. She picked up the tall blue pitcher of sour buttermilk, and worked its yellow flakes into the soft dough. Bob watched as she kneaded the dough and patted it out on the table. Then she cut out the biscuits with the sharp edge of an empty baking powder can, placed the biscuits just touching each other into the battered pans, and stuck the pans into the oven.

While they baked, Bert took the chipped green plates and cups from the cabinet and set them on the table along with the knives and forks from the drawer. She poured the coffee for herself and Charles and the buttermilk for Bob and Bo. Bo stood at the stove, poking the apples that were caramelizing in the ham fat in the black skillet.

Despite the anxious atmosphere of the house, babies Quentin and Suzie still slept. Charles came in from tending the animals. Smelling like stale cigar smoke from the day before, he snorted and stomped his feet, "Oh Lordy, Lordy," sneezing as he came. Everyone but Bert sat down; she brought the biscuits, eggs, ham and gravy to the table and sat down, herself. Everybody ate and drank. Bert was silent; the boys shoved and giggled; Charles alternately made jokes and stared out the window.

After breakfast, Bert made the school lunches of fried ham and biscuits, and the two boys ran down the hill toward the Templeton school. As Bert watched them from the front porch, she pictured Mary Virginia and Kas also laughing together and leaning into the wind as they walked the two blocks to the high school from the big room they rented in Jane's grandmother's house. How much she missed them!

Bert gathered the eggs while Charles shaved over the washbasin in the kitchen, then Charles went off to the barn to milk. The babies woke up and Bert cleaned them and fed them. She rebuilt the fire in the front room, emptied the pee pots, then made the big bed in the front room and the boys' in the dining room. She pumped the water and heated it for the dishes. The babies in the kitchen with her, she washed the dishes and started the vegetables for dinner. She sorted the laundry and did enough sprinkling to iron the week's clothes and sheets. Back in the kitchen, she separated and stored away the milk, saving the cream to be churned later. She went out to the yard again for ham, sliced it, fried it, and made biscuits for the noon meal.

Charles came in from the barn, washing up at the cold water of the pump outside. As they ate, she and Charles talked about the wind, the cattle, and the chickens. Still, she could not talk about Bob. Charles went back out to the barn. Bert washed the dishes once again and began the vegetables for supper.

She cleaned up the babies and put them to sleep again. She started the flatirons heating on the back of the stove in the kitchen, set up the ironing board, spread a damp sheet over it, and tried to make herself think about what she could do about what was happening to Bob.

What could she do about him? She had learned she couldn't argue successfully with Papa about him. Not that she wouldn't argue. Though she wasn't much of a talker—Bert was often nearly tongue-tied when it was time to talk—she was one of the few people in the family who would argue with Papa. She had tried arguing again last Friday afternoon, and it had done her no more good than it ever did when it came to Bob.

Friday had been cold and dreary, with the wind howling outside the windows just as it was this afternoon. It was Bert's favorite time of day. Quentin was on her lap in the rocking chair in the front room, and Suzie was playing in the cradle. Bob and Bo, just home from school, were by the fire. They were drinking hot chocolate, Bob sitting on the stool with his feet on the hearth, Bo squatting and poking at the red lumps of coals with the poker.

They were telling her about their day at the Templeton school with their teacher, Miss Ida. Bert was interested in their learning, and she had loved teaching. She would go back to it in a minute if she could. Furthermore, Miss Ida, who had taught Mary Virginia and Kas, too, in her one-room schoolhouse, was Bert's friend. Miss Ida was funny and happy, and she had a husband who worked hard and was good to her. Miss Ida had often saved Bert's life by taking Mary Virginia home with her to spend the night when Bo and Bob were little.

In the middle of one of Bo's stories, Papa had roared up the lane in his fancy car disrupting everything and bringing Kas and Mary Virginia home for the weekend to the House on the Hill as he did every Friday in winter. In the fall and spring, the girls had to live with Papa and Grammar and ride their horses into town if they were going to go to Sturgis High. In the winter when it was too cold to ride the horses to town and back, they lived in town.

All this had been Mary Virginia's doing, not Bert's. From the House on the Hill, Mary Virginia and Kas should have gone to high school in Pride, but Mary Virginia wouldn't do it.

"I'm not going to that dinky little high school in Pride," she had shouted at Bert and Charles when she graduated from Templeton. "Do you think anybody will even know who I am over there?"

"And how do you think you are going to get there, young lady?" Bert had shouted back.

"I'll live with Grammar and Papa, that's what I'll do," she answered.

"And what makes you think they'll take you in?" her mother wanted to know.

"Because I already asked them. We've got it all arranged. You won't have to do one thing about it!"

From that point on, Mary Virginia pursed her mouth, crossed her arms over her chest, and refused to say a word unless spoken to directly. Though her father gave her the second of the only two whippings of her life, she wouldn't budge. In the end they let her have her way. Kas followed her two years later. Bert only accepted it because Papa took them home with him on Sunday nights after church and brought them home again for the weekends on Friday afternoon.

This is how it happened that, on the previous Friday, Mary Virginia and Kas had gotten out of Papa's car with their clothes and books and had disappeared into the parlor where they slept before Bert could make it to the door to meet them. Bert had known from their behavior what was about to happen. She had been angry at them as they rushed past her, though she knew she shouldn't expect them to back her up against Papa.

Papa had run up the wooden front steps behind his granddaughters shouting, "Where's my boy?" Cold air blew in around him, and the wind wrenched the door out of his hand and slammed it open against the wall in the hall. In the parlor Mary Virginia and Kas could hear the front windows rattle.

"Son, are you ready to come with me?" he called again. Papa was in the house, past Bert in a flash. Ignoring Bo entirely, he had his hand on Bob's shoulder before she had time to turn around.

"Yes, sir," said Bob. He jumped up, leaving his half-drunk chocolate on the floor beside his stool, and ran to the dining room table to root for his clothes.

"Just get your nightshirt," Papa called after him. "Leave the rest of your clothes here. I'm taking you to Sturgis to Holt's in the morning to get some decent things for a change. You shouldn't be wearing that old stuff your mother puts you in."

"You can't take him," said Bert, who had come up behind her father. She was prepared for Papa's announcement, and she had practiced in advance what she intended to say. This time, she intended to speak to her father without Bob or Bo being drawn into it in any way.

Suzie slept and Quentin whimpered as she held him on her hip, while Bo just sat there through the whole thing, never turning around, staring into the fire. She was worried about Bo, too, but she couldn't do anything about it now. She would speak with him later.

She spoke softly into Papa's back. "You can't take Bob anymore, do you understand?" Her voice was perfectly level, perfectly firm. "I won't let you take him. Bob is not your son. He's mine, mine and Charles's."

Papa had turned around in surprise to look at her. It had been a long time since he had heard this tone of voice from her, and he didn't like it. She kept on, unintimidated. Too much was at stake to risk losing control of her own temper.

"Papa, if you love Bob, you have to see that you are ruining him. He doesn't know what he's entitled to or where he belongs, this house or yours. He doesn't need clothes the others don't have, can't you see that? It isn't good for him, and it isn't good for the other children, either." She stopped, and Papa glared down at her in silence. Quentin continued to whimper.

"What are you talking about, woman?" Papa had said, at last. He squinted his eyes as he did when he was crossed, looking hurt and mean at the same time. Bert had whispered. He made sure to speak loud enough that the children could hear him without difficulty.

"What do you mean, Bob doesn't know where he belongs? Of course he knows where he belongs. He belongs with me. He's my namesake, that's what he is. He's mine, and I want him. If you don't like it, you've got nobody to blame but yourself, and you know it. You named him, you and that Charles Wesley of yours. Why'd you name him after me if you didn't want me to do things for him?"

Bert pressed her lips together, trembling with anger. She remembered very well why she had named Bob after Papa. After the birth of three daughters, Charles had begun to worry whether he ever would have a son. Charles was beside himself with happiness when Charles Ray was born. Her sisters and her aunts, too, still talked about the way he had gone down to the barn and jumped and whooped with joy. Of course, she named her first boy Charles Ray, after his father. However fed up with Charles she ever might be, Charles deserved it.

Papa had raged around the house like a mad man.

The baby hadn't even been two days old when Papa first came to see him. Bert had been sitting up against a pile of pillows, nursing him in the bed in the front room. Charles had just come in to check on his new son when Papa had driven up, storming. Grammar had just told him his first grandson's name.

At the sight of his father-in-law Charles had thought up a chore to do in the barn. Bert had had a difficult labor and a hard delivery of his fifth baby, and she was absolutely sick of both men. She'd told Papa then that if he would go away and leave her in peace, she would name the next boy after him.

Now here they all were, right now in 1933, still paying for that one scene when Bo was born. Last Friday afternoon, Bob had stood between Bert and his grandfather, his mouth opening and closing and turning his head toward one and then the other in bafflement and resentment at his own mother.

"Why don't you want me to go, Mother?" he had whined with wily innocence.

"You know I'm Papa's boy, don't you? Just because Charles Ray don't have nice things, you don't want me to have them, either." Bob had bounced up and down on the balls of his feet, watching her.

She had felt like smacking him. "How dare you say such a thing to me, young man," she had answered. "You go ahead and go," she had answered him. "You go ahead and you have your way, but whatever you do, don't think you aren't going to pay for this, you or your grandfather, either one."

She had scared him at last; she could feel his fear and his confusion. She had never spoken to Bob that way before. Bert had gone into the kitchen then, refusing to see them off. She hadn't wanted to look at Bob before he went; if he was afraid of her now, well then, good. She would let him see what that felt like for a while.

After they left, she went back to her mending, utterly silenced by her own anger and confusion. Kas and Mary Virginia stayed in the parlor. Bo had slipped out of the house in all the chaos to go for a walk with the dog in the fields.

She was as confused right now as she had been then. Bert had loved her father, and standing at her ironing board on the Monday after that terrible scene, she knew she still did. She knew he loved her, too; that was the trouble. There was no man in the world like Papa, and there never would be. She had wanted a son named after him, and furthermore, she had wanted her father to do for Bob the very things he did—to buy him clothes, to take him places, to show him off. Caught between two older sisters and a brother and two babies, Bob needed every bit of attention he could get.

Still, Bert had no illusions about her original motives for letting Bob go off with her father, and they filled her now with shame and anger. It had suited her at first to have Papa come to take Bob when he had been so little. However tired she might feel now—and she felt almost beside herself with exhaustion most of the time—she had never been able to cope when Bob had been little and she had been even more worn out and sick than she was now.

The thing that scared Bert so bad she couldn't even talk about it was what it was doing to Bob now. What she had said to Papa on Friday she meant. Over the last few months, with every trip to Papa's, with every night Bob spent in her mother and father's house, Bob felt more and more uncomfortable, more and more out of place in the House on the Hill. Right under her nose, as surely as she was losing her child, her child was losing his home and his family, and there was nothing she could do about it.

All of a sudden, Bert smelled something she shouldn't have smelled. She looked down at Charles's one Sunday shirt spread out on the ironing board before her. Snatching up the iron, she saw that she had scorched the shape of the entire hot iron into the back of the shirt. In one of the corners away from the point of the iron, the cloth was burned all the way through. The rust-colored threads at the edge of the scorch were frayed and separated.

Despair filled her. She could no longer keep herself from knowing what she had tried not to know for years. It was not just Bob she was losing. She had lost, or was losing, or would lose all her children, and Papa had a hand in all of it.

Bert was overwhelmed with grief. She could hardly stand, hardly move. Like an old woman, she picked up the heavy iron and set it down on the side of the stove. She left the ironing spread out as it was all over the kitchen and crept through the dining room and into the front room. Quentin and Suzie were still asleep, but she needed to be near the babies she still had.

In the front room she had intended to sit in the rocking chair by the fire, but once there, she found herself unable even to sit up. The children asleep, she decided she might as well get back in bed. As she took off her slippers and slid down under the heavy covers, she finally remembered her dream of the night before. She had dreamed again of losing Caroline, of her baby's dying.

Caroline had been the second of Bert's children, born in the House on the Hill when Bert was twenty-five. Mary Virginia was a baby herself at the time, only eighteen months.

Bert had been worn out by continual vomiting throughout her pregnancy with Mary Virginia, and she hadn't been glad to find herself immediately expecting again. She could hardly stand to have the vomiting resume again so soon. Still, Bert had wanted this child with her whole being. Soon, she found herself talking and singing as much to the new baby she could feel growing inside her as she did to the child playing on the floor at her feet.

Then, one hot morning in late summer three months before Caroline was due to be born, Bert had a premonition. She had just finished the wash. She had dumped the wash water out of the two wash buckets and put out the fire she had heated the water on. She had put away the lye soap, the corrugated iron washboard, and the washtub. Now she was exhausted. With her big belly she had bent and stooped and stretched and lifted until she could hardly move. Her back ached, her hands hurt, and sweat ran down her face in the absolutely still heat.

She was almost through hanging out Mary Virginia's diapers, and she was looking forward to sitting down with a glass of tea before she had to cook dinner. Then, without a bit of breeze, the diaper she was pinning to the line stood straight up in the air, stiff and flat as a stone. At the same moment, Caroline gave a terrible lurching kick inside her. Bert had sat right down on the bare ground below the line of wash, sickeningly afraid.

Three months later Caroline was born. There had been no trouble with the birth, and she was a sturdy baby who didn't cry much and slept well from the first day. Then at the end of November of that year the great flu epidemic of 1918 overtook Union County. Little Caroline was eleven days old when she, Bert, and Charles took sick. Bert and Charles lay in bed with a high fever, coughing and vomiting for days.

Though Bert's mother came every day, for some of the time daily there was no truly conscious adult in the house. Mary Virginia, only a year and a half old herself, had sat on the floor for days in the high-topped shoes Papa had bought her, turning the pages of the Sears and Roebuck catalogue and talking to herself. Bert remembered that, as she remembered her mother there, bathing her face with cold rags, but she couldn't remember much else, not even the moment when Caroline died.

When the baby died, Charles hadn't even been conscious, and neither of them could go to the funeral. She supposed that that was why she kept having those awful dreams in which she was present at the funeral. In her dreams she was always on the high hill in Sullivan, standing by the open grave in the falling snow between her father and husband and weeping because she couldn't see Caroline's coffin anywhere. The tombstone was already in place, and from where it sat on the snow, the small stone lamb on top of the tombstone turned its stone eyes to her, bleating.

Bert would never get over it. She lay in the bed in the front room of the House on the Hill in the faint light of the afternoon, and the image of the lamb and the memory of her lost baby and her daughters in town and her son Bob and Charles and her father all ran together in her mind until she fell into a deep and helpless sleep.

Sometime later, Bert was startled awake by the heavy sound of Charles's work boots stomping up the porch steps to the kitchen. She was sitting up in bed and looking around in confusion by the time he had scraped his feet outside the door and come through the dining room to the front room. The clock on the mantle said ten minutes after two. She had not heard it strike; she had slept much more soundly than she had expected. From where she sat in bed, she could see Suzie looking like a doll asleep in Nacky's cradle, the dark red baby quilt mounded up over her body. Quentin was sitting on the floor next to the hearth, playing with a pile of shiny coal he'd taken out of the hod to stack between his legs. His hands were filthy and he had a black rim around his mouth.

Charles came into the room and looked around. "Good Lord, woman," he said. "What are you letting that baby do? What are you doing in bed in the middle of the day, anyway?" Charles picked up Quentin and carried him into the kitchen before she could answer. From the front room Bert could hear the sound of water splashing and Quentin wailing.

By the time Charles came back with Quentin, Bert was up and shivering in the creaking rocker. She wasn't truly awake, but she had shaken off enough of her sleep to see that Charles had something on his mind, and that, for a change, he was prepared to talk about it.

She stopped him before he started. "I don't want to wake up Suzie. We'll go into the kitchen and then you tell me what you're thinking about in there," she said.

Charles didn't answer, but he followed her back into the kitchen

100

where he'd just been. He set Quentin down on the floor. The two-year-old ran to the dented truck he had inherited from his brothers, and drove it away from his parents around into the safe space between the back of the stove and the wall.

"Be careful back there," Bert called to him. "Don't touch the stove."

Charles hadn't noticed the ironing stacked around the kitchen when he'd been in with Quentin before, but he noticed it now. "What's this stuff doing all over the place with you in bed, Bert?" He spotted the shirt on the ironing board in front of him. "You didn't go to bed because you scorched my shirt, did you?"

"You know me better than that, Charles Wesley," she replied. "Ironing never sent me to bed in my life."

"Well, what is it, then?" he wanted to know. "What were you doing?"

There was a long silence. Bert and Charles had never talked about painful things together even before Casey County, but since then they almost found such talk indecent. Pain and confusion were like the cross, there to be endured, not talked about. Now their lack of practice and their shame divided them from each other like a thick curtain.

Bert broke the silence first. "You tell me why you came in the house, and then I'll tell you why I went to bed."

Charles bucked himself up. "Your father's been here to see me. He left just now before I came in."

Bert drew in breath. "How did he get here?" she asked. "I didn't hear the car."

"He came on old May across the fields," Charles answered. "I reckon he didn't want you to know he was here till after he left."

Charles got up from his chair and stomped around the kitchen, restlessly adjusting a pot on the stove with one black-nailed hand and patting the pile of ironed sheets with the other. He couldn't sit back down.

Behind the stove Quentin made the little boy sound of engines revving up. "Bert, we've got to talk," Charles said.

Bert looked at her husband. Whatever it was Charles wanted to talk about, it was going to be even more serious than she had feared. "What do you want to talk about?" she replied, suddenly irritated. "I thought we were already talking." She took the scorched shirt off the ironing board and began to pick at the burnt threads around the hole in the back.

Charles ignored her irritation; he cleared his throat and blew his nose into his handkerchief. "You know how your father won't ever let me forget that this farm is his farm and not ours, that this house is his house and not ours?"

"Well, then," answered Bert, cautiously. Quentin came out from behind the stove and up to her. He put his hands on the side of her leg and looked into her face, then, when he saw that he couldn't get her attention, he went back out of sight where he had come from.

"Well," Charles went on, "he's decided to buy the Harris farm from Mary Beth Harris now that George is dead. One of her brothers wants it, too, so she's raised the price on him. You know how he can't stand for a minute to have anybody beat him out at anything. He's determined to have that farm, but it turns out he needs more money than he can put his hands on right now. The long and the short of it is, he came to tell us he won't wait any longer for us to pay him the rent from the farm for last year."

"He won't do what?" Bert asked, incredulously.

Charles's voice rose. "He knows we don't have that money. He's known all along we just don't have it. How can he ask us to do this? Everybody knows last year was a bad year for farmers. He knows it himself; he's a farmer."

"Charles Wesley, there's not a soul in Union County that doesn't know that," Bert answered. She could hardly believe it even of her father. He knew how the awful clay soil on their farm had turned hard and the top flaked off like pie crust, while all around the House on the Hill pools of water had stood breeding mosquitoes in the ditches by the road.

Charles looked down, his voice low. "When I reminded him of that, he said I was going to hell, and it served me right. The Lord was punishing me because I spent all my time at the races."

"Well, it isn't true," Bert snapped. She hated to see her husband like this. Not that Charles Wesley hadn't on occasion visited the racetrack in Henderson. He had, and whatever God was going to do about it, she wasn't about to forgive him all that soon. Still, it was not Papa's place to criticize her husband.

Besides, he really had kept away from the track last year. Even with the grudge she held against him, she appreciated what it had cost him to do it. Charles had spent last summer all alone in the fields, bored and demoralized. He had fainted three times from the same allergy to the sun that had flattened him on his Pa's farm in Casey County, and he was still consumed by hay fever.

Suddenly, Bert was struck by a new thought. "Charles, why did he come to you and not to the two of us, together? You're not through telling me, are you?" She laid the shirt down on the table beside her and looked at Charles intently.

Charles turned his head away from her to answer. "When I started to argue with him and tell him he knew we couldn't pay, it seemed like he wanted to change the subject. He started to talk about his grandchildren, going on and on about how fine they are and how much he loved them. Then I figured out where he was going."

Charles paused and took a deep breath, keeping his eyes away from his wife. "Your father said he wouldn't press us for the money if you would just leave him alone about Bob."

Bert leapt to her feet and knocked the ironing board over. Quentin jumped and whimpered.

Deliberately, she lowered her voice. "This whole thing is about Bob, isn't it? I knew it, I just knew it! Me leave him alone about Bob! How can I leave him alone about Bob? He don't love Bob one bit if that's the best he can do. Bob is being taken away from his mother and father, and Charles Ray is being hurt, and all Papa can think of is getting what he wants."

Bert sat back down. "Why did he talk to you, anyway, and not me? What did he think he could get you to do if I weren't in on it?" She knew the answer before the words were out of her mouth.

Bert was burning him up with her eyes. Charles looked down again and hugged his chest with his arms.

"Go, on, tell me," she urged.

He cleared his throat again and dropped his arms to his sides. He had sense enough not to look at her. "Well, I told him I'd get you to ease up a little. That's what I said at first."

"Papa said that wasn't enough," Bert burst in. "He wanted Bob to come down there and live with them."

She smashed her fist into the table and let out a sob of rage. Quentin began to cry quietly, but he stayed behind the stove.

"Were you just going to give him Bob, then, as though he's no more to you than a good pig or a fat calf?" She sobbed again."What kind of a father are you, who won't even fight for your own boy!"

Charles interrupted her before she could say anything else.

"Of course I don't want to give him Bob. I love Bob as much as you do; you know I do. But think about it, Bert. It's not just the farm; it's the House on the Hill." Charles sneezed again and blew his nose.

"Where else are we going to live? Except for that year in Casey County, we've always lived here. Every one of our children was born in this house; you were born here , and all your sisters and brother were born here, too. It's our house; it's your house. Bert, what do you want me to do?"

Bert was silent. How she had hated this old house when Papa dragged her and Charles back from Casey County to it! She had hated it when the roof over the front room had gotten a hole in it, and the rain was filling up a bucket on the floor almost faster than she could empty it, and Charles didn't want to get up on the roof and fix it. The house had almost made her sick with hate when Mary Virginia declared she wouldn't live in it and go to school in Pride. She had hated it when Caroline died in it.

But Charles was right. It was her house. Slowly, Bert looked around her worn-out kitchen and through into the cold dining room beyond it. She turned and looked first out of one and then out of the other of the two curtained kitchen windows and then out the door to the porch at the same sights she had seen almost every day since she had been a child.

She knew this house and the land around it as well as she knew her own body. She could have stood with her eyes closed and named every crack on its walls and ceilings. She could have put her foot deliberately on the exact spot that made each floorboard creak. She knew where the windows leaked air and just how much force it took to make the front and the back doors slam. She would recognize the peculiar smell of the fire in its grate in the front room if she were in China. Nothing in its parlor was hidden to her; nothing in the little room off the back. The privy and the chicken yard were hers; the Easter flower bulbs she had planted, the pear tree and the apple trees and the maple trees in front, all were hers, and she loved them.

"Charles," she said at last, "this time I'm going to out figure my father, if it's the last thing I do."

Charles didn't answer. His wife sat perfectly still. To her husband her face was as blank as a wall. Charles stood and watched her silently for a long time while she thought. Quentin had come out from behind the stove. Now he knelt quietly on the floor building houses of his own with blocks and corncobs.

Outside, the wind had died down, and for the first time that day Charles noticed the sun was out. The sun coming in the kitchen windows cast long shadows on the floor and up the side of the wall where the kitchen cupboard stood, and dust motes floated in the pale yellow light. The clock Bert and Charles had received from Aunt Lucy as a wedding present was ticking on the mantel in the front room. Charles could hear its ticks blending with the familiar sounds of the house creaking and groaning. He would have supposed the sun made the house do that, but he'd noticed its noises before in all kinds of weather, in all temperatures.

Soon Charles Ray and Bob would be coming up the road, home from school. He pictured his boys in the trees at the bottom of the hill, laughing and calling "Mother, Mother." In his mind, he saw them running past the fence he had left to rot all these years, up the front steps of the house, and into the banged-up door. He imagined himself later this very day coming in from the barn, walking up the back steps at suppertime, to find his wife silent and his children noisy as they jumped up to greet him coming into the kitchen.

All of this filled him with sadness and kept him thinking, but he didn't think, then, of the hard times in the House on the Hill that had not been of his own doing. He thought, rather, of what he now could see were his own failures—of what he had done to Bert; of caving in to Papa; of the times he had gone out when Bert had had her gallstone attacks; of his inability to make a go of farming; of the days he had spent at the race-track. He was filled with despair. Bert had blamed him for all these things, and she had been right.

As for Bert, she turned her attention for the first time in a long time to her husband, not to his failures, but to her husband himself. She thought of that year in Casey County after she and Charles were married. She recalled, now, how much Charles had loved to teach school—

not that she had ever really considered what he did as teaching. She didn't tell herself that she had loved him then, but she sat remembering Charles before they had married, as he had been when she first knew him, handsome and full of fun, lightening the air around her by his total lack of Papa's terrible pushing and pulling energy. She had married him for the very ways he hadn't been Papa.

She thought about Charles's Ma and Pa; it was still amazing to her how they had never bullied or forced Charles to do anything in his life he didn't want to do, and she wondered for a moment if that was what had gone wrong in their lives, why Papa had had such power over them, why she had had to work so hard, why she and Charles and the children were all so poor.

She had often blamed Charles in her mind for their troubles, but she recalled, now, in this moment of danger, what she had heard all her life: "there is none righteous, no not one," and she suspected that this meant her, too. She had never been able to make herself think directly about hard things like Papa stealing Bob, and now, here they were. If she'd been able to face up to it, maybe she and Charles could have talked to each other and thought of something together.

All that was past, now; now she had to think about Papa. Papa was determined to take Bob, and he was threatening to take the house if she didn't let him do it. She had no intention of letting Bob live with Papa and her mother; but even if she did, she knew now that in the end it wouldn't save the House on the Hill for them or even make it more secure. Letting Bob go would only encourage Papa to keep after them as he already had for all these years until he owned her and Charles and the children entirely, body and soul.

She had to face the fact that as long as her father had anything to do with it, the House on the Hill would never be safe. He would never give up control of it. This house was built upon the sand just as surely as the one that Jesus talked about in the parable. What she needed now was a house built on a rock, a solid rock. She needed a sure foundation, and she needed to save their lives.

It came to her all of a sudden what Jesus had meant when he said that the woman who tried to save her life would lose it, but the one who was willing to lose her life would save it. All those years ago in Casey County, Charles had tried to save his life and hers, too, by giving in to

Papa when he offered them this house, and whatever she had told her-self over the years, it had suited her.

Now it seemed to Bert that there was only one thing left to do. She would have to save their lives, particularly Bob's life, by losing her own. She would have to trust that maybe, in some way she couldn't quite imagine, what was true of lives would also turn out to be true of houses, even her house, so that in some form she couldn't even foresee, the House on the Hill might come back to her.

The light in the kitchen had begun to change; the children would be home soon. Bert sat quietly a few more moments watching the light as she accustomed herself to her decision.

"Charles?" she said, at last, but Charles was lost somewhere in his own sadness, and she had to call him again. "Charles?"

Finally, Charles looked at her.

"Take the car and drive to Papa's and tell him Bert's decided," she said. "As soon as we can, we're leaving the farm. We're moving away from this place, out of the House on the Hill. We'll find a place to live with a big garden I can take care of, and you'll get some other work. Go now, and tell him."

With that, Bert pushed her chair away from the table, picked up Quentin, and walked to the front door to watch for Bo and Bob before Charles could as much as reply.

As for Charles, he was stunned. He sat there for a few more minutes, trying to make sense of what she had told him. It hadn't occurred to her to give him any of her reasoning, and it never occurred to him now to ask. If they had talked about it together, they might have recognized the truth—that she and he could save their souls from Papa by giving up the House on the Hill, but it was going to be harder than that to save their child.

A few minutes later Charles got up from his chair and walked out the backdoor past the barn and the chicken house to the edge of the field by the road. Waiting at the front door, Bert watched him look down the road in the direction of the school, then walk back to the car.

She saw him open the door and sit sideways on the front seat for a few more minutes, his feet resting on the running board. Then, without looking back at her, Charles started up the engine and drove down the road toward Papa's.

CHAPTER SEVEN

Power

You know, Panny, power is a funny thing. I was sure I knew what it was when I was a little girl, or at least what it was good for. Power was what stronger people used to make weaker people to do what they wanted. God exercised power over human beings. Men exercised power over women, especially wives; grown-ups, especially parents and teachers, exercised it over children; boys, especially athletic ones, exercised it over girls.

What I thought of the moral status of power, however, was another matter. Whether people had an actual, cosmic right to power by virtue of being grown-ups or husbands, parents or boys, I couldn't have told you. I only knew that half of me accepted as inevitable and right the structures of power that ruled my life. Everybody knew that men—ministers and policemen, doctors and dentist—and certain women—teachers and nurses, secretaries and mothers who were their henchwomen—were, after all, in charge of the world, and that the authority of even atheist fathers like mine was founded in the absolute rights of God. What else but the weight of universal divine law could have been implied in Daddy's "because I said so," the standard reply to my occasional risky question, "why do I have to?"

The other half of me, however, the rebellious half, could never accept the idea that any person, even God, should have a right to tell me what to do only because they were able to hurt me if I didn't submit. I hated my father's power over my mother, and I hated the power that my mother wielded over me on his behalf. Though I'm afraid I did believe in the inevitability of it, I raged against the idea that such power could ever on principle have the authority of God or the weight of the universe behind it.

If my mother felt any ambiguities about such power and its distribution when I was a child, she never let on to me. In those days before my father left her, her concern as a good woman of her time—which was the late forties and very early fifties—was that I learn to accept this power and submit to it as necessary, as she did herself. Her response to my indignant question "why do I have to do dishes when Freddy doesn't?" always given in an outraged, how-dare-you-ask-it voice, was "because he is a boy and you are a girl."

She kept giving the same answer, too, even after my father left her and I was a teenager. She used to tell me regularly that I should "be sure and marry a man who is smarter than you so that you can at least respect him, since you'll have to do what he says."

Oh, Panny, how very much I wanted to believe with a single heart what she and everybody else in those days told me. In fact, I don't think there was much I wanted more than just to be able to accept what everyone I knew seemed to think was right and then be peaceful with it! With my entire child's heart I longed to be able to be a good girl, to be obedient, quiet, and submissive to God's and my father's male power, to not challenge that power with unsuitable questions, to want to play indoors nicely with dolls rather than wanting to take part in the boys' games outside, to be docile, to want to grow up to have a life like my mother's.

No wonder I devoured so eagerly stories from the library of pliant, willowy, long-haired girls, attractive girls who helped their mothers and did what their fathers told them, girls who were rewarded for their submissiveness by being loved by their fathers and their future husbands. Identifying with these heroines gave me hope that one day I might be this way myself. The real fact of the matter, however, was that in my heart I knew better. I continued to be mesmerized by these stories over the years for the same reason I found irresistible Bible stories of children rescued by God from pits and altars, and fairy tales with dragons, witches, and fairy godmothers. They offered me a glimpse into an alternative universe that was impossible for me to live in but which I craved.

For years, as a child and as an adult, I continued to long to be a "good" woman of the sort I had heard about. What else could I do? I didn't know that I had any alternative: there was no "women's movement" as there is today, and I had not yet noticed the difference between what Mama told me to do and what she did herself, nor in spite of being your namesake, did I notice that you never told me these things at all.

So, in my desire to be good, caught between my fear of what would happen to me if I found a way to submit and my dread of what would happen to me if I didn't, at eighteen I married a man—a boy, really—who was just the sort of man I thought Mama wanted me to marry because he had two outstanding characteristics she had taught me to admire in my father. Like Daddy, he was smart and funny, and I was convinced that, like Daddy, he would exercise proper male authority over me.

Both of us were too young to marry, and so there were rivers of unhappiness in our marriage from the beginning, but you always knew this, didn't you? No one could have lived with my complex, depressed, and exhausted intelligence, resentful rebellion, and confusion over what it might mean for me to be a woman. In spite of plenty of evidence to the contrary, I experienced myself as powerless at the same time I believed that I was a "bad" woman because I had failed again and again serenely and lovingly to accept a husband's power with respect to his wife as right.

I am not sure, Panny, how long it was after my divorce before I fully realized that, when it came to questions of power and powerlessness, neither my judgments on my life as a "bad" child nor on myself as weak and helpless in the unsuccessful years of my first marriage were accurate.

I do know that my first real inkling of the disparity between how I had judged myself and what my actual strength was came in a moment of almost-insight many years before my divorce, the summer Anna Grace, my daughter, your oldest great-granddaughter, turned three years old.

It came to me during a typical afternoon in those hard times. Anna Grace had awakened early that morning, as she always did, talking and singing to herself in her crib.

I had been awakened several times in the night already, and I was worn out from teaching and working on my dissertation as well as from being wife, mother, and housekeeper. Still, I staggered out of bed, in my usual puffy-eyed, achy morning condition, and helped Anna Grace down the stairs, all the while trying my best to keep her quiet.

The bulk of my morning was spent sitting on the gold rug in the living room building blocks with Anna Grace and reading over and over *The Tale of Peter Rabbit.* I prepared lunch for the three of us, after which she took a short nap. At last I had a little time to work in an exhausted stupor on my own dissertation.

Anna Grace spent the latter part of the day before supper with Rachel, the dark-haired teenaged baby-sitter who came in several afternoons a week while I worked two more hours on my research. During the time with Rachel that day, Anna Grace did what she liked to do best, drawing and coloring and telling herself stories about what she drew. At the end of the afternoon after Rachel had gone home, while I was having a cup of tea that was intended to give me the energy to cook supper, your great-granddaughter presented me with the picture she had drawn.

Panny, when she brought it, it was clear from her grin and her sparkly eyes that it was supposed to be the picture to end all pictures. Tired as I was, I tried to give it my complete attention. I examined it closely, turning it first one way, then another. The trouble was, no matter how I looked at it I couldn't understand what I was looking at. I could make out a tree with a bird's nest and a bird in it to the left of the picture, along with a house with smoke coming out of the chimney toward the right. In the center, however, there was some enormous round, brown, three-yellow-toed, two-footed animal I couldn't name just standing there. While I was puzzling over what it could mean, Anna Grace was turning self-satisfied circles round and round me; the hem of her red dress stood out like a ballerina's.

"This is a very nice picture," I said to her when I finally gave up hope that I would ever figure her art work out by myself. By now she was jumping up and down; her pigtails were bouncing as she giggled and clapped her hands. "Can you tell me what it is a picture of?"

The giggling increased, along with the jumping. She pointed to the nest and its contents in the tree in the left-hand corner of the picture.

"That is the daddy bird," she said; "he is very, very little and he eats worms." Trusting and unsuspecting as I was, I nodded my head as though I knew what was coming.

Then she put her finger on the large unidentified animal that hulked disgustingly in the middle of what she'd drawn. "That is the mama bird," she explained. "The mama bird is as big as a house and it eats cows!"

Do you know, Panny, for a few moments I was so taken aback I couldn't do anything but stand there looking at the picture with my mouth hanging open. I had no illusions about who the giant, cow-eating bird in Anna Grace's picture was. It was I, her mother! In those bad old days of the 1960s, when the worst thing a woman could be was "strong," when every good wife detested a strong woman, and every psychologist blamed her for ruining the lives of her children and husband forever, the judgment her picture rendered on me struck me, symbolically speaking, as terrible. How could she see me as powerful like this—I, who, I believed, had done a fairly good job disguising my ambivalence from her? What had I done to my female child, I wondered, to appear so strong? I certainly never saw myself this way! What was she going to have to pay for what seemed to her to be my strength in her own later life?

Then I looked at Anna Grace as she continued to dance around me, laughing, and, at least for a moment, I came to my senses. It made me happy to think that she saw me as big and powerful next to her normal-sized father, however I might perceive myself.

I picked her up and hugged her hard as she wrapped her legs around my waist. "It is a very nice picture, Anna Grace. You can grow up and be just as big and strong as your Mama, " I said to her. "Would you like a hamburger for supper?"

Though I still would hardly describe myself as a cow-eating woman as big as a house, I do recognize and take real pleasure in my own strength now in a way I never could when I was younger. I certainly no longer think of myself as having been a bad child or a weak woman because I couldn't accept what I was told about power, men and women, and their place in the world. In fact, considering how much I wanted to be loved and accepted by the adults in my life, I see now that it took a strong child, and then a strong woman, to resist all that stuff about being female which was forced upon me in those days, even if my resistance did leave me feeling deceptively weak and depressed.

I still want to be seen as good and loved, of course, and it still hurts me when I'm not, but that is another matter. Weak I wasn't then, and weak I wasn't later when with a single-minded focus I resisted all the pressures on me to quit graduate school and be the woman I was expected to be. Strength has been what I've needed in order to take the risks I've taken in the years since to have the things I've wanted in life. I've taken plenty of risks and I've had plenty of strength to take them, too—strength that I can count on in myself that has nothing to do with exercising power over anybody else.

Certainly, this strength is far from heroic. Sometimes, it seems to me, it has been more the strength of weeds, like the thick root of a dandelion boring stubbornly down ten feet through the hard dirt to thrive. It has been an absolute single-minded focus that keeps me writing now, day after day, no matter what else is going on in my life. It is endurance, but it is also the power to renounce something I want—like rest or peace—for example, for what I want even more.

What a long time it took me to recognize how false was my old way of understanding God's power as a kind of bullying ability to get people to do what God wants because God is bigger and smarter than human beings! How many years before I was able to abandon the thought that such a bullying divine power underwrote what I believed to be the legitimate power of men over women! How long before I could see that God's power has no need of slaves of any kind!

But I don't believe there was ever a time, Panny, when you didn't know what it took me so long to learn. I think you were always strong. It was this enduring strength that enabled you to take the risk to choose a man to marry who was as unlike your father as any you could have picked out for yourself, a man who broke every rule your family set but who wouldn't dominate you or lord it over you. He appreciated you, too. I remember him saying to Mama, Aunt Kas, and Aunt Suzie, when you were eighty-five years old and on one of your worst high horses, "You girls will never be half the woman your mother is."

It was this that enabled you to stand against what your bullying father wanted for you and move away from Union County, in spite of your flattening, back-breaking depressions. It was also this strength that kept you fighting Papa and his mental illness and, let's face it, his meanness, year after year until you flung away the very house you and most of your children were born in, in exchange for your freedom from Papa and the well-being of your son Bob.

Panny, as a child, seeing you draped only in the wet, dirty rags of the depression I shared with you then, I wasn't aware of any of this about God or about you or the strong house you actually lived in, and I'm sorry. You, the woman whose namesake I was, were a woman of power, and I needed to know it. Seeing as I'm still your namesake, I need to know it even now. It puts the floor under my feet, and a fire in my stove.

CHAPTER EIGHT

Making Jelly

esus, lover of my soul, let me to thy bosom fly," Bert sang slowly. "Mary Virginia," she interrupted herself. "Take those jelly jars out of the steamer and line them up on the table. I knew we should have started this jelly earlier. It's hot as Hades in this kitchen. Oh me, I don't know what's the matter with me these days. I just can't work like I used to."

Bert and Mary Virginia were in the kitchen of the O'Nan house, the white frame tenant farmer's house on the other side of the main road into Sturgis they had moved into two years earlier when they left the House on the Hill.

Across the flat fields that lapped up against the O'Nan place on the kitchen side, the harsh morning sun poured through the open window above the sink. The black stove filled the kitchen; its broad top radiated heat, barely muffling the coals inside it. Though the backdoor stood wide open, the steam from the recently boiling grapes condensed in tears on the green paint of the walls and hung in the room like a cloud.

Bert hadn't expected to be making grape jelly this summer. There had been so many grapes at the House on the Hill that they had hardly known what to do with them, but no vines grew behind the O'Nan house, where they lived now. Last year she had been too angry and proud to accept any of the fruit her mother had offered them. This year she was still angry, but she had accepted three bushels of cloudy blue grapes from her mother's arbor. In spite of herself Bert had been glad to get them. She was enjoying her work; today her complaints were more a matter of habit than they were of substance.

Hands purple and hair drenched to the roots with sweat, Bert had just finished pouring cooked grape juice and skins from the pot through the layers of cheesecloth lining the sieve that sat above the second, smaller pot on the stove. She was encouraging the juice to run through the cloth, leaving behind the pulp, skins, and seeds of the cooked grapes.

Bert was filled with pleasure by the sight of the juice. At the same time, Mary Virginia was making it obvious that she had no intention of sharing that pleasure. Today she hated her mother's hymn singing, and she was in no mood for conversation. Taller than her mother by a head, she let her shoulders slump ostentatiously.

Bert glanced at her daughter and shook her head. She wasn't about to give in to Mary Virginia's huffiness. She had reminded her repeatedly that they were making jelly today, and still Mary Virginia had come in after everyone else had gone to bed. Bert had intended to get her out of bed this morning along with everybody else. As it was, at the last minute she had taken pity on her, letting Mary Virginia lie there another half hour while she started breakfast. Mary Virginia had not been grateful.

As Bert's wooden spoon mashed at the grape mixture in the bottom of the sieve, she glanced again at her daughter's sullen face.

"Maybe we should have made some grape marmalade this year, Mary Virginia, like we used to," she said. "What do you think? It's more work than jelly, but it's good."

Bert picked up the bag of pulp and skins and slowly squeezed it into the sieve with her hands. Juice oozed out of the cloth in clots and splashed through the sieve.

Mary Virginia didn't answer.

"Do you remember the grapes at the House on the Hill?" Bert went on. "The ones over the back porch were so pretty this time of the summer. Remember how good it tasted with angel food cake in the winter time?"

Mary Virginia refused to be drawn out. She was struggling to lift the hot jelly jars out of the enameled pan without dropping them from the tongs or burning herself. She could barely get her breath in the steamy kitchen. She shouldn't have had to get up so early, she thought resentfully.

Mary Virginia knew she was being unfair to her mother, but she just wanted to be left alone. She couldn't bear to have Bert mention the House on the Hill so casually. Losing the house was the worst thing that had ever happened to her. It was like Grammar's Beautiful House burning down, only much worse. It was impossible; it was her house, where she'd been born, where all of them except Bob had been born. She still couldn't understand why they had moved out of it, what it was that had made them leave.

She thought about the House on the Hill almost all the time. She knew everything had not been wonderful there. Being at Grammar and Papa's as much as she had, she'd been out of the house as much as she'd been in it. When she was honest with herself, she admitted that she'd usually been glad to be gone. There was so much work to do when her mother was sick, and she was sick most of the time.

Still, they'd had such good times there. Her mother had been different, then. She had let Kas and her dress the cat in her good baby clothes right in the kitchen. She'd told her to climb the rafters in the barn to find the baby birds in the dove's nest high up in the roof. She knew she was being melodramatic, but sometimes Mary Virginia imagined that life in the House on the Hill had been like the preachers described the garden of Eden. She wondered if she would ever get over losing her house, if she would ever feel safe again.

In the heat of the kitchen, Mary Virginia thought about the ice cream her mother had made for them every summer Sunday on the back porch, under those grapes her mother had asked her about. Week after week, while the green clusters ripened above their heads, the children took turns cranking the freezer in its ice and salt inside the wooden churn. She remembered how the crank in the churn would go more slowly as the ice cream began to set. She saw her mother as she scraped away the crust of ice and salt from the top of the canister, then lifted out the paddle to set it in a soup bowl for the children. In her mind, she watched as Bert repacked the canister in ice and covered it with newspaper while the ice cream inside got firm enough to eat.

Now they hardly ever had ice cream. It was no good; there was no use trying to escape it. Mary Virginia hated their life as it was now. They couldn't keep their own cows here, and the milk they got from Great-aunt Lucy across the way had already been skimmed of its cream.

Mary Virginia recalled the dripping taste of the first bites of soft cream. Her grief made her angry. "Of course, it's hot," she answered at last. "It's supposed to be hot. I'd think starting right after breakfast would be early enough for anybody."

Mary Virginia's voice trembled as she went on. "And you've been saying you can't work as hard as you used to all my life. Grammar says it all the time, too. I'm sick of hearing it from both of you!" She banged down the jar she had picked out of the steamer and wiped around her face with the hem of her apron.

Surprised, Bert put down what she had in her hands, rinsed them and wiped them on a rag. Mary Virginia was far more upset than Bert had thought.

"Mary Virginia," Bert said, "tell your old mother what the matter is."

"It's this house," Mary Virginia answered. "I can't live in this house! I hate it!" She began to sob.

The O'Nan house was the sorriest house she'd ever seen, so sorry dogs didn't want to live under its porch. It was nothing like the House on the Hill. There were no shade trees around it, and hardly any flowers or bushes to make it look as though it belonged where it was. Leading into the two square front rooms, it had two ugly white front doors, one on each side of the cramped porch. The other two rooms sat behind them, the same size and shape as the front rooms. There were no added-on places, no halls, and no privacy. Rather, each room opened directly and skimpily into the others in such a way that everybody—Mother and Daddy, Mary Virginia and Kas, Charles Ray and Bob, when he wasn't at Papa's, and Quentin and Suzie—all lived on top of each other like writhing puppies.

She hated the house and she blamed it for all the chaos and anxiety in their lives since they'd moved into it two years earlier. It was a weak house, unable to do what a house was supposed to do. The very way the flat black fields came up against its peeling walls made her wonder if, some night after the moon was gone, the malignant dirt wouldn't topple the house right into the road in front of it.

Mary Virginia was humiliated by it. She knew she was better than this house, but how would anybody else know if this was where they lived? Grammar had always said to her, "Don't grow up and marry a hired hand," and now, here she was living in a hired hand's house. It angered her and puzzled her that her mother never acted as though she minded. How could she hold her head up when she visited Grammar and Papa? How could she live across from Aunt Lucy's big house her great-grandfather Wynns had built as though it were nothing?

Recently, Mary Virginia had been wondering if her mother even noticed how poor they were. She knew Bert had never stayed inside that much. Except when she had her babies, her mother had always been an outdoor woman who spent more time in the garden than in the house. Though the year they moved it had been too late for a garden, the next year Bert had planted a vegetable garden and not only filled the table for the summer but the root cellar for the winter as well. Even that first year she had knocked together a chicken house out of some old boards she'd found, put up a chicken wire fence, and got herself some hens.

In actual fact, Mary Virginia hadn't seen any evidence that her mother knew the difference between where they were now and where they'd been. As she thought of the enormous heap of clean laundry on the dining room table in the back room where she slept now with Kas and Suzie, tears of self-pity welled up in her eyes. Her mother hadn't folded up that laundry and put it away even at the end. Bert had stuffed the pile just as it was right into the boxes, carried it from one house to the other, and dumped it out on the same table at the other end.

"Come on," Bert said, gently, "tell your mother what's the matter."

Mary Virginia wouldn't answer. Ashamed of her tears, she turned her back and wiped her teary face on her apron. If her own mother didn't care how they lived, then Mary Virginia wasn't going to care, either. She could take care of herself. She looked at the gold watch Jimmy Innes had given her for her seventeenth birthday.

Bert saw her look at the watch. "It's not just the house, is it?" she said.

Mary Virginia shook her head and crossed her arms. "I don't want to talk about it," she said.

Bert smiled; whether she liked it or not, Mary Virginia had just begun a conversation that her mother had been intending to have for a long time. Now, with the same gestures Mary Virginia had made, she wiped her own face on the hem of her apron.

"Let's sit down and rest a minute, Mary Virginia," she said. "We could both do with a cold drink."

Slowly, grudgingly, Mary Virginia sat down at the crowded table across from her mother. She set her elbows on the table and put her face in her hands. She hadn't meant to be ugly to her mother. She knew she was being awful; she just felt so bad and so confused.

Bert glanced at her daughter. Even with her puffy eyes and her pout Mary Virginia was pretty. Bert had always been proud of her, of her loyalty, of her desire to be good, of the way people liked her, of her fearlessness.

She remembered the time when Mary Virginia had won the gold medal in the county-wide declaiming contest. Aunt Nacky had had her up in the hayloft coaching her every afternoon for six weeks, teaching her how to shout out "Thanatopsis" till they could hear her in the next county. They always said Nacky should have gone to New York and been an actress.

Bert had felt vindicated in front of Papa when Mary Virginia had beaten the Henderson girls, though Bert didn't know what she'd been vindicated against, exactly. Mary Virginia was smart and she worked hard. She was not going to have a life like her mother's, if Bert had anything to do with it. Mary Virginia's life would be better than hers had ever been.

Beneath her stained apron, Bert took a breath, straightened her shoulders, and considered where to start. She pushed the jelly jars to one side, took down two big-stemmed, ball-shaped glasses with the thumb prints in the sides and set them on the table. She went out to the porch, chipped off some ice from the ice box, and filled the glasses with ice and tea from the glass pitcher on the cupboard next to the sink. She stirred three spoons of sugar into each glass then sat down.

Bert took a big swallow of tea.

"Well, Mary Virginia," she said, "I guess you're right. I do say a lot that I can't work as hard as I used to. I know you get tired of hearing it, but I'm just not good for much of anything anymore. I guess I'm just plain tired from all that working on the farm over the years and from having all those babies."

Bert waited. Mary Virginia didn't answer.

Bert tried again from another direction. "It was mighty late when you came in last night. I notice Jimmy's been bringing you home past bed-time every time you've been out all summer."

Mary Virginia looked up, sullen. "It wasn't all that late," she said.

"Too late for me to be lying in bed waiting for you when I've got to get up the next morning and take care of this family," Bert answered.

Furious, Mary Virginia responded without thinking. "You're the one that had all those babies," she said. "Nobody made you do it."

Bert looked at her, surprised. Mary Virginia cringed. She wasn't sure how she felt about having babies herself, but the idea of her mother doing that sort of thing enraged her. She remembered the awful day she had found out Bert was expecting Quentin. Mary Virginia had been twelve years old and sure she knew everything there was to know about life in general and women's lives in particular.

"Mother, how could you do this to me?" she had shouted, pouting out like a two-year-old. "My own mother! Now everybody knows what you and Daddy have been doing. How am I going to go to school? The two of you ought to be ashamed of yourselves acting like that at your age!"

She couldn't recall exactly what her mother had answered back; she was afraid she laughed.

"Mary Virginia," Bert called her from the memory, "there's a lot you need to know that you don't seem to have caught on to. If you're married to a farmer, you have his babies and you work till you drop, whether you want to or not. That's just the way it is. I have to do it. Your grandmother had to do it, too, when she was younger, and if you keep coming in late and you don't watch out, the same thing's going to happen to you before you turn around. Is that what you want?"

"What are you talking about? I'm just trying to have a good time!" she said, her voice rising. "It's because I hate this house. I hate being poor. Nobody in this house ever has a good time but Daddy, and even then, I can tell you don't like it."

Bert put off answering her daughter's accusations. She wasn't about to lose her chance to speak to what Mary Virginia had said about the house.

"I know you hate this house, honey, and I want you to have a good time," she said; "but you're thinking about marrying Jimmy Innes to get away from here, aren't you?" Bert stopped for a moment; Mary Virginia didn't reply.

Bert went on. "What kind of a house and what kind of a time are you going to have if you marry him? You'll live in one house after another just like this, and you'll have his babies and work yourself to death worse than I do. He wouldn't save a penny if his life depended on it; just look at the watch on your arm. He'll never be a provider. Everybody in the county knows his daddy's not a worker; he stays in bed till seven o'clock every morning of the world."

Bert went on, "His family never has amounted to anything. Not a one of them would have a book in the house if they had to."

Mary Virginia ducked her head. This was private. Why did Grammar and Papa and her mother have to think they were better than everybody else? Her daddy always told her she was as good as anybody and better than nobody.

"Where's Daddy today?" she asked, suddenly.

Generally Bert answered this question evasively. This time she answered truthfully. "At the races in Henderson. It's not like he gambles, you know; he just goes for the company and the excitement, but I don't care. From the day we got married it seems like he's always been someplace else when I need him. You're old enough to know it. You get yourself a man who will be there when you need him. You marry a man who will work, who won't let money run through his hands like water. Don't you marry a man who farms for somebody else, either."

Mary Virginia was shocked. She could hardly believe her mother was saying what she was hearing.

"Your father never could farm," Bert went on. "His own mother always said not a one of her boys would work with his back if he could figure out a way to use his brain." She paused. "Of course, your daddy was going to be a teacher. He wanted to be around people. He never wanted to be by himself in a field all day long. He wasn't a farmer when I married him, you know. That was Papa's doing."

Mary Virginia ran her finger under Jimmy Lee's stretchy gold watchband where it had been pushed up on her arm for jelly making. She'd known her father had been a schoolteacher when her parents got married, but this was the first she'd heard of Papa making him quit. Was this why her mother fought Papa all the time? Mary Virginia knew better than to ask about it. The grown-ups never let children know that kind of thing, and even if they did she wasn't sure she wanted to know the answer.

"What makes you think I'm about to marry Jimmy, anyway?" she asked instead.

"Because you come in with your mouth funny from kissing, and you think I don't notice," Bert answered. Mary Virginia looked away.

"And because I remember when I was your age." Bert hesitated. "That old urge will get you, sure as the world. Nature wants babies. The first time I saw your father, I just about went crazy."

Mary Virginia flushed. Even though she was almost grown up, she hated to think that not just her father, but her mother, too, had once been interested in that kind of thing.

Another memory from the House on the Hill came back to her. It was some time after Quentin was born. Her mother and daddy were sleeping on the Murphy bed in the parlor, and she and Kas slept on a corn-shuck–filled mattress in the little room off the porch, as they always did in summer. It was storming. Sharp claps of thunder alternated with bursts of vivid lightning, and the rain threw little pebbles sideways against the window glass. As she got up to close the windows, Kas had heard strange sounds coming from the other side of the wall.

Kas shook her awake to listen. Mary Virginia had known at once what she was hearing. She had jumped out of the bed and pounded on the wall.

"You stop that right this minute," she had shouted to them both. "I know what you're doing in there!" Instantly, the noises had ceased.

At the table Mary Virginia shifted in her chair uncomfortably. Suddenly, she couldn't stand to think of herself doing any of this with Jimmy.

"I might kiss Jimmy," she said earnestly, "but that's all I'll ever do." Her voice took on a hint of injured righteousness. "You know you raised me to be good. Besides, Grammar told me women who like that kind of thing are disgusting," she added.

Bert groaned. It was true that Grammar never had trusted that any good could come out of human bodies touching each other. She hadn't even liked holding her own babies. Her grandmother had been suggesting all Mary Virginia's life that even married women didn't have any business giving in to "that sort of thing." Ever since Bert could remember, whenever Grammar had seen a woman she knew was going to have a baby, she would say, "Look at her! She ought to be ashamed of herself!" Then she would make a noise through her nose and end with, "Some women just can't control their passions!" Why Bert hadn't ever entirely believed her own mother, she didn't know.

Bert looked at Mary Virginia in frustration. This was the first conversation they had had about how women act with men, and now she was having to argue both sides at once.

"Mary Virginia," Bert said gently, "I know you love your grandmother, but what she told you isn't right. She used to tell me the same thing when I was a girl, but it's 1935. She's an old woman, and that's the way her parents raised her. I've heard Grandma Ginny say the same things; she thought women who wanted that kind of thing were 'common' though she had enough children of her own. There's no telling what Grandpa Sam thought. After all, he was a preacher."

Mary Virginia shifted in the chair uncomfortably.

"I know there's nothing wrong with having babies, Mary Virginia, and there's nothing wrong with married people liking laying in the same bed together, either."

She kept on talking, though she could hardly believe she was saying these things to her own daughter. "Married women can't help having babies, anyway. Your Grammar talks like it's a wife's choice, but look at her. She had six babies herself, even though I've heard your great aunts say she never would have married in the first place, if it had been left up to her."

"What do you mean, 'if it had been left up to her,' mother?" Mary Virginia interrupted.

Bert went on as though she hadn't heard her. "I know what I've heard the preachers say, but I don't know that I believe all that much of it. I've read the Bible since I was a little girl, and it says in the Bible that a man and a woman ought to cleave to each other. It says it in Genesis, and Jesus said it, too, as plain as anything. Now, Mary Virginia, I know you are a Christian and you still believe in the Bible, even if you are a Methodist. I think Jesus means for women to be happy with their husbands, and I don't care what anybody says."

Bert paused; Mary Virginia was too astounded and embarrassed to answer.

Bert went on, "I'm just worried you wouldn't be happy married to Jimmy Innes."

Mary Virginia anxiously drank her cold tea in its big sweaty glass. She didn't know what Bert expected her to say. She'd certainly never heard her mother talk like this before. Even now, Mary Virginia didn't know whether Bert was saying what she really believed or if she was just trying to get her to break up with Jimmy because she didn't think the Inneses were good enough for her.

Bert didn't give her any help. She wondered what her daughter was thinking as she sat there at the table in the hot kitchen.

"You don't love him, do you?" Bert guessed at last. Mary Virginia didn't disagree. "I didn't think so. You don't even care that much about kissing him." A light brown sediment of sugar lay on the bottom of the nearly empty glass. Bert swirled the sugar back up into the remaining tea and drank it down.

Mary Virginia sighed; she had done her best to be in love. Her friends at school all were crazy to be in love. Whatever her mother said about him and his family, Jimmy was a nice boy who could marry her and take her away from the O'Nan place. He certainly was in love with her. She'd wanted to be in love with him, too, like the women in the magazines she read at the drugstore.

But her mother was right. She didn't love him, and she had only let him kiss her because she was pretending to love him. Now she admitted to herself that he bored her to death. No wonder she couldn't even stand him touching her half the time.

She looked down at her arm, at the thin gold watch Jimmy had given her for her birthday. She had felt so grown up when she had unwrapped the little box and he had slipped it over her wrist. She had liked the idea of her watch.

Her pleasure was over. For the first time she noticed how its stretchy metal band was eating into the fleshy part of her forearm where she'd pushed it up for kitchen work. It was sinking into her flesh and pulling at the hair on her arm. She drew the band off over her hand and laid it on the table. She could see where the watch had left a red, indented pattern of interlocking links around her arm. She rubbed her arm and looked at the watch before her sadly.

"No," said Mary Virginia out loud, "I guess I don't love him." She sighed again. She would never sort it out now—what it was she wanted, what she was supposed to want—if her mother told her one thing and her grandmother had already told her another.

The sun had risen high enough that it no longer shone directly in the window, and the remaining steam had melted away through the back door. It was cooler in the kitchen, now, and the glare of light on the walls had softened. Both of them were silent, but it was a different kind of silence than what had been before.

"Mother," Mary Virginia said at last. "There's not a thing that I can do around here but marry some man like Jimmy Innes. I don't want to marry him; I don't want to marry a man like Daddy, and I don't want to marry a man like Papa, either. I don't want to spend my life having babies and washing clothes till I drop in a terrible old house like this one. I don't want to marry a farmer, no matter what. What am I going to do?"

Mary Virginia had come out where Bert had intended. Bert sat quietly a few more minutes to make sure Mary Virginia thought about what she'd just said; then she stood up from the table and put the glasses in the dishpan in the sink. She set the pot of grape juice for the jelly back on the stove and considered what she would say.

"Well then," said Bert, "let me tell you what your father and I have decided."

It seemed to Bert that Mary Virginia was off to the Spencerian Business School in Louisville before she knew it. Her daughter had accepted her and Charles's decision without argument. Charles made the arrangements with the Wesley cousin in charge of the school within a week. His secretary would find her a place to live where she could do a little light work in exchange for her room and board. Bert wrote to Grammar's sister Aunt Gertie. She replied that they were thrilled that Mary Virginia was coming, and she wished so many of them were not already living in their little house that there was no room for her with them.

Mary Virginia's senior year in high school looked pretty much the same as the others; she was in Sturgis or at Grammar's during the week and at home on the weekends. She wore the same dresses, sewn herself on her mother's old treadle Singer sewing machine and ironed with the same flatirons heated on the stove in the kitchen. She rolled up her hair in the same way on the same rags. Sunday mornings she attended the Methodist church in Sturgis with her friends Jane Shaeffer and Laura Belle Smith; Sunday nights she went with them to Epworth League. She passed the time after school drinking soft drinks and leafing through magazines at the round marble tables in Sauer's Drugstore in town. She wore Jimmy Lee Innes's watch on her arm, and every Friday night she went with him to the Sturgis High ball games and dances. She was voted by her class Most Popular Girl and Girl Most Likely to Succeed for the second year in a row.

In many ways Bert thought Mary Virginia had become again the same happy favorite of her aunts and grandparents she had been before they'd left the House on the Hill. Her self-confidence was back. Certainly her sullen anger and unexpected rages against her mother were past.

At the same time, Bert also felt that her daughter was not the same. Whether the difference came from the prospect of her leaving home to go so far away, or whether it was from something else, Bert couldn't tell. Bert had no illusions about Mary Virginia coming back to live in Union County once she was gone, and she wondered whether Mary Virginia realized it.

Still, for whatever reason, from the time of their conversation Mary Virginia began to come in earlier at night. She spent a lot of time outdoors by herself. Now, too, when her brothers and sisters started talking about the House on the Hill, Mary Virginia would often join in.

Sometimes Mary Virginia would walk around the house, absently picking up a rose vase or a glass paperweight with a picture in it. In those moments Bert often wondered what her daughter was thinking, but she never asked and Mary Virginia never told her.

Two days after Mary Virginia graduated from Sturgis High, she left with her father for Louisville in the new black Buick Charles had gone to Morganfield to borrow from her Aunt Blacky's husband, Mack.

They spent the day before she left filling the black-and-white-checked luggage set Grammar and Papa had given her for graduation. Bert and Kas did the packing, putting in the rayon career-girl dresses and the cotton house dresses Mary Virginia had spent the winter sewing, along with the silky underwear and nightgowns Aunt Nacky and Aunt

Ginny had bought for her in town. Mary Virginia's sweaters, white blouses, and wool skirts, her winter coat, and the shoes from Grammar went into the larger case. Her hats they packed in the matching hatbox.

Packing day was hard for everybody. For Bert it was the worst, for she knew without a shadow of a doubt that there was no way Mary Virginia, once gone, would ever come back to live at home. Had she done it for Mary Virginia, she wondered now, or had she done it for herself? Would some husband in the city really make her daughter's life easier than hers had been? She wondered why she hadn't tried harder to send Mary Virginia to college instead of business school.

The morning of the day they packed was the hardest of all. Right after breakfast, Charles mumbled something about chores for Papa and went off somewhere in the truck that had carried their things from the House on the Hill. The two younger children stayed in the house, alternately whining and banging around. Bo and Bob kept out of sight. Kas, hardly speaking, never let her sister out of her sight. Restlessly she refolded and rearranged what had been set in the suitcases a dozen times already.

As for Mary Virginia herself, she hardly knew what she felt. She dropped an open bottle of White Shoulders her friend Jane had given her for graduation right into the smaller suitcase. (Fifteen years later when she returned to Sturgis the faint smell of it was still there.) She hoped to be strong, resourceful, smart, and popular. Contradictorily, the magazines she read told her that, in the world into which she was going, she would also "be swept off her feet by the man of her dreams" and marry, and she wanted that, too.

As she packed, once or twice in the midst of her excitement the real meaning of her going away hit her. She wasn't yet in a position to know the enormous width of the gulf that separated the reality of her new life from what her mother believed that life would be. Still, at some deep level, Mary Virginia was full of dread. How would she be able to live, she wondered, far from the only people in the world who knew her and loved her?

In the afternoon the house was full of shrieking, laughing aunts who came to see her off with stories of the adventures of other, earlier aunts and grandmothers, and the brothers and sons of earlier aunts and grandmothers who had gone places and taken risks. They talked about their own great-grandmother, the grandmother of the terrible Grandma Nack, who had broken, one by one, an entire barrel of dishes on the floor, which her husband had brought all the way from Pittsburgh on an Ohio River steamboat. She'd thought they were ugly; she had told him he should have been ashamed of himself, and sent him back for more. They reminded her again how Grandma Ginny's mother, still unmarried, had traveled during the Civil War all the way to Chicago by herself to nurse her future husband who was suffering with smallpox in a Union camp for prisoners of war. They told again of Great-uncle Bill who had won fifty silver dollars in a rodeo in New Orleans on his honeymoon, riding a bucking bronco while his bride cheered him on. They even mentioned in passing Cousin Swear-to-God Brooks, who had married at fourteen and moved away to bear innumerable children she couldn't support, only to return in a wagon once or twice a year so that Grammar and Papa could fill it up with good food from the farm.

Along with the going-away stories they carried with them, the aunts brought presents, too. Aunt Nacky had a novel, a book of Shakespeare's sonnets, and an outrageous hat covered with flowers as big as oranges. In an act of dramatic self-sacrifice, from her own neck Aunt Ginny unwrapped a long, sea-green scarf with fringe on the ends to wrap around Mary Virginia's. Aunt Blacky, who, like Aunt Ginny, wanted to think of herself as generous but was actually tight, handed over two jars of homemade sweet pickles wrapped in red tissue paper. Aunt Subie, whose husband kept a hand on everything she spent, brought pale orange Japanese lanterns she had grown in her yard and dried over the winter. Grammar, who had really come to supervise, brought a patchwork quilt of maroon and black and sky-blue wool and two new pillows she'd made with down plucked from the white geese that wandered in her yard.

Grammar and the aunts left before supper, raining advice.

"See the world, Mary Virginia," Aunt Nacky said as she stood grinning in the road outside the house. "Learn a lot."

"Be sweet now," Aunt Subie said, kissing her on the cheek—Aunt Subie who had married the man Papa had told her to marry, and who had sobbed out loud all through her own wedding. "Remember to be careful."

"Don't go and get yourself kidnapped now," said Aunt Ginny. When she was twenty years old Aunt Ginny had gotten lost in a corn field, hiding from the imaginary gypsies her wicked sisters had told her had come to carry her off.

"You send that car back with Charles no later than the day after tomorrow, you hear, Mary Virginia?" said Aunt Blacky.

Grammar was the last to say her good-byes, and her advice was the longest. She took Bert's daughter's face in her hands and looked sharply into her eyes. "Mary Virginia," she said, "you are the oldest grand-daughter, and your mother's firstborn to boot. You're a Wynn; remember who you are and do us proud. And toot your own horn, too; nobody else is going to do it for you."

Grammar dropped her hands; Mary Virginia swiped at her eyes with the back of one hand. Grammar stepped back, out of the range of Mary Virginia's arms, and reached into the pocket of her gray skirt.

"Take this handkerchief and blow your nose," she said. "Don't forget your Grammar and don't forget your clean hanky either," she added. Without touching her further, she reached up and gave her grand-daughter a quick kiss on the cheek. Then she turned her back and went down the steps.

They had an early supper, but it was a long time before Mary Virginia went to sleep that night, and once asleep she slept restlessly. She had strange dreams, and in the high bed the two of them still shared, Kas moaned in her sleep and kicked. Sometime before the dawn Mary Virginia gave up the effort and carried the pink milkglass lamp to the kitchen. Quietly, by its familiar light, she dressed. Then she blew out the lamp's flame and walked out into the dark fields that surrounded the house.

A half hour later when she came back to the kitchen, her mother was deviling the eggs, doing up the Mason jars of sweet tea, and frying the chicken. The children came in while the ham was cooking and the bis-cuits were baking, and Charles went out, hawking and sneezing, to milk. Through it all, Bert was silent and Mary Virginia, too, turning the ham and frying the eggs without speaking.

When it was time to go, Bert went out and stood on the front porch to watch Charles pile up Mary Virginia's luggage by the rear end of Uncle Mack's car. She was barely aware of the gray-blue of the early morning August sky, or of the corn in the flat fields surrounding the house.

130

Faintly, Bert smelled the honeysuckle that grew beside the porch, and the sound of a dreary rooster on Aunt Lucy's farm across the road crowing up the hens made her head ring. Soon she found herself imagining the sun dazzling and dancing off the hood of the car as Charles and Mary Virginia drove through Owensboro.

Susie, standing down by the front bumper of the big car, interrupted Bert's musings. "Mother, why does Mary Virginia have to go away?" she asked. Susie thumped her bottom against the side of the car.

Bert tried to pretend she hadn't heard Susie's question. Susie had been asking the same thing for days. Bert could barely stand it. She was so on edge herself her skin was crawling; she could hardly stand to feel her hair against her face or her skirt against her legs.

"Mother," Susie called out again, louder. By now she was sitting on the front bumper, scuffing her feet in the gravel. She squinted her eyes and held up the raggedy hem of her yellow dress to her face. Bert wondered irritably what she was doing with her skirt.

"Susanna Wesley," Bert said at last, "put your skirt down and cover your knickers this minute. You want people to think you're one of those Hadley girls? You know Mary Virginia's going to school. What do you want to keep asking me for, anyway?"

Susie hopped off the car and ran up the steps. She wrapped her arms around her mother's waist. "Mother, that's not what I mean," she said. She looked up into her mother's face, searching. "I mean, why are you making her go away?"

Bert didn't know how to answer. Mary Virginia was not going to work herself to death on some pitiful farm. She was going to be somebody; she was going to make something of herself and show Papa for her, once and for all. Of course, she wasn't about to say any of that to Susie; she'd hardly say it to Mary Virginia. Neither did Bert know how to respond to Susie's grief or to her own anger at Susie's talking back.

Bert looked down at the child for a moment without speaking. Unbidden, a picture formed in her mind of Papa shouting, trying to shame his grown children into silence when they asked about something he considered was his business. Bert didn't want to act like Papa. Gently, she unlocked Susie's hands and pushed her away.

"Susie, Papa Charles and I have our reasons," Bert said. "You are six years old. Children don't need to know about the things grown-ups do.

Mary Virginia doesn't ask questions like you do. Now, you just be happy with what you know." Before Susie had a chance to answer, Bert hugged her and sent her back down the steps.

Down in the road, Bert could see that Charles had just opened the back end of the car. Her stomach was in a knot. Bert turned her head toward the checked suitcases lined up side by side by the rear bumper. The new quilt from Grammar and the new pillow she had made for Mary Virginia from her geese sat tied up in a bundle on the top of her daughter's hatbox. Susie was bending over the bundle, poking at the knot with a stick.

It was getting late. "Mary Virginia," she called back into the house. "I know you've got everything you need. It's almost five-thirty. You'd better come on. The sun's going to be hot as fire on you."

The door banged open; it was not Mary Virginia but rather Bo and Quentin, side by side.

"Mother," Bo said when his eyes lit on Bert, "why is Mary Virginia going away?" He asked it as though he had just now thought of it.

"Mother, Mother." Quentin butted in. "Is she going to live in a house like us? Do they have houses in Louisville? When is she coming home?" Tears ran down his face. "Where's Bob? Why isn't Bob here to say good-bye?"

Papa had come the night before at bedtime to make his own good-bye's. "Mary Virginia, you be careful in that big city," he had said to her, gruffly. Standing in the kitchen, he had taken a wad of bills out of his pocket and put them in her hand. "Here's a little something to tide you over till Christmas."

Then he'd called into the two front rooms, "Where's my boy? Bob, you get yourself in here and come on; I need you to help John Bundy tomorrow morning." Bob had come running, and Bert had been too tired to fight either of them.

Out on the porch, Bert sighed. Grateful even for this particularly unpleasant change of subject, Bert took out her hanky and squatted down beside Quentin to blow his nose. "Bob's not here because Papa came and got him after supper, that's why," Bert answered.

Quentin sniffed again. "I want Bob. I don't see why Bob always has to go home with Papa. I don't like it when everybody goes away."

"I know, I know," Bert answered. She hugged him hard, rocking him in her arms. "Now's the time," she said, "now's the time," and finally, "you run on and see what Susie's doing."

Kas came out next, her arms full and her eyes red. Watching her, Bert wondered how Kas would manage without her sister. They were like twins who had been together through everything. They had chased each other behind the House on the Hill. They had argued over who worked harder on the chores. They had shared the same teacher at the Templeton School and the same bed in the room they rented in Sturgis while they went to Sturgis High. Bert could hardly imagine Kas without Mary Virginia.

"Mother, I'm putting their dinner on the floor of the backseat. I put in coconut cake from last night for dessert, and two dishcloths for napkins." Kas sighed. "I guess they'll stop at the picnic table by the gas station on the other side of Owensboro."

Mary Virginia came out at last, dressed in what Grammar had told her was a businesslike brown-buttoned, green-and-white-print rayon dress that she had worked on all winter. A spit curl of brown hair poked out from under her wide-brimmed sailor hat on the right side of her forehead; the rest of her hair had been rolled into pin curls around the nape of her neck. Unaware of the painful feelings around her, Mary Virginia radiated energy and self-confidence. For a moment it bucked Bert up to see her oldest daughter so full of herself.

"I'm ready, Mother," Mary Virginia said. "Is Daddy about ready?"

"Yes," said Bert. She gave her a kiss. "Don't forget to hold your shoulders back," she said.

Quentin ran over to his big sister and threw his arms around her legs. "You be good, now, while I'm gone," she said to him. "You'll be a big boy when I see you at Christmas."

She turned and gave Kas a last hug. "If you need anything, let me know," Kas whispered in her ear. "If you need me, I'll come."

Mary Virginia opened the backdoor of the car and placed her hat on the gray plush backseat of Uncle Mack's humpbacked black car. Bert waited while she situated herself in the front beside her father, then she kissed Mary Virginia's cheek through the open window. "You work hard now, Mary Virginia," she said. "You work hard and make me proud."

Bert walked around to Charles's side of the car and patted him on the shoulder. "Charles, remember, you be back by dinnertime tomorrow," she said.

As Charles pulled the car out into the road, Mary Virginia turned to wave good-bye through the oval back window. For a long way down the road she could see her brothers and sisters waving their arms at her from the porch. Her mother, however, didn't wave; rather, she stood stock still in the middle of the gravel road, her hands clasped together under her apron, watching the car go as though it were the last sight she would ever see.

CHAPTER NINE

Home

$\mathcal{D}$o you know, Panny, I would have been hard-pressed when I was a child to tell you what the word "home" meant to me. Oh, I knew what I'd learned about it in my reading books at school. "Home" was supposed to be a red brick house with a garden of foxgloves and roses around it and a white picket fence surrounding that. "Home" was where a happy family lived, a family with a father who returned there at night in a hat and suit to play with his children, and a mother who wore lipstick, an ironed white apron, and high heels while she vacuumed the rugs. This description of "home" didn't fit our apartment and the people in it very well, anymore than it fit the city dwellings or families of the other children in Oakland Gardens in Bayside, New York, where I lived.

I knew the word "home" well enough in its common usage, though, and I used it just the way everybody else did. Everybody had a home; it was where you were when you weren't someplace else. "Home" was where you went after school or you had been playing at somebody else's house. It was supposed to be the place where you uniquely belonged, the place where you were wanted, the place where you were safe.

All this being true, I nevertheless remember often feeling confused about whether I really had a home, or if I did, where it really was. Partly, this was because, before Mama and Daddy were divorced, I hardly ever felt comfortable at home. How could I? I could never forget how I disappointed them. In the case of my young daddy, it was because he held such impossibly high standards in the areas of obedience, schoolwork, intelligence, neatness, creativity, and general character, none of which I was capable, even if my continuous depression had not made them impossible for me. As for my poor mama, not only did she have standards of female hard work, competence, and cheerfulness herself which she had brought from Union County and which my temperament and depression ensured that I would fail to meet. Daddy, whom she adored, also held her responsible for the correction of my failures, and that often made her tense and irritable with me. It's hardly surprising, therefore, that I had a hard time believing I belonged where I found myself.

I suspect a lesser part of my confusion over where my home was, however, also had a gentler, more mundane cause: when Mama and Daddy and I moved to New York from Cincinnati, we lived for a while in Nanaw's house.

Do you recall Nanaw? "Nanaw" was what we children called my other grandmother, my daddy's mother. Oh Panny, I loved my tall, blond, curly-haired, lily-of-the-valley-scented grandmother so much, and I loved her house in which we lived, because she played with me and thought that I was wonderful, and because everything in her house seemed so pretty. To this day, the recollection of her bathroom with its deep purple tiles, its purple sink and toilet, and its little white guest towels, which she had embroidered with purple and yellow pansy faces, fills me with a double sense of well-being and painful nostalgia. Leaving her house to go with my parents into an apartment confused me from the start; it never felt like moving into our own home so much as it seemed like going into exile.

Still, though neither my parents nor Nanaw could have helped it, I don't really believe that it was either my feeling of failure with respect to my parents or my feeling of exile with respect to Nanaw and Nanaw's house that ultimately caused my confusion over where my own home was. I think, rather, that it had something more to do with the charged and painful way Mama herself characteristically used the word "home" that underlay my difficulties.

"Mama," I remember calling out one winter day after I'd fumbled with my key, then flung open the door at the foot of the stairs that led up to our little garden apartment in Oakland Gardens. "Mama, I'm home!"

I needed comfort. I was in the fifth grade and as usual, I had had a terrible day at school. I was starving for a snack, I was lonely, I was anxious about the money I couldn't put off asking for any longer to pay for a field trip coming up soon, and I was looking in dread toward a spanking and a yelling-at from Daddy in exchange for the predictably terrible report card I would be bringing home at the end of the week.

"Mama, I'm home," I called out a third time as I tore off my mittens and the heavy wool coat children wore in those days and ran up the stairs into the little room that served us as a combination living and dining room.

In spite of all my noise coming in, Mama didn't seem to notice me at first, though she could hardly have failed to hear me come in. As I entered the room, I saw that she was sitting in the dark by the stairs at the table on which we ate our meals, a torn envelope and several pages of a pale yellow letter spread out in front of her. She looked tired and sad in the worn-out gray sweater she did her housework in. I could tell as soon as I saw her that she wasn't going to be able to give me either the attention or the comfort I craved.

Still, though she didn't want me to raise any of my hard questions or tell her about anything that had gone wrong during the day, Mama made the attempt to welcome me, as she always did after school. She raised her head and smiled at me absentmindedly for a moment as I stood in front of her with my coat trailing on the floor beside me. "Hang up your coat and change your clothes," she said. "Then, if you're hungry, go and get yourself an apple and a glass of milk out of the kitchen."

As usual, having been too anxious at school to eat my lunch, I was truly hungry, but I needed some reassurance from her before I could find myself a snack. I sidled around to her and tentatively put my hand on her shoulder. "What are you doing, Mama?" I asked.

As Grammar would have done before her, as you know very well, Mama shrugged off my hand. Then she sighed, and without raising her head again, shuffled through the pages on the table in front of her. "I'm reading a letter from Panny," she answered. She sighed again, this time deeper and louder. "I just want to go home so bad," she said in her

Union County accent so alien to the language of New York City. "I'm so homesick I can hardly stand it."

The blood rushed to my head, and my heart began to pound in anger and fear as it always did whenever Mama spoke this way. It was scary enough to see that my mother wasn't invincible, but rather was vulnerable to things that happened to her in the same way I was. It was even worse to hear Mama talking about wanting to "go home"!

How could she say this to me, I wondered, as though I had no feelings? If she said she wanted to go home, she was also saying quite clearly, without using the words, that she didn't think of where I lived with her as her "home." What could it mean that she didn't? Since she was my mother, if the place she lived with me was not her home, how could it possibly be mine? Wouldn't my home have to be where her home was?

It was a further, excruciating problem to me, Panny, that if her home wasn't with us, I wasn't a hundred percent sure where she thought her home actually was. On the basis of this sort of thing about "going home" that she would periodically say all through my childhood, I would have thought home was with you on the farm in Kentucky. Certainly, "going home" was what I heard her tell her girlfriends she was doing when she took my brothers and me to stay with you and Papa Charles during our summer vacations every year. "Going home" was what she said she was doing after she and Daddy were divorced when we lost our house in Delaware and moved in with you on your farm. There was never a time when she didn't talk about "going home" in this way; for that matter she still talks like this when she wants to visit her sisters, my aunts Kas and Susie, in Union County, even now that you and Papa Charles are dead and your old house has been torn down to the ground.

What confused me was the fact that we were never long on the farm in Union County before I would realize that Mama didn't truly feel herself to be at home there, either. Since she looked and talked and acted differently in Kentucky than she acted "at home" with Daddy in New York, I wouldn't notice this at first.

Soon, however, that would change. As you, her aunts, and Mama's sisters fried chicken, made the iced tea, and baked the rolls for the first big family dinner of our visit, everybody—except you, of course—would talk about local people and happenings I could see Mama didn't know about. Mama would go silent, and I would suspect that she was feeling as much like an outsider in this place she thought about as "home" as I was myself.

It was only after dinner that Mama would seem to find her place again and join in the conversation, when the women were once again putting away the food and cleaning up in the kitchen. This is when the serious laughing would take place and they would begin to tell "do you remember" stories about Grandma Ginny and Grandma Nack, great-great aunts and uncles long since dead, about Grammar's Beautiful House, the One That Burned, and, most of all, about life in that long ago given away, rickety, mythical house both generations had been born in, the House on the Hill.

Talk about a feeling of exile! However much you yourself may have hated the House on the Hill, Panny, for Mama it was absolutely the lost home she longed for, existing in her memory with more color and more power than any home it seemed she could ever actually live in again. It was, and still is, I suspect, the one house in which she belongs, the house where she felt herself to be safe and happy and loved. Surely, it is the one home that can never again be given away or that she can never again be sent away from.

Standing as a child in your kitchen, a wet dish towel in my hands, useless and forgotten by the women around me, I hated this imaginary House on the Hill that was my mother's home, which I believed I would never see for myself. It was only many years later, after she had inherited the house on Willow Avenue and many more years into my happy second marriage, that I realized that this was not the case. This is because, without my even being aware of it, Mama had transferred her most vivid memories of life in that house to me in such a way that, when I began to write this account for you, I found that I could no longer tell her memories from my own.

It is a funny thing about family houses. Though, apart from a single brief visit after the house had been remodeled and occupied by strangers, I've never set foot in that house, the shape and size of its original rooms, the furnishings in each of them, the light coming in its windows, the appearance of the trees that surrounded it, and the people who lived in it and visited it, have come to live within me, too, with quivering intensity. It seems wonderful to me, a scary and amazing gift, that the House on the Hill has become my home, too, although like Mama I could never live in it in person. The House on the Hill for me is no longer the place from which I was excluded by my own exacting and particular family. It has, instead, become my own, the place that shelters me and haunts me, a place all other places are measured by, a place that I can never leave.

CHAPTER TEN

In a Hired Hand's House

The last three hours of the night Mary Virginia and Charles were to arrive back home in Union County for Christmas, Bert was so tense with anxiety that she was nearly beside herself. Setting the table for supper in the kitchen, she had dropped a dinner plate and broken it on the floor. Several times one of the children had asked her a question and she forgot what she was saying in the middle of the answer.

Part of Bert's anxiety was natural; she missed her daughter and she didn't want to wait any longer to see her. The bulk of Bert's anxiety, however, had nothing to do with missing Mary Virginia. Rather, it lay in Mary Virginia's letters. Recently Bert had become convinced that there was something wrong with Mary Virginia that her letters were concealing.

Not being a worrier, it had taken a long time for Bert to reach this conclusion. Once a week since Mary Virginia had left, Bert had written her daughter to keep her in touch with the family left behind in Union County. Once a week Mary Virginia had written home about her classes at the school, the school building itself, her teachers, her friend Frances, the Methodist church she went to on Sundays, and the room she stayed in in Miss Beryl's house. In general, the letters had been positive. Although Mary Virginia made it plain that homesickness was getting her down, everything she wrote confirmed Bert's decision to send her to the city.

Bert couldn't put her finger on when it was that she began to wonder whether there wasn't something wrong in the letters, nor on what it was that had made her wonder it. Neither did she know the moment when she went from wondering to knowing that Mary Virginia's regular letters were concealing more than they were telling. Based on her own letters home her last few weeks of school, she believed she had guessed what Mary Virginia was hiding. She decided to confirm her guess. Two weeks earlier Bert had written:

Dear Mary Virginia,

Here it is almost Christmas, and as usual, I'm just not ready for it. I've been making aprons till I'm blue in the face—today a green for Subie and a yellow for Blacky. Last night I made a light blue one for Ginny and a red one for Nacky, though what I'm making them aprons for, I don't know. The only thing Nacky cooks is fudge, and Ginny would starve to death before she could get a meal on the table.

It's so cold here I nearly froze hanging out the wash yesterday. Your father went out in the woods when the children got home from school and chopped down a cedar. It's a pretty little tree, but we haven't had time to get it up yet. We'll put it up before you get home. Suzie and Quentin are cutting out pictures to hang on it right this minute.

A.D. is courting Kas to beat the band. Half the time she walks around like she doesn't see the ground in front of her. He seems like a nice boy, though. I always did think Miss Clella was a good woman. Her sister married Holden Smith. He's a second cousin of Papa's on his mother's side. Maybe you'll find yourself a beau in the big city, too.

Well, Mary Virginia, work hard and be good. Soon you'll have a job and have some money of your own. We can hardly wait to see you.

Love,
Mother

Mary Virginia had written back:

Dear Mother,

I was so glad to get your letter today. I'm so homesick I don't know what to do. Frances is going home on the 19th. I can't figure out how she stands it at the Y. Her mother and daddy can't come to see her, either, and she is only 16 years old. (I guess I ought to write out the numbers like they teach me to at school!)

I'm sorry I haven't been able to go over to Aunt Gertie's yet for dinner. They asked me three times, but I just can't seem to get there. I haven't been able to go shopping for Christmas yet, either. I hope I'll have a chance before Daddy comes to get me. I've still got nearly all the money Papa gave me before I left. It seems like forever till I get a real job.

Well, I have to finish this now before I leave school. I am so tired I hardly know what to do. Kiss the children and Grammar and Papa for me. I'll be home soon!

Love,
Mary Virginia

The letter told Bert plainly that Mary Virginia was tired, that she had no time to herself at all, and that she could hardly imagine having a good job. Her failure to say more only confirmed Bert's suspicions. She remembered perfectly well how carefully she had concealed Charles in her own letters home all those years ago.

Still, Bert recalled that with Charles, she had been so happy she was silly; there was an edge of unhappiness in Mary Virginia's letters that her mother could not possibly have read into her own. If Mary Virginia was seeing a man, there was something that was not right about it. She shuddered to herself to think of what that might be.

Worrying over those letters while they waited in the early winter darkness made Bert wonder now for the first time about her own mother and what it had been like for her twenty years earlier once Bert had married Charles and moved to Casey County. It had never occurred to Bert before to ask herself what her mother had felt about her own daughter's leaving and even about Bert's dreadful sickness with the baby she was expecting.

Bert rocked uneasily and thought. Had Grammar scrutinized her letters for what was left out in the way she did Mary Virginia's? Her mother hadn't displayed a bit of worry in what she wrote. On the other hand, as Bert thought about it now, her mother would have known that if she had written what was really in her mind, Bert wouldn't have wanted to read it.

Staring at the Christmas tree while she rocked and wondered about Mary Virginia and about her mother, Bert had a new thought. For all these years she had been blaming her father for the way he had tricked and bullied her and Charles into leaving Casey County to bring them to the House on the Hill. What if she were wrong? Her father, after all, hadn't come alone; her mother had been with him.

Grammar must have been frantic when she saw Bert in that house in Casey County, lying in the bed in one of her spells, too weak from throwing up to move. Papa, on the other hand, didn't ordinarily see enough around him to even notice what was going on. Did this mean that leaving Casey County and moving into the House on the Hill hadn't been her father's idea, but her mother's all along?

"Oh Lord" Bert sighed and rocked some more. This was something she'd never be able to find out now. It was too much. The children, settled around the fire, looked up at her before they went back to listening to the story Kas was reading. Bert's sighs were part of the weather they'd grown up with: they were as used to these exclamations that seemed to burst out of their mother as they were to clouds forming in the sky.

Bert was so far buried under her own musings that when Mary Virginia and Charles arrived at nine o'clock she almost didn't hear them. The children were the first to see the car's lights. She only really came back to herself as they jumped and shouted, "It's Mary Virginia! It's Mary Virginia!"

The lights grew brighter. Gravel crunched outside, and the two heavy doors of the Buick slammed. The children swarmed, mashing her up against the car and hugging her. "Mary Virginia, Mary Virginia, see if I've grown," laughed Quentin. "Tell us what's it like in Louisville," demanded Bo. Suzie pulled on her skirt. Bob hung back a little, as Kas smiled and smiled and didn't say anything.

The light from the windows didn't shine on the dark place by the Buick where Mary Virginia stood. Bert couldn't see her face, but when she reached to link the girl's arm with hers and draw her into the house, she thought for a moment her daughter had become all bones.

"Come in, Mary Virginia, and get warm," Bert said, leading her through the door. "Let your old mother have a good look at you." Bert reached up and turned Mary Virginia's face toward the light. Under her eyes were black pouches as deep as the suitcases. Her brown hair was long and shapeless, and her skin dull and white like an old woman's. Without her coat she looked even thinner than Bert had thought.

"Here I am, Mother. Do I look good enough for you?" Mary Virginia said before she burst into tears.

"What's wrong, Mary Virginia?" Bert asked. She wrapped her arms around her and shooed back the children. "Are you sick?"

"No, no," answered Mary Virginia, quickly. She drew in a deep breath and brushed at her tears with the back of her hand. "I'm just so tired I don't know what to do."

"Tired," Bert repeated. She pushed Mary Virginia away to look at her again. Her guesses must be right. There was only one thing that made Bert as tired as Mary Virginia seemed to be, and it made her throw up and lose weight, too. Charles and the children underfoot, however, she could hardly ask.

For now, Bert didn't even hint at what she'd guessed. "I can see you're tired," she said to her daughter, instead. "You go to sleep, and we'll talk about it in the morning."

"There's nothing to talk about, Mother," Mary Virginia protested; she'd kept her secret this long; she wasn't about to give it away now or tomorrow, either. "I'm just so tired I'm half sick." She smiled an apologetic smile with a hint of stubbornness to it.

In spite of the fight that was coming, she was so glad to be home she hardly knew what to do. She looked around the small room, at the cedar tree with its lead tinsel and its homemade decorations, at the red fire and her mother's braided rug in front of it, at the flaking, silvered mirror in its tarnished brass frame. She saw the familiar furniture she had longed for in Louisville, worn by these people she loved and whom she knew without a single doubt loved her in return, and every muscle in her body let go at once. "I think I need to sleep," she said. She kissed Bert goodnight, climbed into hers and Kas's bed in the back room by the kitchen, and slept.

Soon after Mary Virginia went to bed, Bert tucked in the children and she and Charles climbed into bed themselves. They didn't talk about how Mary Virginia looked before Charles fell into his usual instant sleep. He'd already told Bert everything he knew, which was that Mary Virginia had dozed most of the way home in the car. Charles wouldn't have noticed any more than her father would. In that way, he wasn't any different from any other man she'd ever known.

Bert, for her part, lay awake half the night thinking and worrying about what might happen—or fail to happen—to their daughter now. She wondered who the man was who had gotten Mary Virginia in trouble. It couldn't be Jimmy Lee Innes. Grudgingly, Mary Virginia had written that she hadn't even gone out with him when he'd come up to see her. Had she met someone at school? Mary Virginia'd never mentioned any other man in her letters, Bert was positive, but that didn't mean there wasn't one.

Perhaps this unknown man didn't want to take responsibility for what he'd done and marry her. On the other hand, what if he wanted to marry her but Mary Virginia didn't want to marry him? Should she and Charles make her do it? Bert had hated to think of a woman yoked to a man who wore her out and made her miserable. Bert had never forgiven Papa and Grammar for making Subie marry. Now, Subie was in town at her husband's church every time the doors opened. It was good to go to church, but there was such a thing as overdoing it. There was no doubt her sister did a lot of good, but it was hard on the babies and it didn't make her happy.

She and Charles would just have to find a home for unmarried mothers in Louisville. Bert knew the Baptists ran one because she supported it every year when there was a missions appeal at Pond Fork. If Mary Virginia went to that home, though, Brother Kinsey would be bound to find out and tell someone at the church.

She shuddered to think of Grammar hearing the news from some gossip in a sunbonnet. Whatever they decided to do, Bert would have to tell her mother herself before she found out from somebody else. Of course, Grammar would have a fit and talk about sin, but it couldn't be helped.

Maybe she should write for help from Aunt Gertie, Bert thought. She didn't want to tell Papa's sister because she might tell Papa herself and Papa would tell Grammar, but Aunt Gertie'd become a Catholic when she married Uncle Al. Everybody knew about Catholics; Catholics must have a lot of homes for girls like Mary Virginia.

Poor Mary Virginia. She could just strangle her! Whatever they planned and whatever they did, Bert wasn't going to be able to protect her daughter very much from the real consequences of her foolishness. Even if Mary Virginia kept her secret from her grandmother and later had a chance to marry, she couldn't lie to her husband. And what man would ever marry her when he found out what she'd done?

The last thing Bert thought about before she finally drifted into a restless sleep was the irony of it all. She had sent Mary Virginia off to school to make something of herself so that she could have a good life and not have to work as hard as her mother had. Mary Virginia'd been her hope, her chance to do it over again right. Poor little thing, now look at her.

The next morning, long after Charles and the children had eaten, Mary Virginia came to the table looking for the coffeepot. It was eight-thirty. Mary Virginia had slept like the dead, and she didn't look much better now than she had the night before. Her hair was brushed but straggly as she hunched herself up at the table in her old pink chenille bathrobe with the pocket torn down the side.

Her mother handed her a cup and saucer and poured in some coffee. Bert had decided to talk to her first thing. She needed to find out what was what, so they could figure out what to do about it.

Bert sat down at the table with her. "Mary Virginia," she said, "I've got to ask you some questions. Pay attention, now."

She looked at Bert in surprise. Why was her mother so upset just because she'd lost a little weight? "Wait, Mother, let me drink some coffee," she said. "I haven't even had my breakfast yet." She'd never seen her mother exactly like this, and Mary Virginia was still so tired she couldn't think straight.

In the front room Susie and Quentin heard their sister's voice and rushed through the door into the kitchen, followed by their two big brothers. "Mary Virginia, Mary Virginia, come and see the Christmas tree decorations we made!" they screamed.

"Bob, Bo, you're grown-up," Bert ordered. "I know you haven't seen Mary Virginia yet, but just take Quentin and Suzie back into the front room and do something with them a while." As they began to protest, she added, "And don't you argue with me one minute." At that, the look on the faces of the two big boys changed from excitement to speculation, but at Bert's frown they left fast enough, the two younger ones in front of them.

Mary Virginia sat through this with her hands wrapped around the cup. She stared out the window into the gray, cold sky where images of the pleasures and safety of her childhood Christmases were presenting themselves before her, one by one.

"Mary Virginia," Bert brought her daughter sharply back to the present as she sat down again at the table. "Now, Mary Virginia, you can't fool your mother," she said. "Tell me what is ailing you. Are you sick?"

Mary Virginia tried to clear her head and pay attention. "I don't know; I don't think so," she answered.

"You don't look like you're eating very good," Bert went on. "I said, you don't look like you're eating very good," her mother repeated. "Are you throwing up much?"

Mary Virginia replied without thinking, "I eat as regularly as anybody, but why on earth should I be throwing up?" Mary Virginia was confused and hurt. She knew she looked bad, but she hated for anybody to say so. Bert had already told her she looked thin, and she had counted on her mother not to push her to talk about how she got that way. After all, she was only trying to protect her mother from what she didn't need to know.

Bert raised her voice and interrupted her daughter's brooding. "I've worked all my life and there's only been one kind of time I've been as tired as you look."

Mary Virginia wondered what on earth was Bert ranting about now. Didn't her mother know she hated it when she got like this?

Bert saw that her daughter, for some reason, wouldn't hear what her mother was clearly asking her. She would have to try another approach. "Mary Virginia, when was the last time you got the curse?" she asked at last.

Mary Virginia was startled, too taken by surprise not to answer. "I don't know," she said. "Maybe September."

Bert sighed, her fears confirmed. "It's a man who put you in this way, isn't it? You might as well tell me about it."

"What? A man? What man?" Mary Virginia asked. "What are you talking about?" She had caught on at last to what her mother thought. First she was stunned, then she was furious. If her mother wanted to think that about her, then she could think it all she wanted. Mary Virginia wasn't about to tell her any different!

Bert was too upset herself to take in Mary Virginia's shock. All she noticed was that Mary Virginia hadn't denied a word of what she'd said. "Well, we won't talk about it now," Bert said. "We're getting you to Uncle John this minute, then we'll figure out what to do with you. Get your coat and let's go."

"We won't talk about it now!" Mary Virginia mocked Bert under her breath. Whatever else Bert was worrying about, she didn't have to worry about being slowed down by Mary Virginia telling her anything. Mary Virginia was so mad, nothing on earth would make her tell her mother now what was wrong with her. Still, she thought Uncle John really might be able to help her some way or other. She did feel awful, and she did wonder why it was that she hadn't gotten the curse in three months.

Mary Virginia put on her coat. "Watch the little ones," Bert called as they went out the door.

Uncle John was the town doctor. He was also Papa's brother, actually Mary Virginia's great-uncle. His office in town was on the front of his fine house, and so, while he was examining Mary Virginia, Bert went on through and visited with Aunt Ella. Uncle John and Aunt Ella had no children of their own. Aunt Ella was bedridden with some vague ailments, but she liked company, especially family company. Bert sat on the little chair by the bed, ignoring the bottles that covered the tabletop by the head of the bed and trying not to think about Uncle John and Mary Virginia. As she went on about the hard winter, and Papa and her mother and her sisters and brother, Bert managed to keep herself composed enough to carry on a conversation without disgracing herself.

After a long time, Mary Virginia and Uncle John came on back to find her. Mary Virginia seemed calmer, but it irritated Bert that John appeared to be smiling. He took the two women back to his office to talk.

"Well, John, I'm waiting," Bert said before either of them could speak. Uncle John stopped smiling. Mary Virginia crossed her arms over her chest, stubbornly.

"Bert, your daughter's plumb worn out, and that's all I'm about to tell you," he said. "Anything else you want to know, she'll have to tell you herself. I've given her a tonic, and we've had a long talk about what she might do to make herself feel better. I know what you've been worrying about, too, so you can just stop it. Mary Virginia's a good girl. There's no boy involved in this," he added. "You trust her."

Trust her. Ha! thought Mary Virginia to herself. Her teeth clinched and her chin jutting out, Mary Virginia stood next to John, looking at the ceiling.

Trust her! Bert would have if she could, but she was too mortified and proud to ask Uncle John anything else. What did he know? Maybe there wouldn't be a baby, but that didn't mean some boyfriend of Mary Virginia's wasn't responsible for her condition. In her experience, women didn't get so worn out as this by themselves. If only Mary Virginia would just break down and tell her!

As for Mary Virginia, she thought about everything all the way home. She could taste her mother's humiliation and desperation so strongly right now that she could hardly sort out what she felt herself from what her mother felt. Still, she was hurt. How could Bert have thought such a thing about her own daughter when it was she who was only trying to protect her mother!

Well, Mary Virginia had paid enough attention in church and listened to enough family stories over the years to know that she couldn't expect appreciation from anybody for her secret protection of her mother. That was what went with self-sacrifice, and self-sacrifice was just part of a Christian woman's lot. Certainly it was a part of a Christian woman's love, and as mad at her as she felt right now, Mary Virginia knew she loved her mother. In spite of her mother's betrayal, Mary Virginia couldn't break Bert's heart by telling her mother what was wrong.

At ten o'clock when they returned, Bert went to begin peeling potatoes for dinner. Mary Virginia couldn't be with her mother just yet. She stripped off her good dress in the back bedroom and changed into her old clothes, then she put on her coat and an unmatched pair of Kas's mittens, wrapped a scarf around her neck and walked out into the half-frozen winter fields.

It was no use; she was trapped. Beyond that, she was too confused to

150

see, and too exhausted to think. Though the crows flew up from the fence posts, and the little cedars raised up their branches like flames, the walk through the black earth of the sleeping furrows brought her no comfort.

By New Year's Day, when Charles drove Mary Virginia back to Louisville, Bert had still learned nothing. She resolved to give her a little while to settle back in at school; then Bert would pay a surprise visit to see for herself what was making Mary Virginia so secretive. Things, unfortunately, did not work out as Bert had planned. For five solid weeks, from the day after New Year's until the end of the first week in February, each of the children got sick, with everything from chicken pox (Quentin and then Susie) to scarlet fever (Bo) and influenza (Bob). Kas, who was living in town Monday through Friday anyway, was the only exception. Bert postponed her surprise visit.

Then, on the second Friday of February an uncharacteristically thin letter arrived from Mary Virginia. Bert opened it with trepidation. The letter, which was on paper that looked as though it had been crumpled, then at the last minute smoothed out, read as follows,

Dear Mother:
   I hate February. It is dark and gloomy, and the weather is just as awful as it can be, damp and cold and dreary. I miss everybody so much I can hardly stand it. I just wish I could come home and sit by the fire in the front room of the House on the Hill.
   I'm am so blue today I don't know what to do. I'm sorry to hear you're so worn out, yourself, with everybody sick.
   I can't write any more now. Don't worry about me, I'll be fine. Give my love to everybody,

                                        Mary Virginia

This was an alarming letter. For one thing, it was the first time Mary Virginia had ever voluntarily mentioned the House on the Hill since the day they had moved away from it. For another, she had never before come right out and admitted to her mother how very unhappy she was. Although Mary Virginia still didn't say what was wrong in Louisville, this time she hadn't even pretended that everything was fine.

Sick children or no, Bert needed to go to Louisville. If Grammar and Papa thought they owned Bob, they could just take care of him. The rest of them would have to do the best they could without her. She would drive up the next day, see Mary Virginia, and spend the night with Aunt Gertie. She would leave early Sunday morning and be home too late for Sunday school but right on time for church.

"Work, for the night is coming," Mary Virginia sang. "Work through the morning hours." Before she had come to Mrs. Simpson's, Mary Virginia had loved this song, which she associated with her childhood school. It had always made her feel noble and purposeful and Christian. Standing on the hard concrete floor with Mrs. Simpson's wet towels flapping in her face, she didn't feel either noble or purposeful. She simply felt worn out and humiliated.

Today her Saturday had started out like all her other mornings since she'd come to Louisville to school. At six o'clock the old lady whom she thought of as her torturer had brought her out of a deep sleep by pounding on her door.

"Mary Virginia," the old lady had called out in the high nasal half-drawled Louisville accent Mary Virginia hated, "get up; time's a'wasting. You need a good breakfast if you're going to get your day's work done."

There were many aspects to Mary Virginia's misery. To begin, trained by her grandparents Papa and Grammar to despise all those who worked on the farm or in the home of someone else, without even thinking about it what Mary Virginia heard Mrs. Simpson say was, "Mary Virginia, you worthless hired hand, get out of that bed and fix me a hot breakfast. Who do you think you are, lying in bed like the queen of Sheba? And don't you dare forget to wash the dishes and sweep up afterwards, either!"

Toiling away in the basement, Mary Virginia hated herself for letting her life be controlled by a nobody old woman who hadn't ever even set foot on a farm. It was bad enough being ordered around by somebody Grammar wouldn't invite in through the front door back home in Union County. But the fact that Mrs. Simpson never lifted a hand to help herself made Mary Virginia's humiliation infinitely worse. Mary Virginia was working for somebody she couldn't even respect. As far as she was concerned, Mrs. Simpson was bone-lazy, too lazy to feed herself in the sight of food. Mary Virginia's shame over allowing herself to be no more than the hired hand of a woman who wouldn't even work was infinite.

Mary Virginia bent over the laundry lit by a single bulb dangling above the soapy sink and tried unsuccessfully to reflect on why she was so passive in this place. It was partly her shame, but she knew it was also exhaustion, which was the second major component of her torture, though she wasn't sure exactly where the exhaustion had come from. She had certainly worked at least as hard at home in the House on the Hill. She supposed she was worn out from the combination of school work, an inability to get even a few hours off a week to herself, and her terrible diet in Mrs. Simpson's house. Past these little bits of insight into herself and her predicament, however, she'd never been able to go.

Deliberately, she turned her mind back to what she was doing. This morning, she noticed, the knuckles on her hands were already red and sore. She tried to brush back the hair that had fallen in her face with a wet forearm. The hair stuck to her wet skin and pulled down further. Aggravated, Mary Virginia lifted a heavy sheet out of the soapy water and let it drip for a moment before she started wringing it out with her hurting hands.

"Work while the dew is sparkling, work 'mid springing flowers," she took up her song again as dirty water ran from her hands down her arms and into her armpits. She hadn't lived with Mrs. Simpson during last spring's flowers, but she figured she'd certainly worked hard enough while the dew was sparkling on all those Saturday mornings of last summer.

For an instant she admitted to herself what she hadn't a moment ago: that there was something about herself that was keeping her in Mrs. Simpson's basement. There was her own fear of what would happen if she asked for help from her family. It was unthinkable to her that she should face what she was convinced would be her grandmother's scorn for her if she found out that her granddaughter had become a servant.

Even more, however, was what had kept Mary Virginia from admitting to her mother at Christmas what had really been wrong with her: she found it simply impossible to disappoint her mother's expectations for her. All her life she had carried her mother's burdens inside her as her own. There were the physical hardships of her mother's gallstone attacks, the weakness and nausea of her pregnancies, the sickness of her exhausted depression. On top of all that there were her mother's devastated pride; her fatalistic stubbornness in the face of her powerful father and her hapless husband; and her grief over her lost baby, her lost son, and her lost houses.

Though in that family of no words, her mother had never told her so, even before she had set out for Louisville, Mary Virginia had known that by sending her away, Bert intended that her oldest daughter vindicate and set right her mother's life by having a better life than hers. This Mary Virginia had passionately thrown herself into doing. How could she call on her mother for help now? There was no way to do it without letting Bert know how she was letting down her expectations and Mary Virginia's own expectations, besides.

Certainly, Louisville had not turned out to be what any of them had expected, though it had taken a while for Mary Virginia to realize it. She had left home with Papa Charles that previous August caught up in the glory of her own vision of good things coming. It had only annoyed her when, before they left, Bert had kissed her as though she would never be coming back.

For Mary Virginia, the glory had persisted throughout the day. She and Papa Charles had broken their trip first by stopping at a gas station to refill the car. They had stopped later for lunch at some blowing pale green trees on a windy bluff above a bend of the Ohio River. There in the shimmering heat, they had eaten the pickley deviled eggs and their fried chicken and had drunk their jars of tea.

While the dew dried up on the little towns they drove through, Mary Virginia had daydreamed of the lives of women in the movies she had seen with her friends and the magazines they had read together. She pictured herself in her new life in Louisville as an independent, efficient secretary joking with her boss in a pleasant office. She smiled secretly as she imagined herself laughing helplessly up into the face of the man she would meet there as he bent her over in his arms to kiss her and ask her to marry him.

Between daydreams, Mary Virginia had counted the See Rock City signs painted on the black barn roofs in the countryside through which they passed. Papa Charles had sung all the verses of the "The Old Rugged Cross," and smoked cigars. Even now she could see her father flipping the thick gray ashes out the window after he had filled the front seat with his smoke.

She and Papa Charles hadn't talked about anything that mattered to them that day, any more than they ever had. For most of the way the only words either of them spoke were the words on the little red Burma Shave signs they read to each other on the side of the road. Now, she wondered what it would have been like to be able to talk with her parents about the unknown life that lay ahead of her. Still, she knew it was as impossible to her as it was to them; she shuddered with embarrassment even to think of it.

In the basement Mary Virginia took a deep breath, twisting water out of the wet fabric; resolutely she tried to turn her mind back to her song. "Work when the day grows brighter, work in the glowing sun," she sang. She was working all right. She had gotten up and made Mrs. Simpson's breakfast and washed the dishes afterward. While the day had grown brighter, she'd vacuumed, dusted, mopped, and cleaned Mrs. Simpson's nasty toilet, bathtub, and sink. Finally, she had made the old lady's lunch.

She couldn't help herself; her mind wandered back to the trip in August. Mary Virginia had been delighted at her first sight of the small white house in the South End where she was to be a companion to Mrs. Simpson, doing two hours of light housework a day in exchange for room and board. The house's blue shutters and surrounding lawn reminded her of pictures she had seen in storybooks.

The end of her daydreams came with her first sight of Mrs. Simpson, who had greeted her unsmiling at the door. She had known Mrs. Simpson was old, but still she had expected someone who would be glad to see her, and someone more fragile.

Mrs. Simpson, who was not fragile in the least, had taken charge of her and her father immediately. "Hello, Miss Wesley. This must be your father, " she had said. "Your room is through the hall and on the left. You tell him to take your things to your room. I am sure that he must need to hurry back. I have things for you to do."

The tone of Mrs. Simpson's voice had given her a chill, which she characteristically ignored. Though dark, the room she had been assigned was large and pleasant; the white chenille spread, which was very much like the one on her and Kas's bed in Union County, felt familiar. Papa Charles carried in her suitcases at once and stacked them in the corner.

After that, her father kissed her good-bye. "Be a good girl, Mary Virginia," he had said on the doorstep. "Work hard and make your mother proud." Before she could even watch him walk back to Uncle Mack's Buick, Mrs. Simpson had firmly shut the door after him.

Remembering now at the sink, Mary Virginia half unfolded the wet sheet, then wadded and twisted it. Water dripping down her front, she unfolded it, folded it, and twisted it again.

"Work, for the night is coming," she sang, raising her voice against her thoughts, "when man's work is done." It couldn't be helped. When she finished the laundry it would be time to go to the store for Mrs. Simpson. Anger churned in her stomach. Mrs. Simpson had gotten rid of Papa Charles because she wanted Mary Virginia to shop for her, and here she was, still shopping for the same pork chops, slaw, and mashed potatoes they always had to eat. She didn't know much about nutrition, but she'd read in a magazine that it was bad for you always to eat the same thing. No wonder, in spite of Uncle John's tonic, her body wouldn't bleed. She only hoped she could have children if she ever had the chance.

But how would she ever have a chance? That she should work only two hours a day was so far from being possible that Mary Virginia could hardly imagine it. Mrs. Simpson controlled every moment of her time. Every afternoon, even now, as she had from the beginning, Mrs. Simpson sat in her rocker by the front window, waiting for her from the minute she got off the trolley from school.

"Mary Virginia?" she would call as she came through the door. "Come here, this instant! Where on earth have you been? You're five minutes late! You've been wasting time again, talking to those silly girls you go to school with." From the start, at this insult to her friends, Mary Virginia would blush with anger.

"You take this money and get yourself to the butcher before he closes," Mrs. Simpson would go on. "You make sure he gives you nice pork chops, or I'll make you take them back, sure as the world." And she would, too; it was a rare day Mary Virginia didn't have to make a second trip to the butcher's to exchange the chops, which were, in Mrs. Simpson's opinion, too fat or too dried up, too thin or too thick. The butcher, who understood all this, would smile sympathetically and take the next two chops from the pile in the glass-fronted case.

Then, every day when she returned from exchanging the chops, Mary Virginia would grate the cabbage, fry the pork chops, and sit down to eat with the old lady. After that, she would wash the dishes and set up the card table and "companionably" play the hearts she'd played with her every single night until Mrs. Simpson decided it was bedtime.

If only she could have a bit of time to herself, just once a week! There were so many other country girls like herself she knew at school who were also working in other people's houses, and all of them had as much free time as they needed to themselves. Unlike them, Mary Virginia hadn't been allowed out with anyone, male or female, a single time since she'd moved in, not even when Jimmy Lee Innes drove up from Union County to see her. She hadn't been to any parties. She hadn't even lingered after school for a soft drink with her friend Frances, much less gone with her to the movies. ("This is your job, girl; you stay here with me where you belong!") In fact, Mrs. Simpson had let her go to Aunt Gertie's for Sunday lunch only once, and even then, she'd made her come home by two o'clock.

Today, over laundry, Mary Virginia could hardly believe Mrs. Simpson hadn't found a way to keep her away from school, too, but thank the Lord she hadn't. Mary Virginia loved everything about the Spencerian Business School. Being fast and smart, she enjoyed the challenge of the work. Mornings, she would hurry to the high-ceilinged yellow room her classes were held in to practice typing on the big black Royal typewriters. She was the best typist in the class, and even in her demoralized state she was proud of it. She wished she had an equal amount of time to put in on the shorthand, but an hour of practicing was about all she could manage between the time when Mrs. Simpson went to bed and when Mary Virginia fell asleep herself.

"When man's work is done!" Mary Virginia sang again, then sighed. The night might come when "man's work" would be over, but as long as she lived with Mrs. Simpson, Mrs. Simpson would see to it her work never was.

How was she ever to get out of it? Mary Virginia laid the wet sheet on the side of the sink, pulled the plug and shifted feet as she watched the soapy water run out.

"Wretched woman that I am!" she misquoted Paul. She filled the tub again with clear water and dropped in the sheet. "Who will deliver me from this body of death?" She swished the sheet up and down in the sink, then answered Paul's question sadly, "Nobody."

How, she wondered again, could it be that she could exercise so little will in the place where she was? She certainly hadn't grown up this way. She thought perhaps it was because, with the exception of her father, she had always obeyed the grown-ups in her life—her mother, Grammar, and Papa.

But these three people loved her and were proud of her. She was somebody at home, the oldest granddaughter of the oldest daughter, and even through her worst periods, Mary Virginia had known that when they told her to do something, she was still somebody to them. They wanted to take care of her, and she wanted to take care of them. They told her to work hard, so she worked hard.

Now it occurred to her that she hadn't been able before to quite grasp that her relationship with Mrs. Simpson was bound to be different because she was hired by Mrs. Simpson to work for her. Even now, when she was trying to think about it, she couldn't get hold of it. Deep down, Mary Virginia expected Mrs. Simpson to want to take care of her and be proud of her in the same way the beloved adults in her life always had. Though she couldn't articulate this to herself at all, she could hardly imagine living without the positive concern of adults; and because she couldn't, she kept hoping for it, and trying to obtain it by compliance with Mrs. Simpson's demands that far exceeded the terms of her employment.

But the fact was, like most employers of other young girls all over the city, the old lady was completely uninterested in Mary Virginia, her "companion." Though Mary Virginia had contracted to work for two hours a day, Mrs. Simpson didn't concern herself with questions of exploitation. She had no interest in Mary Virginia's welfare at all. In Mrs. Simpson's eyes, Mary Virginia was just what Papa's hired hands had been to him, and Mary Virginia knew it. To her, Mary Virginia was a household appliance. Mrs. Simpson not only didn't love her; the old woman hardly even cared enough about her to dislike her.

What Mary Virginia could do about it now, or whether she even should do anything about it, she didn't know. With Mrs. Simpson she was paralyzed. She couldn't imagine herself breaking her lifelong habit of obedience to older adults, and she couldn't conceive of subjecting herself to Mrs. Simpson's vicious tongue if she tried to cross her by asking for more time to herself; yet every shameful day she lived like this, Mary Virginia reflected as she wrung out the sheet for the last time, she was letting her mother down. Her mother had wanted her to have the real life she had never had herself. She had sacrificed and saved to send Mary Virginia to school in Louisville so that her daughter wouldn't be a slave to any man or any farm. And this was how she repaid her mother! It almost killed her to think about the gap between what Bert had wanted for her and what she was actually doing. The only thing she could hope for now was to keep Bert from finding out.

Mary Virginia shook out the sheet, being careful to keep it off the dirty floor, and pinned it up on one of the empty metal lines that crisscrossed the ceiling below the floor beams, the heating ducts, and the water pipes. She knew how worried her mother had been at Christmas when she'd been home. Her poor mother! She wished she hadn't been so spiteful to her.

Enough of that; she wouldn't allow herself to think of her mother anymore today. She would do the underwear and be done. She filled the sink with soapy water and dropped in two of Mrs. Simpson's enormous pink whale-bone corsets. Hundreds of tiny hooks and eyes shone up at her as the corsets floated on the surface.

To chase away her thoughts and buck her up she started another hymn; religion was good for helping you knuckle under to what you had to accept anyway, if it were good for anything!

"When we walk with the Lord in the light of his word," she sang, her hands in Mrs. Simpson's gray underwear water, "what a glory he sheds on our way!" She pushed the corsets under the water again and sang louder to quiet her thoughts. "While we do his good will, he abides with us still, and with all who will trust and obey."

"Trust and obey," she pulled her hands out of the water for the chorus. "Trust and obey," she sang, gritting her teeth to believe it, "for there's no other way to be happy in Jesus, but to trust and obey." She was raised to do it, but she couldn't; she couldn't trust or obey, either one.

At the end of the chorus Mary Virginia heard a fumbling with the doorknob, then the door open at the top of the stairs. "I'm sorry, Mrs. Simpson," she called over her shoulder. "I didn't mean to disturb you during your nap." There was no reply.

Mary Virginia shrugged, in spite of herself feeling guilty for disturbing her, and turned back to the old lady's underwear, reducing her singing to a hum. Footsteps clumped down the stairs behind her; she ignored those, too, as well as the short silence that followed them.

She was totally unprepared, therefore, for the hands that came down on her shoulders and the familiar voice that suddenly spoke in her ears, "Mary Virginia Wesley, what in heaven's name do you think you're doing? I never thought I raised my child to be a fool!"

It was Bert standing behind Mary Virginia in the basement under the hanging laundry. Beside herself with she hardly knew what combination of shame and relief, Mary Virginia turned around and threw her wet arms around her mother's neck, crying and laughing and apologizing all at once.

"Mother, Mother, I'm so glad to see you," she said. "I know I'm a fool! After all you've done for me I've let you down. I'm so sorry. I'm just so sorry!"

Sorry! At last, Bert had seen for herself both what was wrong with Mary Virginia and why she hadn't told her what was wrong: Mary Virginia had been trying to protect her all along. Bert hugged her daughter as hard as she could.

"You little ninny," Bert whispered, patting her tenderly, as Mary Virginia sobbed. "There, there; now's the time, now's the time."

After a long time, Bert lifted the dripping corsets out of the sink and threw them on the concrete floor. Then she took Mary Virginia by the arm and marched her up the stairs ahead of her. As she prepared herself for battle, her mouth went straight across with anger. "Wait in your room, Mary Virginia," she said. "I'll deal with that woman."

Mary Virginia could hear Bert stomping down the hall and pounding on the closed door at the end of it. Out of breath and trembling with fear, she lay on her bed as she'd been told. She heard her mother shouting, then there was silence, and then the sound of someone making many telephone calls.

At last her mother was back in her room carrying a folded washcloth soaked in cold water. "That awful old woman," she only said as she wiped Mary Virginia's face. "Get up and pack your things; you're going to move." She bent down and began to pull Mary Virginia's suitcases from under the bed. "I've got you a new place to stay where you can have a good time and do your schoolwork, too."

The next day, Mary Virginia woke in a different bed in the new room she was to share for the next year with the daughter of a family recommended by the school.

Occasionally over the years it occurred to her to wonder why, after Bert found out her secret, she and her mother never once talked about it. Mary Virginia only knew that it was a relief to her that they hadn't talked. On both sides, what had happened was too private, too fraught with half-acknowledged and ambiguous betrayals, too full of the possibilities of blame ever to be spoken.

Besides, as Paul would have said, there never had been such a custom of talk among God's people.

CHAPTER ELEVEN

Vindication

You know, Panny, the day I decided to let Mama know that I'd begun to write down these stories I am telling you, I was so full of dread that I was almost beside myself. On the one hand, I knew that I hardly had a choice. As the oldest daughter of the oldest daughter of the oldest daughter, it is a necessary act of family piety that I carry in my own body as careful and loving an account of the memories of the women who have preceded me as I can muster. Though no one assigned it to me in so many words, I have known for a long time that it is also my job to honor you by speaking out loud these stories of courage, despair, lament, and strength that have made my children and me who we are.

All that being true, still it seemed to me that I could hardly expect Mama to receive the news of my story writing with anything other than outrage and anger. What else could I look forward to from such a loyal member of a family whose reliable crops of tragedy almost all have sprung from a well-cultivated bed of silence? In the performance of my own duties with respect to memory and hope, I knew very well that just by speaking the words of the stories out loud, by making the implicit explicit, and the unarticulated articulate, I was digging up the very foundations of our apparently safe house: I was laying a very heavy shovel to one of the most fundamental sources of power we wives in our family have always exercised over our husbands, mothers over our children—silence.

I was totally unprepared, therefore, when I told her of this project, for her actual response. "You are writing down the stories? Good!" she said. Her eyes shone with satisfaction and approval. "Good. You can vindicate me. What do you need to know?"

"You can vindicate me!" Can you imagine my mixture of feelings, Panny, when I heard my mother speak these words? I had been prepared to follow through on what I'd begun even if she didn't want me to tell the stories. Still, though I've done it again and again in my life, it is excruciating to me to go against Mama's wishes when it comes to something important to her. Of course, I was beside myself with gratitude for her unexpected enthusiasm.

On the other hand, it also felt to me that all of a sudden, by speaking those four words—"you will vindicate me"—Mama was threatening to snatch away my project to make it hers. I was worried, and I was right to worry, too. Even now, after I have been working on these stories all these years, the question of Mama's vindication keeps coming up again and again in the very places I least want to think about it, often in spite of what I do; and every time it does, in some very subtle ways it pulls against the truth I am trying to tell.

Still, Panny, I'm not sure why I worry about this the way I do. As you know yourself, the theme of the vindication of mother by daughter is not alien to the spiritual houses we are talking about. Though I hardly know about the burdens Grammar must have borne in her generation, it is easy to imagine that from the day you married Papa Charles, you longed to "show Papa," to have your life vindicated before your tyrannical, dismissive father. Knowing Mama as I do, I am sure that from the time Mama was old enough to cringe for you, long before you sent her off to Louisville to set right in her own life what had been wrong in yours, Mama was already doing her best to take upon herself the burden of your life and to vindicate you. No, the theme of vindication is hardly one imported to this story from the outside.

What a terrible, beloved, ambiguous, and bitter idea "vindication" seems to me to be in this family! The religious overtones of the word alone are enough to make me shiver. It calls up the dreaded preaching of Brother Smith in the Pond Fork Baptist Church of my childhood on the work of Jesus—Jesus who lays claims on our souls forever because, self-sacrificially and only partly voluntarily, he carried the burden of the sin, failure, and memory of his people upon his shoulders; Jesus who laid

163

down his own life in order to present the rest of his family righteous and vindicated before a proud, accusing Father.

I remember well the first time I figured out explicitly that one of my own appointed tasks in life was to imitate Jesus and be Mama's vindication in the eyes of all of you as well as in the eyes of my father. It happened when I was nearly twelve years old, about two months after the divorce took place, and Mama moved home to Sturgis to your farm, bringing me and my little brothers, Fred and Wesley, along with her.

Those were the worst months of Mama's life; they may also have been the worst months of mine. My grief and despair over the loss of my father were nearly unbearable.

I had always been afraid of my father's disapproval and his ability to reduce me by it to a well-shamed jelly in a matter of seconds, and my parents' divorce hadn't changed that. At the same time, I was still proud of everything about him that you and the other relatives in Sturgis had in the past seemed to admire, too: his good looks, his infinite supply of funny stories, his omnivorous intelligence, his enjoyment of life, and the energy with which he worked at everything he did. Disapproval or no, I loved him absolutely and passionately. My father was God to me, the stars in the sky, the water in the well, the air to breathe, and the earth to walk on.

In those first months, my very senses could not accept it that he had left, that he really was gone. Night after night I would lie face down on the thin beige rug on the floor of your living room, my body sore with the swallowed sobs and sorrow I was too old to be allowed to speak. Night after night, I would hear the voice of some uncle or great-uncle talking to Papa Charles on the porch, and somehow the Union County accent would transmute itself so that I would think I was hearing the voice of my father come from New York at last to bring me back to my own house. My heart would pound and I would sit up to listen; then the dreadful moment would come as it did every evening when I would realize once again that it was not my father I had heard. My father had discarded me. He no longer wanted me, and he was never coming back.

It was on one of these winter nights shortly after she had put Wes and Fred to bed in the back room that Mama came to fetch me from the living room rug to help with the supper dishes. I imagine now that Mama had had an exceptionally hard day herself, trying, as I had so often seen her do, to hold on to her dignity in the face of the family's various reactions to her divorce—reactions I believed at the time ranged from pity that she had been left by a man who no longer wanted her, through an unspoken satisfaction over the fall of the sister who had thought she was something because she'd gone to New York to live, to a peculiar 1950s Baptist self-righteousness over the fact that she had brought shame to the family by her divorce.

That I was unable, or as she seemed to think, unwilling to keep my own grief to myself in front of you, Grammar, and my various aunts and great-aunts, irritated and humiliated her beyond bearing. Though I didn't understand why my grief bothered her in the way it did, I knew it made her angry. That night when she brought me in to do the dishes, therefore, I tried hard to keep my feelings to myself, but this time she was the one who wouldn't let me.

Standing side by side in front of the sink, our faces reflected in the black mirror of the shadeless window, I remember, for a long time neither of us said anything. Then, all of a sudden, Mama glanced up and caught sight of my uncensored expression as I wiped a plate on a worn linen dish towel. "Now, what's the matter?" she asked wearily.

"Nothing," I said fiercely. I didn't want to answer, but I couldn't help myself. I swallowed two or three times, then choked out, "I miss my Daddy."

Mama made a face that was simultaneously one of exasperation, anger, and frustration. "Well, how do you think I feel?" she snapped at me. "He was my husband!"

I dropped my dish towel on the side of the sink and burst into sobbing I couldn't control. I had always been a child with more imagination than was good for me. Now that I was made vulnerable by my own nearly unbearable feelings, her words had evoked in me not just what I imagined from the outside my mother might be feeling, but the feelings themselves as though they were mine. I was crushed bodily by the burden of my mother's feelings as I experienced her abandonment, grief, and fear, and above all her humiliation and shame, as my very own.

But as if this were not enough for me, in the face of my mother's pain, which had now become mine, I felt something new: I was ashamed that, in the presence of my mother's grief, I should even have dared to take my own feelings seriously, much less have spoken them out loud.

Overwhelmed with a desire to throw myself between my mother and her pain, I sobbed harder. "I'm sorry, Mama," I apologized. "Daddy's leaving us is all my fault," I said. "It was me he didn't want."

It was at this point that Mama began to understand a little of what I had been feeling. She put down the soapy plate she had been holding and dried her hands on my wet tea towel. Then she put her arms around me and began to cry.

"No," she said as she patted my hiccuping back. "It wasn't like that at all. You didn't do anything to make him not want you. It was me he didn't want."

Then, at last, she told me how it was that we had lost Daddy. The previous summer, during the three weeks we had visited you in Sturgis, after thirteen years of Mama and Daddy's shared and happy life together, my father had "found someone else." She was a woman he worked with, Mama said, an intelligent woman with many interests, a sophisticated woman who had fascinated and entranced him.

Finally Mama got to the part that I'm certain she never told you, the part she has never gotten over the whole rest of her life. "Do you know what he said to me when I asked him how he could have done it to me after telling me over and over how much he loved me all these years?" she asked me as she drew away from me and looked in my face.

"No, Mama," I answered her fearfully. I couldn't imagine what I was about to hear.

"He told me he didn't want me anymore because he realized I was stupid and boring!" She began to cry again. "Well, I guess I am stupid and boring," she said. "Your Grandmother Cowan always did say you take after your father and not after me!"

I threw my arms around her neck. "Oh no, Mama," I sobbed. "How could he say that to you?" There was nothing else I knew to answer. Again, I was overwhelmed with shame. I hadn't understood before that she thought I was betraying her by being like my father, but I could see now that if it were true it was horrible, and it was my job to do something about it.

"I'll make it up to you," I sobbed some more. "I'll show everybody. You wait and see. I'll show Daddy, I'll show everybody," I said. What I meant was, "Don't you worry; I'll protect you and carry your suffering, and I'll never let myself be happy again until I vindicate you in the eyes of Daddy as well as your whole family, even if it kills me!"

Panny, what was there about Mama in Mrs. Simpson's house of slavery which seemed to you to be so much worse, even, than the hired hand's house Mother had so hated? Were you appalled when you realized Mama hadn't told you what was happening to her in Louisville because she was trying to protect you from the knowledge that she couldn't set right all your losses, that she couldn't vindicate you by success in the eyes of Papa? What did you think when you saw how she tried to save your life by the exchange of her own?

For that matter, Panny, do you think, as I tell you now, that when Mama appointed me that night to the job of vindicating her before my father and before you all, she could have had even so much as an inkling of what she was asking?

Or could you possibly think any of this could have the faintest connection to whatever it was Jesus did for us in the eyes of his Father?

CHAPTER TWELVE

Higher Education

The August sunlight was bouncing off the Ohio River through the open door to the main offices of the Blue Line Steamers. When it darkened for a moment, Mary Virginia looked up from her typing. It was so hot she could hardly think. Though the windows stood wide open, the humid air in the room was heavy enough that the overhead fan was barely able to move it. Even the backs of her well-groomed hands were perspiring.

"What can I do for you?" she asked the young man who had cast the shadow in the bright room.

"Two things," he said. His voice was businesslike and authoritative. "You can tell Ed Laramy that Mr. Cowan, the salesman from Allied Parts, is here to see him, and you can tell Mr. Cowan you'll go out to dinner with him tonight."

Startled and embarrassed, she dropped her eyes. Who did he think he was? She was not about to go out to dinner with some traveling salesman who showed up at the door of the Blue Line offices. She'd never eaten in a restaurant with a man; until a few months ago when she moved to Cincinnati she hadn't ever even been in a real restaurant.

When she glanced back up, he was smiling in a superior way at her discomfort. Infuriated, she noticed he was good-looking. He had black, curly hair, dark skin, and wire-rimmed glasses. In the heat, his blue shirt was still starched. A suit coat was slung over one shoulder, and a red bow tie lay against his collar.

He was as good-looking as anything she and her friends from Sturgis High had ever swooned and giggled over in the drugstore after school, better even than the men she and her girlfriends at the YWCA dreamed up together in their big tile bathroom on the fourth floor.

She felt like a cat who sits down for a bath in the face of a growling dog. Her mind kept on wandering to the girls at the Y through whose eyes she had just seen herself. She could hardly wait to tell them. How lucky she'd been to have been able to move into the Cincinnati YWCA, on top of getting a good job with Blue Line Steamers!

Of course, it wasn't only luck. She had managed it because Mr. Jackson, the father in the family Bert had fixed her up with after she had left Mrs. Simpson's house, worked for the company. Her first job in Louisville had come through him, and when he'd been transferred up the river from Louisville to Cincinnati, he had also been able to arrange a new job for her there. She knew the Jacksons had thought she would continue living with them in the new city, so she hadn't been surprised by their disappointment when she moved into the Y. She'd been sorry to disappoint them, but she was twenty-one now and almost an adult.

The man before her cleared his throat. "You can call me Fred," he said. She shook herself out of her daydream and noticed the dimple in his chin.

"What do people call you?" he was asking her. "Where are you from?"

"You're a Yankee!" she answered. His eyes were so dark she couldn't distinguish his irises from his pupils. She patted her hair, which she was wearing in what she liked to think of as a sophisticated French twist. She turned sideways in her chair—her legs were her best feature—and sat up straighter.

He came around the side of the desk and stuck out his hand, which she looked at for a moment before she took it and shook it. She'd never shaken the hand of a person her own age in a social situation, but she wasn't sure this was really a social situation.

He laughed. "You're no Yankee," he replied, "and you're not from Cincinnati, either. I'm from New York, myself, born in Manhattan, the land of the Flat Iron Building, the Fulton Fish Market, and Times Square, a real New Yorker like my father before me."

"Manhattan!" she repeated. Some of the movies she went to were set in New York City. Though she would love to visit it, Manhattan was so far away from her own home that she could hardly imagine it.

She pulled herself together at last. "My name is Mary," she said, smiling up at him by now, "Mary Wesley." No more "Mary Virginia" for her; only country girls had double names. "I'm from Union County, Kentucky, myself."

In the end, she wouldn't go out with him for dinner that night, but she agreed to go to the zoo with him the next day, which was Saturday. She figured that once she felt she knew him, if she enjoyed herself, she might get a bite to eat with him afterwards.

He arrived in a borrowed maroon Chrysler soon after lunch on Saturday, nattily dressed in an open-necked, short-sleeved, cream-colored shirt and pleated pants, but unshaven. Dressed in her own new blue sailor dress with its matching straw hat, she had taken one look at him and sent him home. "Fred Cowan, why do you think a girl would go out with you like that? Didn't your mother teach you manners?"

Fred was disconcerted, then he laughed. Though he didn't like girls who laughed at him, a proud eighteen-year-old, he was also young enough to be flattered by attention to his facial hair. "I never have had more than ten or twelve whiskers," he replied: "I didn't think you'd notice."

"Well," she said, "I did notice." She crossed her arms over her chest. "I'll wait right here for you till you come back."

Fred laughed again, annoyed and delighted at the same time. "Don't go away," he called as he pulled out of the gravel lot. "I'll be right back!"

Looking back on that moment thirteen years later, Mary could hardly believe she'd sent him back. She supposed it was because she had not yet fallen all the way in love with him, since it was only early afternoon. Certainly, it was the only time in their many years together, unmarried, married, and then unmarried again, that she wasn't so besotted with him or so afraid of displeasing him that she could ask him to do anything for her, much less hint to him, and maybe to herself too, that she found something about him less than perfect.

But she hadn't yet gotten to such an addled state. At least through three o'clock she was still free, still full of her old self-confidence. Waiting at the Y for his return, she listened to her friends' envious jokes and answered them in kind as they poked at each other with the sharp country laughter that didn't cover up their worries. Would some man choose them? Would they become wives, not the wives of the make-believe men they dreamed about, but wives of any men at all? What if they had to spend their lives as old maids, shamefully by themselves, working as secretaries somewhere, occasionally creeping out to eat alone in some public cafeteria once or twice a year?

Fred returned soon after he left, smooth-faced and grinning. Mary's friends had left him alone the first time he'd entered the lobby; this time he was treated with less respect: coming in the door, he was surrounded by Mary Virginia's friends who had draped themselves over the old green couches to give him the once-over. After a few jokes on his part, some half-smiles and no jokes from Mary, they were on their way.

They left his friend's car in the parking lot in the shadow of the building where he had parked it, and took the trolley to the zoo. The trolley clattered and shook over the bumpy tracks; they had swayed into each other continuously, touching shoulders and hips while they talked.

He asked her her age, and she told him. He asked her about her life at home, and she described her grandmother, Papa, and her aunts in their big house in Union County. She talked about her mother, about her two brothers at home and her one brother in Papa's house, and about her sisters, especially Kas, who was already married and expecting a baby. Mary was sickeningly homesick for them, and she wasn't ashamed to say so. She didn't tell him about the House on the Hill or her grief over its loss, nor about her father who had just gotten a new job as a prison guard at the federal pen in Eddyville. She told him only a little about her indentured servitude in Louisville, understanding instinctively that he would not care to hear about her "feminine" vulnerability.

Fred was charmed by her prettiness, her energy, and above all her peculiar combination of self-possession and deference to himself. Worldly and cynical as he was, her innocence of city ways and the mind-boggling complexity of her farming family were as exotic to him as a tropical island.

When she had asked him in return to talk about himself, he told her, truthfully but reluctantly, that he was eighteen but, untruthfully, that he had been "on the road" for several months now. He talked about his ambitions for his work and for his future, and he told what it was like to grow up in an apartment in Manhattan close to the big Riverside Church near Union Seminary, about running with other boys who also valued toughness, independence, and wisecracks—boys who baked potatoes in garbage cans in a vacant lot, who wove in and out of traffic on roller skates, and who sat around on fire escapes talking into the night. After that came the stories of his family's hiding out from various New York gangsters because his father wrote articles about them for the various New York newspapers. He told her about writing poetry for the literary magazine in Stuyvesant High School, and he bragged about outwitting his teachers. He told no stories, however, about his home life, how it hurt him when his father in his presence called him and his sister his "ball and chain" to his friends. Neither did he talk about his powerful, angry mother and how she would chase him around the apartment screaming at him, "I need to fight; stand still and argue with me!"

Mary Virginia was too young herself to know to worry about his age, and too naive to read enough between the lines of what he told her of his family to understand what his relationship to his mother might mean to his future wife. She only saw that he was a good-looking man who took pleasure in everything he did, whether working or playing, in a way she had never seen in a man before. Apart from his good looks, his stories, and his obvious fascination with her, she was overwhelmed by his voracious curiosity.

At the zoo, they had wandered its shady paths for hours, holding hands as though they had been together all their lives. They were delighted with each other and with themselves, and they continued to talk—or at least Fred did—as they equally admired the pink-footed park pigeons and the emerald-crowned peacocks who unfurled their tails in the grass beside them. In the late afternoon, in the coolness and the emptiness of the big cat house where they had gone for refuge against the quivering heat of an August afternoon in the Ohio River Valley, they had kissed.

A moment later they broke apart and continued up the path. They stopped at the big, bare, straw-covered yard where the elephants were kept. The elephants shook their heads and poked their trunks over the top of the fence as they waited for peanuts from the striped red bags Mary Virginia and Fred had bought from the zoo vendors.

Still silent, they wandered over to watch the seals performing for their supper. Sitting on a bench, Fred put his arm around her shoulder and drew her next to him. Though neither of them spoke, both had envied the slippery seals diving and nosing, rolling over each other, black and cool, through the shimmering waters of their green-bottomed pool.

For Mary Virginia, only one event damaged the day: directly, after the two of them had left the seal pool, they had walked past the little amphitheater up the trail and into the late afternoon shadows of the rustling trees. Suddenly, they had come upon an enclosure of chattering, scruffy baboons. Some were chasing and threatening each other, others sitting close together, concentrated as they combed each other's hair for lice with their long, human fingers.

At first, she had been interested in the big animals with their intelligent faces, then frightened and sickened by the sight—and it seemed to her the smell—of their swollen genitals, and huge, shining red bottoms. Their behinds, which looked as though the fur had been gnawed or licked away in a frenzy, reminded her of the frightening things her grandmother used to tell her about men and their animal ways with women. She didn't want to see what was in front of her; somehow, it mocked her romantic fantasies of swooning in a strong man's arms. She thought about Fred and their kiss. Confused as well as angry, she had dropped Fred's hand and turned her face away from him.

She had been humiliated and hurt by the way Fred had laughed at her repulsion and embarrassment. As far as she was concerned, he had shown himself to her at last in all his male animal crudeness. She only wanted to go back to the Y, to what the baboons had demonstrated to her were the innocent, unrealistic dreams of her friends.

Fred, for his part, didn't know what was wrong, but he took it seriously. He assumed that she was probably upset by his laughter. "Hell, Mary, I'm sorry I laughed at you," he apologized, but she wouldn't look him in the eye.

"It's all right," he said, kissing her on the cheek. "You don't have to look at me." He drew her to him gently and put his arms around her waist.

After a while she reached up and wrapped her arms around his neck. It was obvious that he hadn't understood what it was that had upset her, and she had no intention of telling him. She had learned her lesson well, back home in Union County; for something so personal, so painful as this, between a man and woman, a withholding silence was the only response that would leave her any dignity or power.

They had left the zoo soon after this, swaying into each other in the streetcar all the way back. Though the public physical display of affection violated everything she had ever been taught, she let him put his arm around her.

Self-consciously, in the parking lot in the shadow of the big building they had gotten into the car, aware that they would be alone. A little afraid, they had driven directly to the diner by the river to which Fred had planned to take her. He had hoped that Sally and Ruby, the two gum-popping young waitresses, would be there to call him by name and impress Mary a little. Neither was, and remembering the touchy time at the baboon cage at the zoo, Fred was relieved to find that they were not.

He made up for his inability to show off with the waitresses by introducing her to the chili Cincinnati was famous for, with its exotic combination of allspice, cinnamon, sharp cheese, and cool onions. After they had eaten, he had driven, fast and very badly, to the top of Eden Park. At last, even Fred was out of stories. In the sticky heat the two of them had sat entwined on the warm wall, watching the river below them change from pale blue to the shining black of seals. After a long time, they returned to the loaded privacy of the borrowed car.

Back at the Y an hour and a half later, neither of them could bring themselves to go in until the matron came to spy out what improprieties were taking place in the Chrysler. For once, Mary was too far gone even to be embarrassed.

She had gone in at last, Miss Stillwell all the while hissing with rage at this violation of the rules. "Wait until I write your mother and tell her about your behavior, young lady. What do you think she'll have to say when I tell her how you're acting?" Miss Stillwell stopped on the top step to underline her point. "We'll just see how long she leaves you here once she knows the truth about you, Mary Virginia Wesley!" Mary Virginia only smiled.

When her friends heard her come up the stairs, she refused to answer a single one of their questions. "That's the man I'm going to marry," was all she said. She could hear them whispering and giggling in the hall for a long time after she went into her room.

Her nights of childish fun with her friends were over; over the course of the day, she thought, she had become a woman. Deliberately, as a "real woman," she had given over not only her independence, but the control of her entire person, soul and body—voluntarily and completely—to the man she loved.

She never asked herself then or later how she could take it so much for granted that this decision to give up her life to any man was right. Certainly, she had been told enough times that such a "surrender" was necessary to a woman's happiness by everything she daily heard and read in the city. Still, it was a far cry from the egalitarian way men and women lived together on the farms back home in Union County, and it was very different from what the women of her family had taught her to expect out of marriage. It was the opposite for sure of what Grammar and her mother, Bert, had tried to impart to her by word and by example about what it meant to be a woman.

Nevertheless, her hormones overthrew everything Grammar had ever said. She loved the smell of Fred's skin, the texture of his hair, and the look of his hands. Her deepest longing was to lie down next to him, belly to back, for the rest of her life. All she wanted to do was to iron his shirts, cook his food, have his children.

But such a desire wasn't the result of hormones alone. It followed upon her humiliating indentured servanthood in Mrs. Simpson's house in Louisville. Never again did she intend to be so absolutely alone and without resources. Nor did her experience in Mrs. Simpson's house stand by itself. Though she never let herself actually think it, life under Mrs. Simpson's roof picked up where her life in Union County had left off: with her mother's extravagant sacrifice of the House on the Hill and with her own resulting experience of humiliation and shame in the house of a hired hand.

Fred Cowan, to use the warning words of her grandmother when she was a child, was a "man who ran," a man who knew how to work and would make something of himself. Not only would he love her and take care of her; men who ran made something of their wives and children, too. The giving over of her person, body and soul, to such a man seemed a small price to pay in exchange for a home, for love, and for an end to her shame.

The marriage took place within a month of the trip to the zoo, though the wedding was nothing like the beautiful event Mary had imagined for herself.

Labor Day weekend 1939 was hot, as hot as the day Mary Virginia met Fred, and Mary Virginia was limp with the heat and especially quiet in a way Fred had not yet seen her. As they were having their chili for lunch on Saturday, Fred asked her if there was anything special she wanted to do, any place she wanted to go on Labor Day that would cheer her up.

Mary Virginia had written several letters to Union County over the past few weeks, and it was this correspondence that was getting her down. She hadn't told her mother explicitly what she had told her friends the night of her first date, but she had, uncharacteristically, found herself telling Bert a lot more about Fred and the things they did together than she really intended.

Though Mary Virginia had no way of knowing it, her mother had understood from her first letter that, if Fred would have her, Mary Virginia would marry him, and there would be nothing Bert could do to prevent it, even if she wanted to. Bert had not directly responded to this fact; rather, she had kept her own letters back to Mary Virginia calm, loving, and almost without advice. She wrote instead about Papa Charles's new job at the penitentiary at Eddyville and about the activities of Kas and her husband, A.D., of Mary's three brothers and sister at home, and of Mary Virginia's stolen brother, Bob, at Grammar's.

Bert's concealing letters made Mary Virginia feel more out of touch with her mother, more cast out and hopelessly homesick than ever. When Fred asked her what she wanted to do on Monday, therefore, without even thinking or seriously intending it, she had sighed and answered: "I want to go home."

"Damn!" Fred had replied—he liked to swear; it was fun to jolt her polite feminine sensibilities, and that made him feel more of a man than ever—"Damned if we can't borrow the car again from Dudley and do it."

As besotted as she was, he was looking for a chance to do the impossible for her. He himself was up for an adventure and too self-confident to be put off by the idea of meeting Mary's enormous, powerful family. It didn't occur to him that they wouldn't like him. Having a tough and resourceful German grandfather of his own who farmed in upstate New York, he had none of the contempt of the city man for the farmer, nor did he suffer from romanticism about farming. He believed farmers were men after his own heart. He admired their toughness, their independence, and above all, their ability to work long hours seven days a week.

"If I can get the Chrysler, we ought to be able to make it to Union County in about ten hours, if we drive fast and don't stop," he said.

At this, Mary was too surprised to answer; she hadn't meant to make a serious suggestion. They had only two days left of the weekend, after all, but even if they'd had more time, Fred's driving was so dreadful that she knew she would be taking her life in her hands to drive that far with him. Moreover, Mary was not so sanguine about her family's acceptance of him. She had seen for herself the ways in which they ran off potential beaus—or even friends, for that matter—by making them look ridiculous.

Though it wasn't true of her father, the Wynns thought there were no people on earth good enough to be their social equals—not just Yankees, but people from town, tenant farmers, people from farms smaller than theirs, Catholics. Why should she expect them to accept Fred? At the same time, against the odds, she trusted Fred to stand up to them and win their respect.

The long and the short of it was that Mary was too homesick to turn down this opportunity, however dangerous it was. She hadn't been home since the previous Christmas, and she couldn't stand it much longer. She had answered against her better judgment, "OK, let's do it. We can stay at Grammar's; even if that old Baptist preacher is there, there'll still be room. You can sleep in Aunt Ginny's old room with Bob, and I'll sleep in Aunt Nacky's bed with her." Then, because she was halfway angry with her mother for being so calm when she, Mary Virginia, was in such turmoil from her homesickness, she added, "We'll surprise them all; we won't call Daddy and Mother till we get there."

Fred and Mary had separated shortly after that, Mary to pack and organize food for the trip and Fred to wheedle the Chrysler out of the gullible Dudley. Fred picked her up at the Y the next morning in a smoky darkness and a blowing rain, then they bumper-carred their way out of a sleeping Cincinnati, down the two-lane highway that more or less followed the Ohio River on the Ohio and Indiana side, passing up the bridge to the still sleeping Louisville, and off into southern Indiana.

For Mary Virginia the ride was awful; she may have been foolhardy and she may had been in love, but she wasn't stupid. As the car bounced and zigzagged down the road, she held on to whatever she could grab as though her life depended on it. Though she had known Fred was a bad driver, she had never been on the highway with him before. Moment by moment his driving was proving much worse than she had thought. Every truck they tailgated, every oncoming, Sunday-school going car that swerved honking out of their way, filled her with appropriate terror.

"Would you like me to drive a while?" she asked at last. Knowing it would hurt his pride and make him mad, she had put it off as long as possible, but now she really feared for their lives. "I could spell you for a little. I'm a good driver, Fred; I've been driving a truck since I was twelve years old."

She'd been right about his pride. Fred turned his head from the road to glare at her, terrifying her still further. Hastily, she looked straight ahead toward the gray, rushing road.

"Women drivers!" he said with disgust. "I've never seen a woman yet who knew what to do behind a wheel. All they do is poke and piddle."

Poking and piddling was exactly what she wanted to do. By this time, however, Mary had learned that making generalizations about the weakness and fallibility of women was one of Fred's favorite conversational topics. She had also learned the hard way that if she tried to argue with him about anything, she would feel stupid and incompetent, and be in tears within five minutes. This wasn't something she could afford at the moment, so she tried to distract him from his hurt pride.

She took a deep breath and let it out slowly. "Who taught you to drive and how old were you when you learned? Where did your Daddy keep a car in New York City?" she asked.

He wasn't about to let himself be appeased as easily as that. "Learned to drive a car? I've never had a driving lesson in my life." He laughed.

"Hell, the first time I was ever behind the wheel of a car was a month ago when we went to the zoo. Why would a man need somebody to teach him to run a piece of machinery?" He laughed again. "By the way, my father doesn't have a car; everybody knows that people who live in New York take taxis everywhere."

Speechless with anger at his arrogance and her inability to argue with him, Mary Virginia concentrated on gripping the hand strap that hung above her door with one hand, while she held on to the seat with the other. How could she have ever thought she loved this man?

Fred had no reason to notice Mary's frustrated anger. He was a man. Being free himself to say exactly what he wanted to her, exactly when he wanted to say it, he had no reason to be a grudge-holder. His own self-righteous touchiness was spent. After a while, he reached over to pat her shoulder, and so they drove on in silence.

A half hour later it began to grow darker. Then the rain, which had slacked off for most of the flat parts of southern Indiana, started up again in great sheets, which crashed in opaque waves against the wind- shield. In this new threat to their safety, Mary tucked away her grudge for later. Quickly, they rolled up the windows, but the situation was impossible; even before they had the vents closed, the windows had steamed up and the road before them had become invisible.

Above the sound of the storm Mary Virginia shouted, "This is too much to drive through; let's stop and eat in Dale." She'd been trying by the sheer effort of will to keep Fred driving the car in a straight line as well as to control her anger. It was wearing her out; she figured they both needed to stop.

Fred was tired; he was ready for a stop himself. "OK," he answered. "I know a great place that serves barbecue. Do you think you could eat barbecue?"

"Sounds good to me," she said, grateful that he was willing to quit for a while. By now, if he had suggested they stop and chew rubber she would have been glad to do it.

"Here," he said, grabbing the Indiana map out of the pocket in the door to hand it to her, "see if you can tell how far we have to go to get to Dale."

She turned on the map light, took the map from his hand, spread it out and refolded it.

"I found Dale," she raised her voice above the storm, "but I can't see exactly where we are."

"I love you, Mary," he answered in a sudden rush of feeling.

It was at that moment, before she could call back "I love you, too," that both of them saw the curve in the road in front of them that had been obliterated by the rain. They were going too fast to take the curve, too fast even to slow down to a safe speed. Mary Virginia closed her eyes and prayed. Fred lifted his foot off the gas pedal and, knowing nothing about driving, threw on the brakes as hard as he could.

The tires squealed and the car began its inevitable skid. Fred wrenched the wheel back in the direction of the road as hard as he could. Mary stopped breathing as she felt the skidding car pick up speed. Then they heard a sound like an exploding shotgun. Under the impact of the blown tire, the Chrysler hurled into the air and slammed itself back against the road two or three times.

Fred hung onto the wheel as best he could, to no avail. In an instant, they were off the gravel of the shoulder, bumping and rolling over a thirty-foot embankment they wouldn't have been able to see the bottom of, even if it had been daylight. How many times the heavy Chrysler rolled over they never knew; what they did know was that the last roll was followed by an enormous drop. The car stopped upright with both doors open in a ditch at the edge of a field full of the dark, wet shapes of sleeping cattle.

In the ditch the darkness was complete; neither could see the other. For an unspecified length of time, there was silence.

Mary Virginia came to consciousness first. "Fred?" she whispered as the fingers of her right hand felt the back of her head for the enormous lump that was forming on it. "Fred? Are you all right?" Tentatively, afraid of hurting him if he were still alive, she stretched out her hand toward where she expected him to be.

"Mary?" he answered, wincing as he reached toward her on the seat beside him. "My wrist is sprained, I think, but, oh Mary, you aren't dead!" He was so relieved that she was safe he could hardly speak.

From the sheer release of tension, Mary began to shake all over, then to sob. For an instant he was filled again with panic. "Are you hurt?" he asked.

"I don't know," she answered. Still shaking, she felt the rest of herself all over. Though she was bruised all over and the cuts on her hands and face were beginning to sting and pinch, miraculously nothing was broken. All of a sudden she began to feel around the floor with her feet and then her hands.

"Mary, what is wrong? What are you doing?" He asked, alarmed again.

"It's my new shoes," she answered. "I've lost my new shoes."

At that, Fred began to laugh until he couldn't catch his breath; like the rain outside, relief that he hadn't lost her was sweeping over him in great gusts of joy. This time he pulled her so close to him it made her whimper. "Mary, I love you," he said. "I'll buy you a thousand shoes if you want, ten thousand shoes. Let's get married. I want to marry you before I kill you."

"Get married?" They had never spoken of marriage, but she had thought of nothing else for a month. "Get married?" she asked. "Oh, yes, yes!" Like a drunk at the sort of party she'd never been to, she began to laugh, herself.

"Let's go on up there and get someone to give us a ride into town," she said at last, catching her breath. "Kas told me when I went away that if I ever called her, she'd come and get me, if it were at the end of the world. Well, now's the time; we'll call her and A.D. to come and get us and take us to Grammar's. It's a shame we can't get a license and get married tonight. Brother Smith'll be staying at Grammar's sure as the world."

As it turned out, neither of them had to climb the embankment and flag down a car. A passing state trooper stopped his patrol car to see why there were car lights on in the ditch at the bottom of the hill.

The middle-aged trooper was just what the two euphoric, shaking young people needed. Carefully, he helped them both up the hill to put them in the backseat of his car. He made another trip for the luggage, which he stowed away in the trunk; then he made one more trip to check out the state of the utterly wrecked Chrysler in the ditch.

By the time he brought them to the police station in Dale itself, it was five o'clock. Mary used the sheriff's phone to call Kas and A.D., telling them only where they were, that there had been an accident, and that Kas was not to tell anyone that they were coming. Kas was well enough trained in family silence not to push for further

181

information. She promised that if they could leave the baby with Aunt Blacky going through Morganfield, they would be in Dale by eight.

They got there exactly at eight. Coming through the door to the tiny police station, Kas laughed and groaned at the sight of the bloodied but happy Mary Virginia. Then she turned, still laughing, to the equally battered, happy Fred.

"Who the heck are you?" she asked him, hugging him, too. "I'm Fred Cowan," he said, shaking the huge hand A.D. held out to him, "and I'm going to marry your sister if I don't kill her first." He and Mary looked at each other and began to laugh again.

"Well," said A.D., "if that's the case, we'd better get on the road as soon as we can and figure out how you're going to do it."

They did figure it out, too. By the time they had gone through Evansville, crossed the bridge over the Ohio River, and driven through Henderson on the other side, A.D. remembered that the County Clerk in Morganfield was a member of his Sunday school class in Sturgis. Calling from the gas station on the edge of town, A.D. got him out of bed to meet them at the courthouse to issue a marriage license. At Aunt Blacky's, where they stopped next to pick up the baby, they called Grammar to tell them they were coming and to ask for help.

Grammar was Grammar, prepared for anything. She assured them that the preacher was, indeed, spending the night and that she would have him up and dressed by the time they got there. And they needn't worry about witnesses: with the exception of Aunt Blacky, who would be coming along with them, all the aunts were already there for a Rook party, as well as Cousin Frances from California, Papa's brother, Uncle John the doctor, and Mary's brother Bob, who for all practical purposes lived there.

The two conspicuous absences from Grammar's that night were Bert and Charles, having moved to Eddyville for Papa Charles's job. This being the case, Grammar asked Mary were they sure they wouldn't rather wait until next morning?

No, said Mary. She was unreasonably hurt that they weren't already there for this most important event in her life. Of course, she realized they weren't there because they hadn't known she was coming. What she didn't let herself admit was that she was also angry and embarrassed that her own father wouldn't do any better for himself than to have a job in a prison, and she blamed her mother for going along with it.

No, Mary said, she would call them afterward and tell them her news. She and Fred could see them in the morning.

And this is how it happened. When they arrived at Grammar's and Papa's house at last, they were taken in and hugged and their injuries exclaimed over. They were led to the back of the house to wash up and don their wedding garments. Over her cuts and lumps and bruises, Mary put on her brown and white rayon dress with the jewel buttons she had made before she moved to Louisville. Along with his sprained left wrist and his own cuts and bumps, Fred dressed up in his double-breasted tan suit and brown bow tie he'd inexplicably brought.

The two of them stood up together in the midst of as much of the family as was assembled in Grammar's and Papa's living room. There, in front of the empty fireplace, they exchanged their vows, Fred to "love, honor and cherish," Mary to "love, honor and obey" as long as they both would live. There was no ring for Mary, of course, but she hardly felt she needed one.

Afterwards, while the men teased Fred and the rest of them drank glasses of the thick float and ate the date cake left over from the Rook party, Mary called her mother and daddy to break the news. What they thought of it, whether it wounded them that their own daughter could not wait till the next morning to have her parents at her wedding, whether they were frightened that Mary had married a man they didn't know, or sad that this marriage meant that Mary was gone for good— none of this did they say, nor did it occur to Mary to wonder about it. She and Fred were married, and for that night, at least, nothing else mattered.

Though the wedding itself was nothing like Mary Virginia's fantasies of such events, the first two months of marriage were pretty much as she expected.

As a married lady, Mary went in on the Tuesday after they returned to Cincinnati and resigned her job with Blue Line, effective that moment. She and Fred spent the rest of the day looking for an apartment into which they could immediately move. Shortly after lunch they found what they were looking for in Eden Park, not far from where they had gone to watch the river a month earlier. Partially furnished, with two well-lit bedrooms and a pine-paneled kitchen and breakfast nook, it looked to Mary like a picture in one of the women's magazines she had recently begun to buy. After signing the lease, Fred had helped her shop for some of the bare essentials necessary for life in the apartment.

From Wednesday on, when Fred went back on the road, during the week she was on her own. Those first weeks she performed the ordinary household chores of shopping, cooking, doing the wash, and ironing with energy and enthusiasm. She cleaned like a crazy woman, scrubbing walls, windows, floors, woodwork, stove, refrigerator, tiles, bathtub, toilet, sink. She shopped for kitchen stuff, sheets and towels, and second-hand furniture. She selected fabric for curtains and a bedspread. She measured everything, cut out what she measured with the sewing shears she had bought for herself at the Y, and because she had no sewing machine, she sewed everything by hand with tiny stitches. Fred, convinced that his wife could do anything in the domestic field, admired everything.

At first, this is exactly what she wanted. She longed to be and do for her husband all the things the women's magazines told her men wanted from a wife. She wanted to make a home he could come back to and be proud of. She wanted everything clean and orderly, from the windows to the worktable. She wanted every meal she cooked for him to be tasty and full of vitamins. She wanted his shirts ironed just right and the points of his starched handkerchiefs to stick up sharp in his suit coat pockets. She wanted him to come in the door at the end of the day to find her clean and waiting, hair and dress and shoes appealing. She wanted to be perfect for him—perfectly beautiful, perfectly desirable, and perfectly admiring in all things.

As for the hard work it took to give him all this, it suited her just fine. At a level that had nothing to do either with Fred Cowan or with romance, she was glad for the work. She had come from a hard-working family who, with the exception of her father, despised inactivity. Above everything else, they admired get-up-early, stay-up-late work and the women and men who knew how to do it. Mary liked work; it made her feel that she was doing something significant. When she wasn't working, she felt like nobody.

It also pleased her that much of what she did was exactly the opposite of how her mother lived with her father. Obscurely, as all daughters do, I suppose, Mary set out to "show her mother." She respected her mother and she loved her, but it also made her angry that Bert was so old-fashioned, so full of moans and groans, so carelessly uninterested in making herself desirable to her father. No wonder he wasn't much of a farmer when they lived in the House on the Hill; it was her mother's fault they'd lost it!

This would never happen to her. She had married a man who ran. She would work to be a good wife and please him; she would make herself happy for him, and she would be safe.

And for the first few months this is the way she thought it was going to be. Then, one Tuesday morning, Mary realized that most of the job of setting up the household was done. With Fred out of town as usual until Friday, the only things left for her to do were the daily chores, but she had done almost all of them for the week already. On Friday it would take her half a day to mop and vacuum, dust and cook, and that was it. Even if she worked on her embroidered tablecloth two hours a day and wrote letters to her mother, her grandmother, and all her aunts, between Tuesday morning and Friday evening there was no work for her to do.

There was no work, and she was completely by herself. It wasn't simply that Fred was not there. With the exception of those months in Mrs. Simpson's house, it was the only time in her life that she had had no one to talk to at all. Her family was more than eight hours away. She no longer saw her friends from the Y or from work. Fred liked her family, but he didn't like her friends and he let her know that he didn't want to find them there when he was home.

At one level, she hadn't minded the loss; their lives were so different now that it was hard to imagine what they would have to say to each other. What she really missed was her life at Blue Line Steamers, those days when her mind had had something to chew on and her boss had praised her for her skill and quickness!

For one horrible month, she tried to put the thought of her old job out of her mind. She began to work on elaborate handmade presents for Fred's family, whom she would meet for the first time at Christmas. She tried to make friends with a standoffish older couple in the building by baking them pies and cakes and leaving them outside their door. She attempted to meet some other young women by going to the midweek service at the Methodist church she attended when Fred was out of town.

It was all in vain. She was twenty-one years old, she was lonely, she was so bored she couldn't stand it, and so restless she could hardly sit down. At the beginning of the second week in December, one hour after Fred left for the road, she was on the trolley. She walked in the front door of Blue Line Steamers two hours before noon. In the time since she'd left, three incompetent temporaries had come and gone. Her boss was thrilled to have her back.

Not having decided what she was going to do until after Fred left the previous Monday morning, she could scarcely have told her husband about her decision. It was not until the Thursday evening before his return that she let herself think even briefly about how he might react.

Still, whatever he thought, it was her own life, and surely, so long as she kept his house and cooked his meals, what she did with it while he wasn't in town was her own business. He was a worker himself, and he loved her and wanted her to be happy, just as she loved him and wanted him to be happy in return.

Or so she told herself until four o'clock Friday, when the door of the office at Blue Line Steamers slammed open and Fred Cowan walked in grim faced. She drew back a little as he came around the side of her desk and took hold of the top of her right arm.

"All right," he said to her in a voice so cold it could have frozen the Ohio River outside her window. "Get your coat, and I mean get it now. I don't know what you think you're doing here, but you're going home this minute and you aren't coming back!"

Too stunned by the tone of Fred's voice, not to mention his hand on her arm to answer back, Mary stood up to obey.

At this moment her boss opened his own door and stuck his head out to see what the cause of the disturbance in his outer office was. What he saw didn't please him.

"Mary, what is going on here?" he asked. "Do you need help?"

Before Mary could get in a word, Fred turned to him. "No, she doesn't need help," he said, "and you mind your own business. She's my wife, and I say whether she needs help or not. She doesn't work for you, and don't you forget it."

Her boss was rendered speechless, but Fred went on to speak the words that would continue to hurt and shame her whenever she remembered them the rest of her life.

"You don't tell her what to do," he said. "Nobody tells me what to do but my boss at Allied Parts. I'm her boss; she works for me."

So that was the end of that particular fantasy. Thirteen years later on the night train from Delaware to Jacksonville, where she was going to get the divorce he'd asked for, she remembered it with bitter grief. She could recall nothing of what they had said to each other or done that weekend after she went home with him from the Blue Line Steamers.

What he had done didn't hurt her love for him. On the contrary, the very sight of him continued over all the years of their marriage to make her knees tremble and her heart race, and she continued to want to be for him everything he expected her to be.

Only she knew now that life with Fred wasn't exactly what she had thought it would be. She had believed that marriage would make her a free woman and fill the empty hole in the center of her body that had opened when she left the House on the Hill. Now she understood that she had been free before but she hadn't known it. She suspected that she could work her fingers to the bone out of love for Fred Cowan for the rest of her life, but he would never see her work as any more than what she already owed him. She should have known it; everything she read in her women's magazines and heard from her friends told her that a wife had better regard herself as a hired hand in her husband's house if she wanted to please him. That's just the way it was, and this time, even if she'd wanted it, there would be no mother coming to rescue her.

On the Monday after Fred had come to get her, for the first time Mary hadn't written home. There was nothing she could have told them that wouldn't have saddened and disappointed them and shamed her even more. Her only course was silence, and so for the next dozen years until society regarded her as fired, that's the way it was.

CHAPTER THIRTEEN

Playing Houses

You know, Panny, during hard times as an adult, I have always dreamed of houses. Sometimes I've known that these dreams have had their foundations in practical difficulties I've encountered living in the actual, solid dwelling places I inhabit during my waking life. Sometimes my dreams have risen two floors or more over the dirt basements of more difficult things that have oppressed my spirit. Living with my first husband over the years in places that were too small for me, I often used to have a hard time telling which was which.

Do you remember where we lived on Pokagon Street in South Bend before Benjamin was born? If you can recall from your one visit there when you were already so old, it was what they call a "Dutch colonial," a sturdy, two-story, three-bedroom, white frame house with natural oak woodwork on the first floor and a single bathroom on the second. The house was nice enough to look at, and it would have been very suitable for most other families with two children or so.

For me, life there was cramped, body and soul. My husband needed the largest of the second floor bedrooms for his study in which to work on his dissertation. Before Benjamin was born, this probably would have been just fine for all of us if it had not been for the fact that the house was so small that while he was working Anna Grace and I needed to be dead quiet and stay off his floor where the single bathroom and our bedrooms incidentally also were. Believe me, Panny, it is hardly surprising that I found that house worse than oppressive; it was as though I had breathed up the whole of my share of the oxygen in it by eight o'clock every morning.

I remember during the three years we lived there that I dreamed endlessly about discovering whole suites of rooms I hadn't known were in it. In one recurring dream I would walk down the steep flight of stairs to the basement with a load of dirty laundry in my arms, drop the clothes in the washing machine, start it up, and finally lean exhausted against the crumbling painted yellow brick wall by the dryer. Always at that point in the dream, a door I had never noticed before would swing open suddenly behind me. I still recall the look of the bright, secret places that were waiting for me there night after night, behind that dream door—a large study of my own, a bedroom with a single bed and flowers on the dresser, and a little room for reading, peaceful and soundless and full of open windows.

I used to discover attic rooms in my dreams in that house, too. On some errand in the top half of the house, I would suddenly see a previously unnoticed trapdoor with a rope handle in the ceiling of the upstairs hall, pull down the handle, and walk up a staircase into a new world where there was space for me to live and air for me to breathe.

The last ten years of that marriage were full of these dreams, and even in the better years that followed—the years of the development of my professional life and my happy marriage to Richard—in every time of transition in my life I have continued to dream of houses.

I've always remembered my significant dreams, Panny, ever since childhood, so it seems odd to me that I don't have any memories of house dreams from that dreadful year Mama, Fred, Wesley and I left my father in Delaware for good and moved in with you and Papa Charles into your old farmhouse in Union County. Certainly the circumstances would have prompted such dreams. Perhaps I had them, but, in spite of what I expect, I simply don't remember.

It's hard to believe I wouldn't have dreamed of a house that first night on the farm with you. I have a clear enough memory of a fitful sleep under the ugly dark wool quilt in that high, heavy bed that stood beneath the back windows where the sink had been when the room had been the kitchen. I remember waking up, too, that first dreadfully early morning to find my mother in the bed beside me, radiating in some incomprehensible manner a combination of utter unconsciousness, devastated grief, and angry, energetic bewilderment.

What it was that actually awakened me that morning I don't recall, if I ever knew. It might have been what soon became for me the ordinary noises of your rocking chair creaking in the silent room next door. It may have been the hateful sound of the mourning doves outside my window, calling out their dreary grief over the dark fields behind the house.

Or what jolted me out of sleep might have been my first real awareness of what was happening to me: even the night before, after the grinding move, the long trip by train, the whole of the time in the car, and all the greetings and cooings of aunts and great-aunts, I still hadn't really let myself think about the fact that this trip to Union County was not one more vacation to visit you and Papa Charles on the farm. I had known well enough that I was leaving behind in the house in Delaware not only the toys and dolls of my childhood — I was almost twelve, after all—but even the furniture of my room, my red stenciled bed, my matching dresser, my chair, and my cut-out mirror. Before that first morning, though, I hadn't really let myself acknowledge what all these leavings were about to mean.

Something in that first Kentucky night shocked me from unawareness to hyperawareness, and I wouldn't be surprised if that "something" weren't one of the familiar house dreams I came to associate with my later years. Whether this was really the case I couldn't say. What I can say, however, is this: I woke up that morning believing, without a shadow of a doubt, in the deepest and most diffuse parts of myself, that from now on I was absolutely alone, not only without a father but without a house for my body or for my soul, utterly homeless in a universe that had not one single landmark in it I could recognize or be comforted by.

This profound sense of homelessness, I suppose, is why that year in Union County I filled the edges of my school notebooks obsessively with complex sketches of the floor plans of imaginary houses, looked for secret hiding places under the bushes in the woods next to your house, and built myself tiny rooms and closets out of Wesley's wooden blocks. I think I was making a home for myself in the alternative universe of my mind.

Almost always these building projects were secret activities, but once, surprisingly, or maybe not so surprisingly, considering what finally happened to him, Bobby Wynn played "house" with me. I wouldn't have played this game with one of my girl cousins, of course. They had real houses of their own, and besides, I was too intimidated and confused by the way their mothers, and especially their fathers, doted on them, petting them and calling them "little girl" and "missy" to be comfortable in their presence.

Of course I wasn't aware at the time of what I know now about Uncle Bob, how he had been stolen by Papa in spite of all your efforts, and how he continued to bluff his way out of his own participation in that theft with his toughness and his demand that his three sons be equally tough. I did know instinctively that there was something about Bobby Wynn, his middle son, that made him similar to me, something about him that was, as they said in those days, "not quite right." He was a boy who couldn't be good, who couldn't be what his father expected no matter how hard he tried, a child to whom his father never spoke without irritation in his voice.

I wouldn't want to suggest by this, however, that the day Bobby Wynn played houses with me I had deliberately decided to seek him out for this game in particular. I hadn't. I had only talked Mama into driving me down the road to Uncle Bob and Aunt Ida's farm that unseasonably warm October Saturday not long after we moved in with you and Papa Charles, because I was anxious and restless in that house of yours where there was so much feeling and so little words. My cousins Charles Stanton, Bobby Wynn, and John Scott were all three younger than I; Mama had been surprised that I wanted to go, and I hadn't been sure what I expected to do there myself.

It was mid-morning, I remember, when Mama drove on past Pond Fork Baptist Church, turned down the lane, and dropped me off. Aunt Ida was in the kitchen in her beautiful low, antique-filled, long-windowed house. (Was I actually there for that magical house, and not really for my cousins at all?) Uncle Bob was busy in the barn with the quarter horses he raised.

191

Customarily out on the farm without playmates other than their brothers, my two blond cousins, Charles Stanton and John Scott, and my black-haired cousin Bobby Wynn, met me enthusiastically at the back door by the kitchen. Free, at least for a little while, of the controlling attention of the grown-ups in our lives, we children quickly established ourselves in the big half grassy, half bare-earthed space under the live oak trees between the house and the barn.

It was a beautiful morning, full of the interesting smells of a dry, soon to be hot day on a Kentucky farm in fall: sweet hay, manure, yellow dust, a chicken yard, and the acrid odor of some drying weed. The sun, I remember, was early enough to cast the long dark shadows of autumn on the ground among the trees, but strong enough to make us squint when we looked up to see the great white puffs of clouds that stood in contrast to the dark blue sky.

Do you remember Uncle Bob's concrete horse trough that stood beneath the biggest live oak? Surely you do; it was four feet deep at least, its thick, straight sides about the length and width of an ordinary bathtub. Long green moss grew like grass on its inside walls, but you couldn't see the moss unless you put your face down close enough to look through the reflecting surface of the water into its nearly opaque depths. That day I was fascinated with the tiny body of water, and I was ecstatic when Aunt Ida let us strip down to our underwear and sink ourselves, dreaming, up to our necks in its strange black water.

Later, after we had dried off with some old striped towels from the clothesline behind the house, we dressed and moved our games to the barn. Charles and John Scott, tough and full of the proud, aggressive energy they'd learned from their father, leaped up the ladder to the hayloft with pretend guns and knives to call each other names, shoot, and jump on each other from the towering stacked bales of yellow hay.

Bobby Wynn was dark-skinned like Papa, ironically, with straight black hair that kept falling down into his dark eyes, but he was small for his age and a dreamer, without the energetic character of his father and his brothers. He went with me into the slat-walled corncrib to help make a little house on top of the dry corn the cattle ate. How we decided to do this or what we consciously thought we were doing, I couldn't have told you at the time, but I do recall that Bobby Wynn and

I, considering the nonaggressive ways of both of us, played what should have been a peaceful game with an amazing fierceness.

We laid down the corncob outline of the walls of our rooms first, waving our hands and arguing over the plan of the bedrooms, kitchen, and living room as though our lives depended on it. After our rooms were completed, we put an equal attention into furnishing the house exactly the way we wanted it, making beds, chairs, and tables from a broken piece of dowel we found in the barn and cut to shape with Bobby Wynn's pocketknife, along with the corn husks we ripped from the hard yellow corn around us.

Except for the tension involved in the laying down of our walls together, it was soothing, deeply satisfying play for both of us displaced children. Inevitably our healing game came to an end, however, when we were struck down by the wrath of God in the person of Uncle Bob and sent once more out into the thorns and sweat of our brows in the real world in which we lived.

Exile from our very small and temporary paradise happened like this. Having filled up our house with the furniture we had deemed necessary for rudimentary family life, we had begun to construct out of corn shucks the father, mother, girl, boy, and baby dolls who would play out their psychic dramas in our home. What we were doing took a lot of concentration; our materials were stiff, and the work needed more eye-hand coordination than either of us had. Focused as we were on what we were doing, neither of us heard Uncle Bob come into the barn or noticed him peering suspiciously into the corn bin to see what we were about. Charles and John Scott, who had come down the ladder to find out what we were doing, had heard him, though, and they were up the ladder and into the loft before we even saw that they were gone.

Some close sound of a throat clearing or an indrawn breath made me look up, and all at once I saw Uncle Bob's face dark red with rage looking at us through the rough slats. In the next terrible minute he was through the door, ignoring me entirely to turn the whole of his scornful adult attention on his eight-year-old son. "What are you doing?" he shouted at Bobby Wynn, his rising voice mocking and desperate, almost tearful. "Playing with dolls!" He grabbed Bobby Wynn by the top part of his arm right below the armpit and yanked him upright.

"You're such a sissy!" he kept on shouting. "You're nothing but a girl! What's the matter with you?" he screamed in a higher pitch. "Why won't you be a boy like you're supposed to, you horse's titty?"

Bobby Wynn whimpered, shock, shame, then cringing despair in his face, as Uncle Bob dragged him off to the house or behind the barn, or someplace else I couldn't imagine, to "whup his hide."

As for me, I was left shaking and crying in the bands of sunlight and shadow that patterned the floor of the corncrib, our house and the homemade dolls that were to inhabit it scattered around me now like so many pieces of trash. Besides the fact that Uncle Bob didn't like Bobby Wynn playing dolls, besides the fact that my uncle had just underlined for me what it seemed to me that my own father believed about the human female, I didn't understand what either of us had done to provoke this violence.

On reflection at the time, all I could come up with was what I used to think in New York when my mother would tell me that I only read books I liked "to escape," and send me out of the house "to play" with the gang of jeering, girl-hating boys who lived in our neighborhood: it was a law of nature that adults would inevitably find something horribly wrong with a child's attempts to create a safe space the grown-ups couldn't get at.

Many years later, in the midst of the cynical unhappiness of my first marriage, I would have given myself another explanation of what went wrong that day: there was no man on earth who could stand the sight of a woman, or a child-woman, setting the terms of her life in her own house, or the sight of another man supporting her while she did it. Considering the men I know now, and especially my generous and gentle husband, Richard, that judgment seems a bit harsh to me today.

At any rate, whatever my offense that summery October day of 1952, when I went into the house to call my mother to come and get me, I was so angry at Uncle Bob and so ashamed of whatever unknown thing it was I was supposed to be guilty of, I could hardly speak. Aunt Ida and Uncle Bob as well as my three cousins were out of sight when Mama arrived ten minutes later. Mama seemed as absentminded as she always was around me then. When I climbed into the car, she didn't notice I'd been crying, or if she did, she didn't ask me what had happened or what was wrong. I hadn't expected it. No one would ever have asked that sort of question in our family, would they?

To this day I've never told Mama or anybody else in Union County what had happened to Bobby Wynn and me in the barn that morning, but I came to think about it frequently and sadly when my cousin met his death driving along the road to his parents' house ten years later.

As certain as the sun coming up over a new field, Panny, when I come to Union County to visit my aunts and my cousins, or at least what is left of them, I dream about Bobby Wynn. In my dreams I redesign the rooms of his life and rearrange the furniture in it, as surely as I sometimes still work on my own houses in my sleep.

CHAPTER FOURTEEN

Asking

$\mathcal{A}$mid the bright light and deep shadow in the upstairs hall of the new house in Delaware, Mary was bending over, restlessly sorting laundry from the wicker hamper and studying Fred's white shirts for loose buttons, ink blots, and food stains. She had left the overhead light off to save electricity, and her brown eyes squinted through a dimness made dimmer by the intense light that was streaming through the window at the head of the stairs. Her unlipsticked mouth was puckered with concentration.

It was hot work, and a hot morning, even for the day after Labor Day. The heat irritated her and the sun wore her out; she could tell both were going to get worse as the day progressed. Considering that Roberta and Freddy were already back in school, it didn't seem right that the weather was what it was. Every year it took her by surprise that summer didn't end with the first day of school.

As she pulled a brown knit shirt of Freddy's from the bottom of the hamper, sweat dripped off the tip of her nose and made a dark spot on the shirt. In her uneasiness, and having even less patience with her own fallibility than usual, she muttered to herself as she wiped her face with the back of her hand and tossed the spotted shirt into its appropriate pile.

"Here I am, thirty-four years old, a grown woman, the mother of an eleven-year-old, a seven-year-old, and a baby. Anybody would think I'd have learned by now that Labor Day never is the end of summer!"

In the dark part of the hall amid the dirty clothes, Mary stood up, put her hand on her hip and straightened her back, frowning and shaking herself. She pushed away from her face the front edge of the old silk scarf that she wore to cover the alternating rows of tight silver curlers and the bare scalp between them. She was uncomfortable all over. Her feet hurt, and the short sleeves of her baggy brown cotton housedress were bunched up painfully under her arms. She pulled out her sleeves, then yanked on the sides of the skirt to straighten the hem.

She glanced down at her feet, noticing with distaste the calluses on her shiny red toes as they poked out of the split seams of her penny loafers. She shrugged her shoulders: she could change her clothes, but right now it would simply take too much effort. Besides, she certainly wasn't about to do the laundry in her good shoes. She already intended to have a shower and clean herself up before Fred was supposed to come home—though things being what she was afraid they were, she didn't imagine it would do much good.

Mary took a deep breath, let it out, and bent back over the tan wicker hamper as she began again to sort the dirty clothes into their familiar, stale smelling piles. As she checked the pockets of her husband's shirts for scraps of paper and coins that would hurt the washing machine, it passed through her mind that there was an irony in the fact that it was Fred's laundry—his boxer shorts, his seven white shirts and seven handkerchiefs all needing to be bleached, starched, and ironed—which not only made up the smallest of the piles of clothes around her, but also meant the most work for her by far.

Certainly, compared to his, the rest of the laundry didn't need much attention. The children's and her white things, pajamas, underwear, nightgowns and socks—none got any particular care outside of a little ironing. Neither did the load of diapers, sheets, and towels, which she had already hung to dry on the clothesline strung above the muddy yard behind the house, nor did the pile of children's dark play clothes, her own housedresses, and Fred's socks and weekend shirts she was about to take to the basement.

She was in a hurry to get to the new washer, and she was working fast. She was working fast, of course, because fast was the way she always liked to work. In spite of Fred's gift of the washing machine, neither the twelve years she had spent in New York City, nor the last year they had lived in Delaware, had erased her Union County farm woman's contempt for lazy women who didn't "know how to do," or, rather, who knew how to do but took twice as much time as they ought to.

It wasn't that Mary thought women had to be working every minute; she herself sat down for a little while almost every afternoon and had a cup of tea before the children came home. Still, she had a hard time with the rest of her neighbors, who drank coffee together in the middle of the morning while they told each other the most inappropriate and personal things about their husbands. Though she couldn't say why, exactly, that they listened to soap operas on the radio while they did their chores also irritated her. How did they think they could make something of themselves while their kitchen floors were sticky, their windows were dull and greasy, and their baseboards dusty?

Mary was working fast because it was the way she liked to work, but she was also hurrying because Wesley was taking an unaccustomed morning nap. Having quickly glanced at the clock as she ran upstairs after doing the breakfast dishes, she figured she could do at least one more load of laundry. She would take his playpen outside and hang up the clothes in the backyard later. Now, if she got on it, she ought to be able to scrub the bathroom floor before the washer stopped and the baby called to her. She was working fast because she liked to, therefore, and because, as she told herself, she was trying to beat Wesley's nap.

Still, there was a third reason today in particular for what was, even for her, the frenzy of her work: Mary was trying to get away from the one sickening, terrifying fact in her life that soon she could no longer pretend not to know. There was something seriously wrong between herself and Fred. Something was broken that had never been broken before. She had been aware of it for a month now, ever since she and the three children had returned from their annual summer trip to Union County.

Even while they were still in Kentucky, a secret part of her had begun to suspect that something was going on with Fred. During those few weeks she and the children visited Panny and Papa Charles, Grammar and Papa, her aunts, her sisters, and her sisters' children, Fred had abruptly begun to stay out late, working. At least, "working" was what he said he'd been doing the night she tried to call him after they'd gone to the Union County Fair.

Ordinarily, she never phoned him from her mother's house, but this year the visit to the fair had been unexpectedly difficult. Every summer the fair with its carnival was the high point of the children's trip, and though the loud noise, the human and animal smells mingled with the odors of greasy foods, and the general chaos always wore her out, she liked going with the children to watch their excitement.

There had been nothing at the start of this year's visit that was all that different from the other years. She'd left Wesley with his grand-mother Panny, and she, Freddy, and Roberta had driven Papa Charles's Buick over to her sister Kas's so they could ride to the fairgrounds with her, A.D., and the children's four cousins. They'd gotten happily into A.D.'s red pickup, three adults in the hot cab and six children horsing around on bales of hay in the back. (Fred would have had a fit if he'd known she was letting them do something so dangerous!)

As they drove through the concrete archway that led to the grassy fields where everybody parked, her heart was lifted unexpectedly by the glittering yellow lights of the Ferris wheel which turned the night sky above it the color of ripe blackberries. The honky-tonk music of the fairway and the announcer's voice calling out the results of the last horse race on the track filled her with pleasure. The slight breeze blow-ing through the window of the truck felt good on her bare arms, and the intoxicating smell of the crushed summer grass they drove over was that of new hay.

Her surprising euphoria lasted most of the evening. It was only later when it was time to pry the children off the midway and take them home that she found herself all at once oddly worn out and sad. Trying to make sense of her change in mood in the truck full of sleepy cousins, she remembered how she felt as she and Kas had walked through the crowded tents to see the blue and red ribbons lying beside the winning exhibits of handwork, fudge, rolls, pies, and canned goods. Most of the winners had been made by the women of her own family, her sisters, her mother, her aunts, and even her niece.

She didn't understand at first why the sight of all these prizes hurt her; she was proud of her family and she certainly wasn't jealous of their success. It was only later, after she, Roberta, and Freddy had left Kas's and gone on back to her mother's, that she figured out the cause of her pain. Somehow, in the course of admiring the ribbons at the fair, for the first time it had become clear to her very soul that Union County no longer was her home. She had become an outsider in the midst of her own family.

It wasn't that she'd never thought of this before; she couldn't say why it struck her now the way it did. Wherever she was, she had always loved her family with a desperate homesickness. As the oldest daughter and granddaughter, she never forgot that she was responsible for them. She had hated being away. Over the years she had tried to share a common life with them. She sewed dresses from the patterns they sent her, baked and canned the things they cooked, and grew what old-fashioned flowers of theirs she could. Even in the apartment in New York she had gone out nearly every morning with her fork and trowel to coax up zinnias, asters, and marigolds from the two narrow strips of hard gray dirt beside the front stoop.

The evening of the fair she had come home knowing, really knowing, that she no longer shared a single life with them; her life was not like theirs. She could write them all a thousand times a week—Monday was her day for letters—two thousand times. It was no use. The fact was, she no longer belonged in Union County, and everybody else knew it too. When her sisters, her aunts, even her mother got together and talked about their lives, the people they knew, and the things they did, they talked around her or over her head. She was not one of them anymore. It hurt.

That night she had waited until the children were in bed and asleep to call Fred. She wouldn't have dreamed of trying to talk to him about what she was feeling, but she did need the reassurance of the sound of his voice. She needed him to remind her that in spite of her loss, she had what she wanted, a husband she loved, children, and a house of her own.

Though it was an hour later in Delaware when she placed the call, Fred hadn't answered the phone, nor had he answered it the next night, no matter how many times she tried to put the call through. Three days later she finally got him before breakfast. He apologized for being so hard to reach. He had not been home the first two nights, he said, because he'd been working late, the other night because he had been baby-sitting for the fancy long-haired dachshund of some woman he worked with while she was out of town. When Mary called, he'd been taking the dog out for a walk. It was a smart dog, and he liked it.

Mary hated the idea of a dog in her house—and she hated the yellow dog hairs it had taken her two weeks to vacuum up once she was home—and she didn't know what to think about the rest of what he told her. Still, early in the morning and far away on her parents' farm, she was so relieved to hear his voice at last that she didn't push him or ask any further questions.

The trouble was, now that they all were back, Fred was still working at night more often than he was home. Over the last three weeks he had telephoned nearly every afternoon after she had already started cooking to tell her that he was sorry he couldn't be there for supper and that she shouldn't wait up for him.

She could hardly stand it. She missed him, and his absence made her both profoundly sad and excruciatingly anxious. Still, when she told him she missed him (she kept the rest of her feelings to herself), uncharacteristically, he brushed her off. Instead, he gave her an account of his new habits she couldn't argue with—not that she had ever been able to argue with him successfully.

"Remember, you were the one who wanted me to take this job in the advertising agency," he would say, sometimes indignantly, when she cautiously brought up the question of his absence.

Though she knew he wasn't being fair, she could hardly argue. However tired she had been last year from Wesley's birth, however hard it was for her to leave the security that had accrued to her during the six years they'd lived in their small garden apartment on Long Island, she had, indeed, wanted the move. For the two or three years before they left New York, Fred had been restless and unhappy in his job. Considering his energy and his competitiveness as well as his enormous capacity to make any work he did interesting, Mary knew that his unhappiness was serious.

He wasn't bored easily. Even during World War II, in the world's most tedious job at the wartime factory in which he worked, he had taken an innocent delight in secretly redesigning the gear-cutting equipment to which he had been assigned, so that he consistently cut half again as many gears as any of the other men who worked there. When his fellow workers were resentful because the boss demanded the same productivity from them, he had treated the whole thing as a joke.

But her observation of Fred's diminished ability to enjoy life was not the only reason Mary took seriously his complaints about his job. In the past, only on the rarest of occasions had either of them ever talked directly to the other of any but their most positive emotions. Apart from his ongoing irritation or anger with the children, whatever feelings of hurt arose, of unhappiness, homesickness, incompetence, or helplessness, he, like she, kept them to himself. The fact was, after thirteen years of being in love with him, what she most wanted in the world was that he be happy. That he was miserable enough to speak to her of his unhappiness frightened her and made her desperate to try anything that would help him.

All this meant that when he would remind her that she had wanted the move as much as he had, she would have to agree.

"You're right," she would say, sick to her stomach with fear, "I wanted you to be happy."

In these difficult conversations, however, he rarely left it alone at that. He would remind her that he had never done this kind of work before. He was going to have to excel at it if he were to succeed, but there was a lot in the office that he could only learn on his own time after everyone went home.

She was certain what he said was true. At the same time, she tried to accept that the new people he worked with were of a different sort from the folks he'd been with either in New York or in Cincinnati in the early years of their marriage. Both colleagues and clients probably did take it for granted, as he said, that a man who wanted to get on in the business must put the business first and do what he was asked. This was why he had had to keep the dog that weekend while Mary was gone. He'd been sorry about the chewed leg on the coffee table. She must expect that from now on, Fred would need to be available to go out evenings to entertain clients and talk business. It was only too bad, Fred told her, that she couldn't go with him.

If he had said this to her six months ago, Mary would have believed he meant it; she didn't now. She did know that in all the years of their marriage he had never had such a high-powered job as this one. A high school graduate, by joining the firm in Delaware, he had moved into a world populated with people who were not only college-educated, but educated in such fancy schools as Harvard, Princeton, and Yale.

She herself was from Union County, Kentucky, the granddaughter of a Wynn and the daughter of a Wesley, and she wasn't impressed by these big-city, sophisticated business associates of her husband. Indeed, when she ran into them at the unending cocktail parties Fred told her they needed to attend, what mostly struck her was how loud they were, how much they drank, and how full of themselves they were. Their half-leering compliments on her figure, her face, and her clothes were offensive. She didn't, however, share her opinions with Fred or with anyone else.

Furthermore, it was obvious to Mary from the way she heard them talk about him that Fred's colleagues were impressed with his self-confident intellectual energy and easy abilities to charm and entertain. Why her husband would let himself be impressed in turn by their hot-shot educations and memberships in the local country club was more than Mary could begin to fathom. Unless she had seen it with her own eyes, she never would have believed that the fact that they laughed at his jokes, took him out to lunch, and treated his words as some kind of oracle would go to his head.

It worried her. Late nights at work, needing to keep other people's dogs, missed meals—all this she could have taken in stride if she really were convinced that they were no more than a requirement of his job. Not for nothing had Mary heeded her grandmother's unspoken advice to avoid a man like her own father, and Grammar's spoken advice to "marry a man who ran." Fred was a hard worker; she expected it of him as she did of herself. It was something important they shared between them. Work was work; whether man or woman, you did it because you wanted to excel at it and succeed, and you did it because work was what life was about.

No, it wasn't any of this other stuff that was causing her worry now. It was something else new in their marriage. For the first time since they met, Fred had taken to speaking to her in a way he had never spoken to her before, saying things to her that were positively mean. As she stood now in the darkened hall beside the empty laundry hamper, she thought about his words last night, how they had first hurt and terrified her at the same time they made her so mad she hardly knew what to do.

She had been both apprehensive and happy when he'd called that morning to tell her he would be there for supper, but she tried to set aside her anxiety by concentrating on the tasks at hand. She washed the windows in the living room and dining room, and before the children came home, she made him a coconut cream pie, his favorite dessert. At five o'clock she got Roberta to watch Wesley, then dressed herself particularly carefully in Fred's favorite red cotton knit dress that showed off her figure and emphasized the size and brownness of her eyes. After that, she put on the expensive earrings he had had made for her for Valentine's Day the year before. Opening the pale blue box, she couldn't help herself from re-reading the card he'd put in with them. For a moment the words, "To my wife, the most beautiful woman in the world," filled her with such longing and sadness that she had had to sit down.

An hour later when she went to meet him at the door, she was collected once again. He bent down to let her kiss him, but any other efforts to return her usual affectionate gesture or respond to the tense excitement of the children, who had also been confused by his absences, were minimal. His face, which under normal circumstances struck her as almost unbearably handsome, was frowning now, and his mouth was drawn into a grimace of exasperation. The ends of his bow tie hung down untied on either side of the neck of his white shirt in angry zigzags.

Irritated by their excitement and their noise, he quickly disposed of the older children, as he often did in the evenings, sending them to their rooms until dinner.

He sat down in the chair closest to the door, the wing chair she had finished covering before they'd left in the summer for Union County. Without looking at her, he asked her curtly to bring him a drink. Bending down, he took off his wing tips, placed them by the left leg of the chair, and picked up the paper which lay by his shoes.

The dress, the earrings, the pie—Mary could see they'd be no use tonight. She frowned, her anxiety violating the unspoken thirteen-year-old prohibition between them against speaking directly of anything emotionally painful or dangerous.

"What's wrong?" she blurted out. "Did you have a bad day at the office?"

"Why do you want to know?" he replied. Without looking at her, he opened the paper he'd brought home and pulled it up in front of his face; he spoke from behind the paper.

"You wouldn't understand if I told you. You don't know anything in the world except sewing and cleaning, saving money and keeping house," he said, his voice now emphatic and full of rage.

With the gesture of her mother and grandmother before her, out of sight under her white apron, she clasped her hands together tightly. The blood rushing to her head made her dizzy. She couldn't breathe.

"Do you know what I wish?" he went on.

Her heart pounding with fear and speechless with shock, she shook her head.

He shut the paper, slammed it down on the floor, and stared at the eagle that perched on the top of the big baroque mirror his father had given them last Christmas. It hung on the wall above the hide-a-bed Fred's stepmother had picked out and had delivered the day they'd moved in, both symbols, it had always seemed to her, of Fred's sophisticated parents' refusal to let her furnish her own house according to what she was sure they thought of as her "country hick taste."

"I wish you would be a little more like the women I work with. Why can't you be interested in something besides the house and kids, and be smart and have a little fun for a change?"

She hadn't answered—her shock and pride closed her mouth—but she wondered now, standing among his dirty shirts that waited for her services, how he ever could have spoken to her that way. She left the hamper and walked out of the dark to the sunny window at the end of the hall, absently noting as she looked out, the precise stickiness of the red mud that filled their lawn and the neighbors' where grass would supposedly grow later.

As they had all through the night, the words "like the women I work with" began to roll around in her head like crashing stones. What did he want of her? Of course, her whole life was making a nice home for him and raising his children. Certainly, she sewed and saved money (if she didn't save it, he certainly wouldn't have), cooked and cleaned and did laundry and drove his children to Cub Scouts, Girl Scouts, art lessons, the library, and church—he didn't know the half of it! But even if her time were not filled this way, what else did he expect her to do?

She wasn't complaining about the things she did; she liked keeping house for him and she was proud of her skills when he praised her, but who did he think was the one who had insisted from the beginning of their marriage that she was to be a housewife with no more than a housewife's interests? She wasn't a housewife when they got married. She'd been to school to become a woman just like the women he worked with now. She'd had plenty of interests then and she'd liked to have fun, too.

Who was it who in the first year of her marriage stormed down to the Blue Line Steamer office, dragged her out, and told her boss "she worked for him," now that she was married? Who practically locked her up by herself while he was on the road with his friends? Who was it who never even wanted to hear about the books she occasionally found time to read? Who was it, for that matter, who seemed to call any woman who read anything or had an opinion of her own "a pushy broad"? So why were the women at work no longer "pushy broads"?

And now he was unhappy with her because she had become exactly what he had insisted she be!

She had hurt too much to respond, even later, to his outburst. She simply picked up Wesley, who had been playing quietly on the green wool rug of the living room, carried him into the kitchen and put him in his high chair. She was grateful she had had Roberta set the table in the dining room before Fred had come home; she wouldn't have wanted to look at him or the back page of his paper as she walked between the kitchen and the dining room to do the job herself. As she fed the baby in the kitchen, her stomach was turning over. Her head had begun to ache. Her headache had worsened as she took the roast chicken from the oven and set it on the counter to cool. It had grown worse still as she drained and mashed the potatoes, finished the beans, and set everything on the table.

Thinking of all this as she looked out the second-story window of her own house, she gazed in unconscious bewilderment at the big red cockscombs and the three-foot-tall purple petunias she'd planted by the split rail fence Fred had put in for her in May.

When they had sat down in the dining room at last, neither of the older children seemed to notice anything unusual. Their father was silent and stern-faced. Though he was never normally that way with her, it was often his way with them. As usual, they had tried to handle it by keeping quiet and cleaning their plates. They'd excused themselves at once after finishing their meal and gone upstairs.

It had been a relief when Fred left without explanation right after dinner, though the wakeful hours in bed by herself had been the same familiar hell.

She had begun to cry in great, wrenching sobs when the lights of his car at the end of the road finally brightened their bedroom window. By the time he'd come in, however, she'd wiped her face on the sheet, moved onto her side of their maple bed, and held herself still, pretending to be asleep. When sleep came at last, inexplicably, she dreamed of his beloved and familiar arms around her. It had been a dream of almost ecstatic sweetness, chased away by consciousness.

Now, Mary turned her back to the window in the hall and sighed, remembering the evening, the night, and the dream. She walked back into the shadows, and gathered up the load of dark clothes ready for the wash. A little calmer now, she started down the stairs with the armful of laundry, through the bright living room she was so proud of. The room with its soft gray walls and its green slipcovered furniture and maroon-and-gray-striped drapes she'd sewn herself comforted her at the same time the crown-of-thorns gave her pleasure, blooming among its nonflowering companions below the window in the long plantstand Fred had made for her the previous winter.

By the time she'd walked past the ugly Chinese ancestor portrait Fred's father had bestowed upon her against her will one Christmas in New York, her brief moment of equilibrium was over. At the door to the basement she fumbled the lock, unable to see over the laundry in her arms, and all of a sudden she was desperate. "Why should I work so hard, if Fred doesn't think any more of me than he says he does?" She walked down the stairs into the cool gray odor of her high-ceilinged cement basement.

"What's wrong with me?" This time she spoke aloud. "Don't I have any gumption? Once I get the washing machine running, I'm going to go upstairs, heat myself a cup of coffee, and sit in the living room and drink it. The bathroom floor can just go to hell!"

Lazy women and unreliable husbands be damned! It was a good, strong plan and one she would surely have carried out if she had not gone back up the stairs to the kitchen and found, lying on the floor, incontestable evidence of what Fred had really been doing all those nights when he'd been gone.

As she had carried the clothes through the kitchen, one of his black socks had fallen from her arms; the whole time she'd been in the basement starting the water in the washer, putting in the clothes and adding the soap, it lay there, waiting for her in the full sun which shone through the clean window on the backdoor.

She noticed the sock the minute she came through the door into the kitchen. She didn't even have to bend over to see it. It was covered with the short, gleaming blond hairs of a dog—the same kind of hairs that had been all over the house when she returned from Union County the month before. He had only worn the sock she was looking at yesterday, but the dog was long since gone from the house, the last of its shiny fur vacuumed up from her rugs three weeks ago. Fred took his shoes off every night when he came home, the same as he did last night, but he couldn't have gotten that hair on his feet from Mary's rugs.

As she stood there staring at the alien sock, understanding and unable to catch her breath, she began to tremble. The coffee she had planned for was forgotten. She couldn't bring herself to touch the sock. Somehow, she stumbled to the living room, and collapsed, head on her chest and eyes closed, on the pale green couch by the stairs. Here she sat for a long time, her mind blank with fear and grief, while the Chinese grandmother watched her implacably and unblinking from her place on the wall above the dining room table.

Time passed until at last a faint energy of anger rose up inside her. She went to the telephone in the kitchen. Carefully keeping her back to the sock still lying in the sunlight on the floor, she dialed Fred's number. She was trembling so hard her teeth rattled in her head.

He picked up on the second ring. "Hello," he said, "Orange and Tanner Advertising. This is Fred speaking."

Her voice was low and taut. "I know what you're doing," she said, and she hung up.

Four days and many wrenching conversations later, it had been decided, or rather, Fred had rashly decided, what they were to do. They would immediately put the house on the market, Mary would pack up and go to Jacksonville with the children for what people referred to as "a quick divorce," then go on home to live with her parents on their farm in Union County.

From where Fred stood, it was the ideal plan. Of course it would be a little hard on Mary for a while, he said, but Mary's family were good people, and there were a lot of them to help her out. He intended to send her enough child support that she could get an apartment in town after a while if she were frugal. Besides, she was young; she'd find somebody down there who would want to marry her soon enough.

He wasn't worried about the children. Kas and A.D. would help Mary look out for them, and finally teach them to say "yes sir" and "no sir" as they'd never learned to do with the kind of friends that they'd had in the city. Freddy and Wesley would laugh and play with their cousins in the fresh air, raise prize-winning 4-H calves, and grow up to be like their hard-working, successful uncles. After Roberta's aunts, great-aunts, grandmother and great-grandmother taught her to bake, can, sew and iron like they did, she would marry a farmer and do well for herself.

Children really didn't have feelings like adults did, he reminded her; she'd always told him herself it was what her grandmother used to say. He'd visit the children once a year; he couldn't very well have them come to stay with him and Sally. If he kept away from them (Sally told him it was hard on children of divorced parents to go back and forth between the mother and father) it wouldn't be long before they'd remember him enough to do what he told them to when he called, but they wouldn't miss him enough to hurt.

As for what Mary thought about Fred's plan, for the first few days she was simply too shocked, too frightened, too hurt, too angry, and too humiliated to be able to do much thinking at all.

She was blindly terrified for the children, not for what would happen to them emotionally, but simply for their survival. Over the next six weeks Roberta or Freddy would often come into the kitchen or the upstairs only to find their mother standing there wringing her hands and repeating "how will I ever support my three children?"

She understood, therefore, that no matter how she felt about it, she had to agree to put the house on the market; there was no way she could stay in it even if she had wanted to. She had to care for her children; as she would frequently remind them in the years to come, they were all she had. She had learned in the summer that she no longer belonged in Union County, but her not belonging was no longer relevant. She had to take Roberta, Freddy, and Wesley to the farm to live with Bert and Charles. With no money of her own, not having worked in an office for more than a dozen years, and unaccustomed to making her own plans apart from Fred, what else could she possibly do but that?

For a very long time, that was almost all there was to it. Though Freddy and Roberta spent endless hours together over the next six weeks, puzzling over what was going on in their parents' minds, they couldn't figure it out to save their lives. Why was their father making them go away? Why would they never see him? (Yes, they remembered he'd said he would visit once a year, but a year was so long it didn't really count.) If they were good, would he come back to them? None of these questions would they have dared to ask their father.

Not being afraid of irritating their mother, they did, however, try to find out what they could from her. She would tell them nothing. "No," she answered them when they pushed her, "your father won't come back," and "no," she would add, "it has nothing to do with you at all," but that was it. Mary believed the experts. It was not good for children ever to see their parents disagree, nor was it healthy for them to have to deal with adult problems. The children were unhappy, she could see that and it worried her, but as she'd learned at home, the fastest way for them to get over their feelings was simply to ignore them.

As far as she was concerned, what was happening between her and their father was none of her daughter's and son's business, anyway. She would no more have explained things to them than she would have explained them to her parents, though her mother and father, at least, unlike Roberta and Freddy, would never, ever have asked her anyway.

Just talking to the real estate man, dismantling the house she loved, sorting out Fred's things from her own, sending Roberta's furniture back to her in-laws in New York, packing boxes of linens for Union County, and committing to death every happy memory and every hope for her life with her husband was so painful that she felt she wouldn't have had much energy for talking to Roberta or Freddy even if she'd wished to.

For the fact was, in those last days of her marriage she felt as though she were dying. Time played odd tricks on her, bending and folding back upon itself like a ribbon, so that the nearer past of her earlier marriage, the distant past of her childhood, and her mother's even further past touched upon her present, so confounding her with grief that she continually banged her head on cabinet doors and bumped her hips on tables.

In an odd way, her memories often led her to such a place that she could hardly tell the difference between her mother's life and her own. One day as she worked through boxes in the basement, recalling her pride and happiness in choosing Fred, a man as unlike her father as she could find, she actually seemed to remember her mother's determination to marry Charles, a man as unlike her grandfather as her mother could ever hope to meet. On another day, sorting her own children's clothes and toys for packing, she suddenly looked up from her work and was confused, having forgotten for a moment that she was not her mother preparing to move from the House on the Hill, but Mary moving from her house in Delaware.

Piercingly happy memories of her earlier life with Fred mixed themselves up with what felt like, but couldn't be, actual memories of her mother's. She remembered the first turkey she'd ever cooked for her husband in the same instant she remembered her mother's feelings when her sister Caroline died. Her mother's desperate move to the House on the Hill before she was even born juxtaposed itself in Mary's mind with the first Christmas she and Fred had spent with her in-laws in New York. She recalled the exact quality of the delight she'd taken in Fred's company on a picnic the two of them had had on a trip to the Smokies with the children before Wesley came along, and in the same moment she seemed to recall lying on the floor of the kitchen in the House on the Hill, writhing and green with a gallbladder attack, calling out "Charles, Charles" to a husband who never answered.

Underneath all these other memories lay the House on the Hill. As she dismembered the new house in Delaware, whole chunks of her childhood in that ancient house returned to her, not in some orderly, sequenced fashion, but in waking dreams, in ancient images and feelings that mixed themselves confusingly with the images before her eyes. Cooking with her mother at the cast iron stove in the house her mother had been born in; the smell of the sheets on the bed in the dining room where she slept with Kas and Charles Ray; the sight of purple grapes hanging around the porch by the backdoor; the taste of the chocolate milk Bert made them as they came home from school; the safe sound of the wind around the windows in the winter—memories like these seemed to surface inexplicably from her very body like groundwater.

All these things remembered from the House on the Hill jumbled themselves together in a swamp of memories of Grammar's Beautiful House That Burned, with recollections of the hired hand's house she'd moved to after losing the House on the Hill, of Mrs. Simpson's house where she'd lived during business school, of the various apartments she'd been in with Fred, as well as what seemed to her to be memories of the house in Delaware she was even now in the process of disassembling.

After six weeks of such terrible remembering, all she wanted was to get it over with and go. Soon enough she got her wish. Once the red leaves had fallen from the one small maple tree they'd planted in the yard, the house was stripped and sold, and the boxes put into storage to be sent on later.

On the last day of October, Fred, beginning to return to a kind of sanity, loaded his wife and his three crying, bewildered children into the car to put them on the overnight train to Florida. Filled at last with panic over what was happening to them all, he had awakened the night before, shaken Mary awake, and turned on the one remaining light, beside the bed.

"Mary, don't go," he pleaded with her, urgently, his arms around her; "don't go. I love you. We can fix everything," he said. "Please, give us a chance; you'll see."

She'd only shaken her head and looked at him. Give him a chance? Tears rose to her eyes, and for a moment, her heart leaped out to him for what she still might have. In the same instant, however, the memory of his bitter words and scornful face as he had enumerated her inadequacies as he compared her to the woman at work pushed her away. She loved him. She would always love him and grieve over him, but she had her pride.

Besides, it was too late. Her appointment with the judge in Jacksonville was only two days away. Kas and A.D., having fetched the two of them to their wedding thirteen years ago, were even now somewhere on the road to Florida to pick them up in Jacksonville and drive them back to the Union County from which she had been sent with her mother's hopes. Though Mary knew she no longer belonged there, her mother and father, her sister and brothers, her grandparents and her aunts expected her arrival. Mary met her obligations.

Except for the way it persisted in her own mind and body and in the minds and bodies of Roberta and Freddy another forty years or more, the marriage was over.

CHAPTER FIFTEEN

Fingers

Fanny, that year in Union County after Daddy and Mama were divorced was the one in which I think I really began to grow up. At least, this was when "sex" became a conscious reality in my life. I know you hate this word; do you think you can excuse me?

It was the year I began to develop a figure, as they euphemistically said in those days. There wasn't much to it—I was a skinny child right through high school—but I was simultaneously proud of and embarrassed by what there was. In response to my deviously indirect urgings, Mama bought me a "training bra" at Holt's department store. I have to say that what it was that was being trained is much clearer to me now than it was then.

I also had a Sunday dress I remember picking out almost solely because of the way the wide, shiny blue and gray stripes of rayon converged on my tiny bosom. Those stripes were like arrows flying to the center of a target. When I knew Mama would not be home, I used to take the dress out of the closet I shared with her and admire it. Imagining that I was sixteen and going out on a date, I would throw off my clothes, drop the dress's metal coat hanger on the bed, pull it on over my head, and zip it up the back. I would tiptoe over to the bedroom mirror and scrutinize myself as I stood there, turning sideways and straightening my shoulders to measure and admire my assets.

One morning during recess in the spring of seventh grade, my pride in what little I had was shattered by Roger, the knowing boy with dark brown curly hair and a cynical smile on whom I had a crush. Roger was running through the playground doing something or other at the front of a small herd of laughing, snickering older boys from the eighth grade.

"Hey, Bobby Marie," he yelled, using the baby name I hated. He slapped me on the back as he went past me, "you need to find yourself some falsies!"

I was so mortified, I didn't know what to do. When the bell rang at the end of recess, I somehow got myself in line with the others and went back into class. I could not raise my eyes. At lunch I walked home and staggered into our apartment, slamming the front door behind me.

"Is that you, Roberta?" Mama called out when she heard me.

I dragged myself into the kitchen where Mama was heating soup and grilling our cheese sandwiches. Fortunately, Freddy wasn't home yet, or I could never have told her what happened.

"Mama," I burst into tears. "Do you know what Roger said to me this morning?"

"Nope," Mama answered. "Sit down and I'll give you your soup. What's the matter?" she said, waving a hand to direct me into my chair. "It must have been pretty bad."

Unable to sit, I continued to stand there, wringing my hands. "He said I needed falsies! He said it right in front of the other boys! Everybody laughed at me." I threw my arms around her. She held the soup pan away from her body so I couldn't knock it out of her hands or burn myself on it.

"Do you think I need falsies?" I asked her, looking up into her face.

She didn't understand my humiliation or my shame. She patted me with her free hand. "You look fine to me," she said. "Just forget they ever said it. Now, sit down and eat or you're going to be late going back to school."

You know, Panny, I was always a sloucher, but I think it was from that point that I began deliberately to hunch my shoulders at school and walk as often as I could with my arms folded across my chest. Paradoxically, I also started to do what I knew my girlfriends did; every day when I got to school, my first act was to sneak into a stall in the girls' room and stuff my training bra with toilet paper.

I got my first period not too long after that, and it was a shock to say the least. Mama had tried two or three times to prepare me for it, but it embarrassed me so much I would never let her tell me anything. For that matter, Panny, even in my wildest dreams I can't imagine such a conversation between you and your own mother, Grammar. Even for those times, from what Mama and Aunt Blacky say, Grammar hated everything remotely touching on sex. I wonder now. How did you happen to find out about the bloodily fertile inner workings of women's bodies, anyway?

As for myself, I knew long in advance that something was not right with my insides. I had had a stomachache as well as a headache for several days. My abdomen was bloated. I was also very shaky, and the lower part of my back hurt awfully.

The morning I discovered blood on my panties, I was frightened half to death. I was sure I had cancer and I had gotten it from imagining myself kissing that hateful Roger. I hid a long time in the bathroom, crying. I didn't know how I was going to tell my mother the truth. When I finally came out, desperate with fear, she was sympathetic, helpful with supplies, and surprisingly offhand.

It was later in the day, however, that Mama let me shave my legs for the first time. I was thrilled; among my friends, at least, having smooth legs and talking about how they got that way was what made you a woman. I remember I shaved that night in the bathtub; I turned the water pale pink when I gouged out a big chunk of flesh at the back of my right ankle with the heavy double-edged razor my mother used.

The next afternoon Mama's old high-school friend Jane Kurtz came over—you know who I mean; she used to be Jane Shaeffer before she was married. Mrs. Kurtz congratulated me obliquely as she eyed the bandage on my leg. "Well," she said, grinning. She had a great grin. "I hear you're growing up."

"Yes," I said, as though it happened every day and I had always talked the racy, grown-up talk of women. "Yes, it's true; I got the curse."

Getting my period still didn't mean I knew much else about sex. In my stubborn unwillingness to let Mama tell me anything, I was innocent, or at least ignorant, of the most fundamental knowledge. Wait until you hear this story, Panny. You aren't going to believe it, but I swear I'm telling the truth.

One Saturday that same spring I was over at Uncle Bob and Aunt Ida's having lunch with my cousins Bobby Wynn, Charles Stanton, and John Scott. I don't know why I was there; by now I was sure I was too old and sophisticated to play with any of them.

It was a bright and pleasant day. I remember we were sitting at their enormous Early American table in the kitchen, and the sunlight where it squeezed through the slats of the long indoor shutters was making patterns on the shining wooden floor.

Aunt Ida was fetching and carrying while Uncle Bob and the boys talked farm talk. I don't recall what they were discussing—perhaps the sows having pigs, neutering the bulls, or maybe finding a nest of chicken eggs just hatched in the barn. I hadn't said anything. I was shy and unclear enough about where I fit in that I never said much, particularly around adults.

I was listening all the same, and suddenly their male conversation prompted me to think about something I'd never thought of before. It had to do with humans, rather than farm animals.

"I wonder how a woman's body knows she's married, so she can have a baby?" I blurted out.

I knew I'd said the wrong thing the minute the words were out of my mouth. Aunt Ida looked down at the casserole she was setting on the table as though she hadn't heard me, and Uncle Bob got completely still and covered his mouth with a napkin. My boy cousins, sitting on the bench in a row, squirmed with delight, hardly able to wait to answer my question. Aunt Ida glared at them. "John Scott," she said to the one closest to speaking, "you hush your mouth! You just hush up your mouth!"

Oh, Panny, how could I have made such a mistake? It was not that I knew nothing at all about where babies came from. Do you remember when tiny, drab Mary Kay Seely "got into trouble" in the seventh grade and "had to" drop out of school and get married? Whispering on the playground, my friends had told me all about it. I had heard the same girls talk about how certain kinds of kissing could, as they said, "cause a child."

I think I probably thought that men and women having swoony romantic feelings for each other, kissing, sighing, and looking deep into each other's eyes was most of what sex was. The rest, I believed in some weird way that I never did articulate, had to do with a man and a woman living in the same house together.

Panny, I said I didn't have what I believed articulated; I had enough put together, however, to be able to create my own fantasies. I learned something significant, too, as I tried to act out one of them.

The time I have in mind occurred on a blinding early afternoon in August right before I started in the eighth grade. Freddy and Wesley were out at Aunt Kas's on the farm with their cousins, and I was lying on the couch reading in the living room. Mama came in from the kitchen and said she was going to run over to Aunt Blacky's for a little while. Do you remember? It was when Uncle Mack was alive, and Aunt Blacky still lived out by the drive-in next to Morganfield. I asked to go along. I loved to visit all of my great-aunts who were your sisters. Aunt Blacky's appealed to me especially that day, however, since her son, my cousin Sam, and I were the same age and he would be someone to play with.

Aunt Blacky's house was as hot as a barbecue pit when we got there, even if it was set up on that high hill. Sam was nowhere in sight, so I lay around with Mama and Aunt Blacky in her Florida room, which was all the rage then, drinking iced tea and trying to catch whatever breeze came through the glass slats of the jalousie windows. The brown hassock fan whirred in the middle of the floor, giving the illusion of cooling our sticky skin, and the oscillating fan periodically raised our wet hair and the damp hems of our untucked blouses.

Mama and Aunt Blacky talked, and I had nearly fallen asleep against the background of their words when Sam, with his dark face and straight black hair like his mother's, ambled through the backdoor.

"Well, if it isn't Berta Marie," he said. (Did you know that Sam, Kathleen, and Aunt Blacky still call me "Berta Marie" almost forty-five years later? My other male cousins, who called me "Roberta" in junior high and high school, call me Berta Marie, too, now, when I see them. I wonder why.)

"What are you doing sitting around with the old people?" Sam said to me when he saw me sprawled out in the rocker, my feet up on the hassock fan, so that it could blow up past my sandals and onto my legs. Mama made a face at him, and I sat up.

"Come on outside," he said; "let's find us something to do."

We went out the back at once, leaving "the old people"—Mama was in her thirties and Aunt Blacky, ten years older, in her forties—to doze where they were.

"Let's see, Berta Marie," said Sam from the back steps. "What'll we do, now?"

About that time, across the yard I spotted the four-room house that Uncle Mack's hired hand generally lived in with his family. There wasn't a single chair on its porch, or anything else, for that matter. I looked at it again more closely and saw that it was completely empty. That's when one of my fantasies kicked in.

"Let's go inside that house," I said. "We can pretend we live there."

Sam didn't know what I had in mind, but his father was in town, and he had nothing better to do. "Well, OK," he said without any enthusiasm, naturally enough.

I began playing house from the minute I walked up the steps and through the lefthand front door. Sam following, I looked over my property with the eye of a home-settling woman. I scrutinized the empty front room with its peeling, ivy-covered wallpaper, then walked through it to the worn-out kitchen beyond. In the middle of the room, there was a beat-up green table. By the chipped enameled sink, an old gas stove stood in one corner, the broken door to the stove hanging open. It wasn't much, but it would be ours, a place of our own.

I left the kitchen for the square room to its right at the back of the house. This room didn't appeal to my imagination, though the one in front, which would be our bedroom, did. There were limits to my daydreams, even so. I returned to the front room I'd started from.

There, as I'd heard Mama do enough times, I began to talk to myself, furnishing the room for Sam and me with an imaginary braided rug, chairs, love seat, end tables, and Victorian lamps.

As my pretend husband, I turned to Sam tenderly to ask his advice. "What do you think?" I simpered. "Should we hang the mirror over the fireplace or put it in the bedroom?"

Never having seen me act this way or heard me use this voice, Sam drew back and looked at me with horror.

"What's gotten into you, girl?" he said. "Something's wrong with you. I'm not going to play this stupid game." He stamped out the door in disgust, his brogans thumping on the empty wooden floor like the boots of a grown man.

"Wait," I cried. I followed him out the door and off the porch, in equal parts embarrassed and disappointed.

"OK, then," I said, standing in front of him. "You think of something to do."

He looked at me, grinning. "All right, I will," he answered.

At that, he grabbed my sweaty arms, which were folded across my chest, and pulled them out straight. Rapidly, he slid his hands down my slippery arms to my hands. He wrapped his own calloused hands around my two little fingers as close to the palms as he could get, then he began to bend them sideways to the other fingers. The pain was excruciating.

"Say uncle," he cackled in his high-pitched voice. "Say uncle," he danced around me, taunting. "I won't quit till you say uncle."

My little fingers felt as though they were on fire; flames leaped up and down from the second knuckles and shot through the backs of my hands, through my wrists, into my arms, and up into my neck.

"Say uncle," Sam kept on crying. "Say uncle, say uncle." As my fingers bent farther and farther away from my hands, he sang in the familiar taunt-song melody of children.

I was furious and I was proud. I clamped my mouth shut and didn't let out a moan. I thought of my father and mother; I thought of some unknown future husband and myself. I thought about the bossy boys on the playground who believed they were something just because they were boys.

I wouldn't have given in to Sam and said uncle if I'd thought I'd end up maimed for life. I would never give in. I would absolutely never, ever give in. If he broke my fingers, that was fine with me. It would be worth it.

I didn't given in, either, Panny, and I didn't call into the Florida room for help, though sweat poured off my face in a flood and the fire in my hands flamed white and blue.

I think what broke the deadlock, so to speak, between the two of us, is that Sam simply got bored waiting for me to give up and so he gave up himself. At least, he finally dropped my hands and went off in the direction of the barn, chortling and calling "I got you, I got you," back at me till he disappeared. I knew better and so did he.

Left standing in the yard by myself, I held up my hands in front of my face. My hands looked deformed, the little fingers pointing out at an odd angle. The fingers themselves were still burning as though someone were holding a match to them. They were bright red, and the knuckles ached sickeningly. My stomach turned over. In spite of the heat, goose-bumps were running up and down my arms.

I looked at my hands with satisfaction. They hurt a lot, there was no doubt about it, and they continued to hurt every time I played my beloved flute until the day I sold it at eighteen, shortly after I got married, but there was no doubt in my mind that the pain had been worth it. I was stubborn, and I couldn't be broken.

Panny, though my fingers still stick out at a funny angle, it seems worth it, even now. I'm proud of the girl I was that day, so stupid and brave. I'd do it again in a minute, and I know you and Mama would, too.

CHAPTER SIXTEEN

Another Place

It was late afternoon of the first weekend after Easter. Though it was damp and cold outside, the sun was shining through the dining room windows with the pale, white light of very early spring. Inside her own dining room on Bonnycastle Avenue, Mary was sitting at the slightly rumpled table in a nearly contented state of melancholy. She was drinking strong black coffee from one of her favorite cups, one she'd found for fifty cents in the junk store down from the corner.

It had been a good Saturday. Her mother and her three aunts as well as Kas and Suzie had driven all the way from Union County to Louisville and back in the same day, nine hours in all, just to let her fix lunch for them. The chicken pot pie, salad, and rolls had turned out just right, and the angel food cake with its fluffy white icing had been perfect. There were enough leftovers for the children to have for supper, and Roberta, in her sullen teenaged manner, had promised to heat it up for them. Having come home early on the bus from her weekend job at Grant's, Roberta was in the room she shared with her mother, writing passionately gloomy poems on the old Remington Mary had had since she graduated from business school. From their room across the hall, she could hear Freddy and Wes making car noises on the wooden floor between their beds. Charlie German was on his way over to take her back to his house for the good food he was cooking for her supper.

For once, at least, there was nothing Mary had to do between now and bedtime except let someone else wait on her, and it felt good. She was bone tired. She had gotten out of bed at five-thirty to do the week's laundry, clean the bathroom, and vacuum before she started cooking. Normally, she let herself sleep a little later on the weekends to catch up, but she always got up early during the week. She had to if she were to have a few minutes to herself before she got the children off to school and went down to be a secretary all day. She certainly couldn't get an hour to herself in the evening; by the time she got home at six, cooked supper, and did what she needed to do with the children, she was ready for bed.

She raised her cup with both hands and looked over it at her good dishes which were washed and stacked on the table around her to be put away. She was tired, yes, but she took a certain satisfaction from being tired. Indeed, she was proud of it. As her mother and her grandmother had told her often enough, a woman had to get tired if she were going to have what she wanted in life. A woman had to expect to get tired, a lot more tired than any man, if she wanted a little independence, if she wanted to have nice things of her own, or make something of herself. If she weren't married, it was the only way she could take care of her children, much less see to it that they were able to make something of themselves. That was just the way it was. She'd always heard "it was a man's world," and it really was.

"Roberta, you've just got to learn to work harder. You can't depend on a man being there to take care of you," she tried to tell her daughter. "Look what happened to me."

"Do you think I don't know that?" Roberta would sometimes answer her, anger flaring up. At other times she would only shake her head, an expression on her face Mary couldn't understand.

She could tell her daughter till she was blue in the face. Roberta wouldn't listen. It angered Mary and made her nearly frantic with worry.

Charlie, the man she went out with, the one about to take her for dinner, didn't know what she was talking about, either, but then, he wouldn't. For one thing, he was a man himself, and he didn't want to hear it.

"So, you have to work hard because you don't have any money; if you'd just marry me, you wouldn't have to get so tired," he'd answered her, exasperated. "I'd give you anything you asked for."

"You know I can't do that," she'd replied, looking at him with frustration. He simply couldn't understand that she would rather drop dead of exhaustion then ever again put herself in a position where she would have to ask a man for anything.

Charlie didn't have the faintest idea what it meant to be dependent on anybody. Not only was he a man; he'd never had to ask anyone for anything; he'd never really even worked. Charlie had grown up rich, the only child of a doting mother. He still lived in the beautiful three-storied house that had been built for his parents on Willow Avenue in the 1880s. He was forty-seven years old, he'd never been married, and he lived at home with the same doting mother. True, he cooked for the old woman and managed the family property from his second-floor office at home, but as far as Mary was concerned, that could hardly be considered work.

Still, Charlie was a good man, she thought now as she set the cup down in its fragile saucer. She brushed the invisible crumbs off the tablecloth, put her elbows on its surface, and rested her chin in her cupped hands.

When Charlie was young, he'd been in vaudeville. He had put his supply of magic tricks to good use winning over Freddy and Wes three years earlier when she'd started going out with him. He and Roberta had never hit it off; she thought he was coarse, crude, and a bully, which Mary had to admit he somewhat was. Wesley, however, she was certain, really loved him. Wes would climb in his lap and laugh at his jokes for hours. Considering how far away the little boy's father was and how infrequently he saw him, Mary could only regard this as a good thing.

Besides, Mary enjoyed him, herself. Though she secretly believed he had an overinflated sense of his own dignity, he entertained her with his funny stories. He liked to take her out to nice places, pamper her with presents, and cook her elaborately extravagant meals. Though his gifts made her uncomfortable, and she didn't care whether she was taken out or not, she loved to be in his house. She enjoyed seeing him, a man, cooking. She liked using the old-fashioned silverware and elegant cream-colored, gold-edged dishes, and she delighted in eating on his carved walnut table under the elaborate nineteenth-century brass chandelier that hung from the high ceiling of his dim dining room.

She also had to admit to herself that she got a certain amount of pleasure from the fact that Charlie German believed she was beautiful, and thought of her as "the most wonderful woman in the world." She took these compliments with a grain of salt, but she also knew that she was his closest friend. It was true that she somehow actually liked his crotchety, terrible old mother; he had fallen in love with Mary when she told him one weekend before he went out of town that she would be glad to stop by his house to take care of her while he was away. She'd been looking after his mother during the trips he'd made ever since. Even more, however, he loved her because she loved his house and valued every single old or beautiful or sentimental thing in it.

Still, beg as he would, she absolutely would not marry him.

"Marry another man after your father!" Mary sometimes would exclaim to her daughter, sighing and shuddering when the subject came up between them. "Don't you know there could never be another man for me after your father?"

Roberta thought she was comparing Charlie German's appearance to Fred's, and, Mary had to admit, she partly was. She couldn't help herself. She had never gotten over the effects of Fred's dark good looks, while poor Charlie seemed to her to be as big, round, white, and pompous-looking as a raw Thanksgiving turkey.

Whatever the cause of her feelings for Fred, she couldn't get over him, and it infuriated her. It wasn't as bad as it had been five years before, but it was bad enough. She could hardly bear to see his picture. The blood pounded in her ears and her mouth went dry when the phone rang and she heard his voice on the other end, asking for the children. An expression on Freddy's face or a turn of phrase of Roberta's mouth would bring him close to her in a minute, leaving her overwhelmed with sadness. He didn't want her; he was married again, but she still wanted him. She knew it was bad for her, but she couldn't stop herself.

That she was still in love with her former husband and could not forgive him for it was not, however, the only reason she refused to marry Charlie German. There were two more. The first applied to her thoughts on marriage in general. "I know he loves me," she would say to her suspicious, anxious daughter who would be waiting up for her on the occasional night when she got home after eleven o'clock, "but you don't have to worry. There's no way a woman can be married to any man worth his salt without having to do what her husband says," she would state. "Don't you think I'm going to let some man tell me what to do, ever again!"

The second was specific to Charlie, and it had to do with the petulant jealousy he sometimes displayed toward all three children, but particularly Roberta. He just couldn't accept it that, as far as Mary was concerned, the needs of her children were always going to come before his own wishes. For this, he blamed not her, but the children themselves.

"Why were you so sarcastic with Roberta?" she would push him after he had been particularly snappish. "You'd think you believe you have to compete with her."

"I'm sorry, Mary," he would answer, sighing heavily, his hands spread out wide on his heavy thighs. He tried to put it back on her. "It doesn't have to be this way, you know."

The fact was that, from her point of view, it did: she wouldn't marry him, no matter how she was talked about or how financially unsafe they were. Her life as a divorced woman in a married world was harder than she had thought it would be, but it was hers. She liked him, but she didn't trust Charlie to be less competitive with the children if she were his wife. If his competition continued into marriage, as she was sure it would, she would be stuck.

If he were her husband, he would insist that she go along with what he wanted. As it was, she might be looked down on as a divorcee at church, have to struggle to have enough money to take the children to the dentist, then have the anxiety of raising the three of them by herself, but she was a free woman in her own house, or at least in her own rented apartment, in a way she hadn't felt herself to be since she was a child in the House on the Hill. She belonged to nobody, and she liked it.

Sitting in the sunlight at the table remembering that house she'd lost, she sipped her cold coffee and looked around at her apartment with satisfaction. It wasn't the greatest apartment, she knew that perfectly well. It was the kind of place where doorknobs tended to come off in your hands, closets were shallow and few, and roaches living in the basement for generations waited implacably for the human inhabitants to forget to spray.

Everything in the kitchen was worn out, with the exception of her salvaged-from-the-divorce washing machine, which sat between an unreliable stove and a minimal sink. There was no countertop; in fact, there was not a cabinet in the room apart from the tall white metal one she'd bought in a sale at Sears.

It was a lot better, she told herself than the kitchen in the House on the Hill she'd grown up in. There was plenty of room for her well-loved but scuffed enameled-top table at which the four of them ate their meals. (Aunt Blacky, who was ordinarily tight, simply showed up with it in Louisville one day soon after they'd moved from Union County four years before.) Mary had put up some boards and bricks under the sink for a make-shift cabinet and covered them with a curtain, and there was a small butler's pantry going into the dining room, and so she had a few places to store her things. Besides, it was just a step or two from the washer to the clotheslines out the backdoor and under the walnut tree in the yard. In this respect, she congratulated herself, it was even better than what she had had in Delaware, where she'd done the laundry in the basement and carried it up the stairs to hang it out.

The bathroom was not too bad, either, if she ignored the fact that it was hard to turn off the water in the scrubbed-out sink, the drains tended to stop up, the linoleum had holes in it, and there never was enough hot water to fill the claw-footed bathtub.

Of course, there was the bedroom situation, which, she had to admit, if she looked at it from the children's perspective, wasn't so good. In Fred and Wes's dark room, inappropriately wall-papered with large red cabbage roses alternating with wide, navy blue stripes, there was hardly any room for toys. Her and Roberta's room, on the other hand, was big enough, but they lived on top of each other in a way that was probably not good for either of them. Roberta was excruciatingly messy, and she seemed to have a baffling need to get away from the rest of the family Mary had certainly never felt at her age. Mary herself longed for a place to go at the end of her day at the beck and call of everyone else where she could shut the door and find a little order and peace.

There was nothing she could do about their crowding; whenever she began to worry about it, she made herself remember how happy they had been in the House on the Hill. This was in spite of her and Kas having to sleep in a single bed in the dining room with Bo, who peed on them both every night till she herself was ten years old!

Smiling to herself now as she remembered, she looked around her dining room with what was positive joy. She loved the tall brick duplex with its high double porches. Even if their part of it was too small and falling to pieces around their heads, on her secretary's salary and Fred's child support, they were lucky to have it. The location was just what she wanted. It was on the very edge of a part of town that was full of solid big Victorian houses like the one Charlie lived in with his mother, and only two blocks from her mother's first cousin Dorothy. Though it wouldn't have suited somebody who went for the new and clean, she liked it old. "Old" reminded her of her grandmother Grammar, her aunts, her own mother Bert, and the House on the Hill they'd all, with the exception of Bob, been born in. Even apart from that sense of comfort and safety it gave her, however, the apartment was worth it simply for the living room and dining room.

Today, the room she sat in filled her with special pleasure. The soft spruce walls and the dark honey oak woodwork shimmered in the late spring sunlight that poured gently through the clean windows on the side of the room that faced the couch. It was the same couch her in-laws had sent her and Fred when they'd moved to Delaware six years before, and it gave her great satisfaction that no one, not even Fred, would have recognized it in the new striped slipcover she'd made. The marble-topped battered dresser she had salvaged with her aunts Blacky and Ginny from the junk room of a barn below Owensboro stood against the wall to her back. It had been refinished to a deep golden cherry that perfectly complimented the big mirror that hung above it and the matching dragon-covered platter and serving bowl that sat on top of it.

The appearance of the table especially pleased her today. Ordinarily, she kept it folded down under the windows as small as she could get it, since it was only an ugly 1940s mahogany drop-leaf castoff of Charlie's. Now the table was open wide in the center of the high-ceilinged room, its ordinarily dreary surface still clothed in a deep rose-colored linen tablecloth. A low bouquet of late yellow daffodils from beside the house glowed in a cut-glass bowl in the center, the sharp facets of the glass mysteriously flashing red and blue sparks, as the streaming sunlight failed to strike it.

She loved the cut-glass bowl with her whole soul as she loved every delicate dinner plate, each shining silver fork, and each antique serving piece with which she had set the table. The cut-glass bowl, however, had been magic to her from the moment she had first spied it in the dusty window of an antique shop on Bardstown Road. Though she knew it wasn't really likely, it seemed to her to be a larger version of the tiny Victorian punch bowl that had once sat on the miniature buffet in the upstairs landing of Grammar's Beautiful House, the One That Burned. As she leaned forward to run her fingers over its sharp, zigzagged edge, it spoke to her even now of what was lavish in her grandmother's house, of soft, long gone angel food cakes, transparent jellies and fruit compotes set on white linen cloths, the smells of rolls baking, salty country ham frying, and the extravagant, favored praise of younger aunts.

The living room, she reflected, gave her as much pleasure as the dining room. From where she'd continued to sit at the table, she could see almost the whole of it through the wide archway that separated it from the dining room. It, too, was a gracefully shaped green room—she'd painted it herself—also with a high ceiling and a shining hardwood floor. On the outside wall, flanked by two homemade bookcases, was a big red brick fireplace with an oak mantel, a nineteenth-century pastoral scene hung above it. One on each side of the archway, a square carved love seat and chair, also refinished and covered with rose velvet, from the same barn as the marble-topped dresser in the dining room, faced toward the street in front. She knew the chair and love seat weren't very comfortable, as Victorian things to sit on generally weren't, but the carving especially pleased her. Besides, they weren't the only pieces in the room to sit on. There was a wide sofa long enough to lie down on which she had found at an auction and re-covered with a green brocade in a peacock-tail design. Invitingly, it stood on curved wooden legs under the front window, a marble-topped, carved coffee table in front of it and two small tables with marble lamps on either side of it.

Whatever problems there were in the back of the house, indeed, whatever problems she had with her life, these two rooms never failed to comfort her and make her proud. How glad she was in these sleek, Danish-modern days of the fifties that the carved, ornamented, fringed, and cut-glass Victorian treasures of her youth were out of style! On her secretary's salary, she could barely get the bills paid. She had scraped together every penny she could find, nevertheless, often skipping her own meals to save money, in order to surround herself and her children with the beautiful artifacts of other people's pasts that reminded her so much of her own.

To be able to make such a home for herself and the children, a home that was graceful, that pleased the soul with its beauty—this was nearly as important to her these days as the maintenance of her own freedom. Indeed, when she thought about it, she wasn't sure how to separate them, beauty and freedom, in her mind.

Wherever she was now, however, it was Fred's doing. If Fred hadn't told her how incompetent and boring she was when he left her, she might have just slept through her life. She'd certainly been happy with him, she'd grant him that, but she didn't believe he respected what she could do. Well, she'd showed Fred, she said to herself. With the back of her hand she brushed away the tears that never ceased to well up inside her when she thought of him. She was going to keep showing him, too. She didn't know how, exactly, or what, but she would show him.

She was just grateful that, as far as her own family was concerned, she didn't feel that she had to prove anything to them. She'd been so glad to see them all when they'd come today, especially her aunts! They had praised her as they had when she was a child. She smiled to herself, remembering their conversation.

"Isn't Mary Virginia's chicken pot pie wonderful?" Aunt Nacky had said, with her Cheshire cat smile. "Mary always could make the best crust!"

"Oh," said Aunt Blacky in her high, nasal voice. She was quivering with energy, her dark face turned to one side like a bird. "Mary Virginia has everything so nice because she's such a good hard worker!"

"Mary Virginia's rolls are as light as a feather," Suzie added, while Bert and Kas nodded their agreement.

After lunch Mary had taken them into the living room to drink coffee and eat the high white cake from delicate plates they placed daintily on their laps. Afterwards, they helped her with the dishes, laughing and telling stories of the outrageous doings of their own aunts, great aunts, grandmothers, and cousins. At last, they collected their coats from her bed in the back room and went out the door, patting her face and kissing her good-bye.

"You come to see us soon, Mary Virginia, you hear?" Aunt Blacky said.

"Don't you forget us up here in the big city, Mary Virginia!" said Aunt Nacky, smiling up into her eyes.

"You take care of yourself," Kas added. "Work hard."

"Kiss your old mother good-bye." Bert reached up and hugged her daughter around the neck with a secret smile like the Mona Lisa she resembled. In one of her protracted blue moods, she'd hardly said a thing all day. "It may be the last time you ever see her."

Mary hugged her mother in return. She'd heard these words so many times in her life, they barely registered on her.

Mary smiled to herself again as she remembered her sisters and aunts' typically boisterous, sentimental exit.

She got up from the table and walked into the living room to check the time on the French cloisonné clock Fred had given her for their first anniversary. It was nearly five o'clock. She walked over to the sofa, and set the cup she found still in her hand on the coffee table, pushing aside several yellow pages of poetry Roberta had left scattered there. She kneeled in the middle of the cushion and put her face up to the window. There was no Charlie yet. She let out a long sighing whistle between her lips, unfolded Aunt Blacky's feather-stitched throw quilt off the back of the couch, and covered herself with it as she lay down.

She put her hands behind her head and stretched her back, then turned over on her side, her sister Suzie's throw pillow bunched under her head. How much her aunts, her sisters, and her mother had done for her since the time of her divorce! She could hardly imagine what would have happened to her without them.

She had been so bedraggled and brokenhearted that first night Kas and A.D. had brought her and the three children to Mother and Daddy's she was nearly beside herself. She was exhausted with grief. She was also worn out from the terrible weeks of giving up her house, from the trip on the train to Florida, and finally, from the two days it took to drive from Jacksonville to Union County with Kas, A.D., and the confused and wounded children.

When they arrived, she'd fallen asleep beside Roberta in the back bedroom under a mound of blankets that seemed to be keeping her from floating off, disembodied, to some gaseous upside-down hell in the sky. She'd slept like a corpse. Hyper-alert the next morning, after she'd taken care of Wesley and gotten Freddy and Roberta started on their breakfast, she'd walked out barefoot into the October grass off the back steps just to see if she could still feel anything besides the peculiar, straining pain she carried in her chest and throat.

Fortunately, in Union County no one was about to talk to her about what had happened. Even her parents seemed either to take her presence on the farm as normal, or if not normal, at least, her own business and not theirs. Mary accepted this gratefully as a sign of their support. As though she were paying some ordinary visit, her mother had emptied out the drawers in the dressers in the back bedroom she and Roberta slept in. Bert made up the cot for Freddy and set up a crib for Wesley in the drafty, rattley little room beside it that was the cold cellar when the big room had been the kitchen. She neither inquired about her daughter's plans nor offered advice.

In the first weeks the four of them were on the farm, Mary sunk into the familiar sounds and smells, routines and textures of life in her parents' run-down old house. Though she'd never lived in it as a child, it was a house she knew: her grandfather had given it to Bert and Charles when her father had quit his job as a prison guard shortly after she and Fred had married.

She woke every morning in the big back bed to the cooing of doves, a sound she found at the same time infinitely comforting and melancholy. She did the wash in the elderly washer on the back porch, running their clothes through the electric wringer and hanging them on the metal lines out by the chicken yard. She spent a lot of time in the middle of the day at the back window gazing blankly toward the Dyer Hills, which lay, long and low, at the horizon. She vacuumed, dusted, and moved quickly and silently in the kitchen as she helped her mother cook the country food she'd given up for Fred.

For hours she rocked Wesley, her only child who was too small to ask questions, in her mother's cracked-seated rocking chair she'd bought for two dollars with money from the Red Cross after the '37 flood. "If I had the wings of an angel, over these prison walls I would fly," Mary sang over and over as Freddy stood on the rung of the rocker, his head resting on her shoulder. As for Roberta, she was off somewhere as often as she could be, at Grammar's or Kas's or Aunt Blacky's. In her present state of mind, Mary's daughter baffled and irritated her with her black moods and her insistent, unanswerable questioning.

The rest of her family wasn't prepared, however, to let Mary mope around on the farm forever; it wasn't long before they began to come for her. Mary would come in one morning, Wesley on her hip, to find Aunt Nacky with her mother and father already eating country ham, biscuits, and sorghum at the big, ugly dining room table she'd grown up with. The next morning it would be her baby brother, Quentin, and her middle brother, Bo. Kas would ask them all out for dinner on Saturday and tell her to bring the boys early so that they could stay all day. Susie would fetch her to pick up pecans in the field across the road from Suzie's house. Aunt Ginny would invite her to go shopping in Evansville, and Aunt Blacky and Aunt Subie would pick her up to take her antiquing.

It was a dreadful few months made increasingly easier, relative to what it had been, by the attentiveness of these people of hers who cared so much for her. By late February, having survived the first Christmas in Kentucky, at least in the outlying parts of her person Mary started to feel a little more like herself again. She began for the first time to notice and be bothered by the fact that she was being talked about.

Some, the voices of strangers, were out and out hostile. Once, Freddy looked up from his green beans and ham at supper to ask if it was "true that Jesus doesn't like children whose mamas and daddies had a divorce."

Other voices, the voices of acquaintances, were more ambiguous, more simply nosy than anything else. At least this was how Mary interpreted it when Roberta came home from a friend's house one day wanting to know, "What's a grass widow, Mama? Judy's mother said that's what you are when she was asking me how you were."

Then, there were the anxious, hushed voices of her aunts. She could hear them now, whispering in concern as she came into a room. "Look at Mary Virginia; hasn't she gotten thin!" one would say.

"That husband of hers sure didn't know when he had a good thing, did he?" another would reply.

"Do you think she'll ever remarry?" someone would ask. Mary would grit her teeth.

"Hush your mouth; she's coming," the first would say again, as though Mary hadn't heard everything they were saying already.

Mary couldn't stand it; she knew they loved her, but their pity was humiliating.

The worst that happened, however, was one Sunday in March when she went with her mother and the children to Pond Fork Baptist Church. Though she and the children had generally been attending the Methodist church in town, Pond Fork was the church in the country she'd grown up in. However cynical she'd been in her life about preachers, especially Baptist preachers, she didn't feel that way right now about God. In fact, sometimes she wondered how she could ever have gotten through the last few months without God, who seemed to her to have been loving and present to her in a way God never had before.

That Sunday morning, feeling particularly sorry for herself, as a woman bruised and alone in a world that had no place for her, she wanted the comfort of meeting God in her childhood church, which had been founded by her own great-grandfather, Grandpa Sam.

Mary hadn't known it was the quarterly Sunday for communion, but she had sat in the worn wooden pew, glad to be home in this dearly familiar house of God waiting for the little glass of grape juice and piece of dry bread to be passed to her.

She had been shocked, wounded, and angered when her own brother Bob, who was a deacon, had lifted the plate right over her head so that she couldn't even reach it. She supposed he had decided himself that she wasn't going to be allowed to share in the Lord's Supper. Whether it was because she often worshiped with the Methodists, whether it was because Bob considered her, a divorced woman, to be a sinner unworthy of the table, or whether he was finally getting back at her for going away and living like a Yankee she didn't know and wouldn't have asked if her life depended upon it.

Whatever the cause, however, it enraged her that he, of all people, should think he had the right to decide she wasn't good enough to be one of them at Pond Fork, much less to receive communion. Had he forgotten he was the brother who had thought he shouldn't have to grow up with the rest of them in the House on the Hill? He had had to live with Papa, whose namesake he was, just because Papa fussed over him and bought him things his other brothers didn't have.

It made her furious, furthermore, that he, or anybody else, for that matter, should think he could keep her from communion, even if he did think she was a sinner. It was the Lord's Supper, after all, not his, or any preacher's, either. It was Jesus' meal, and if he didn't think she was good enough for it, well then, in the Gospels, Jesus always took women like her over men like him. If Jesus wanted her, she was quite certain nobody else had a right to turn her away from what he offered her.

Besides, who did he or anybody else think they were to condemn her for the fact that Fred had left her? Didn't they know what it meant for a woman to be in her position? It was as though they wanted to condemn her for having her car hit by a drunken driver!

Her rage—at Fred, at Bob, at Pond Fork, at the nosy, self-righteous people who didn't know a thing about her, even at her aunts, her grandmother, and the sisters who loved her—was just what she needed to get herself moving. No matter how she still might feel, she would play the part of the helpless, cast-off wife no longer. It was time to get on her own two feet and take care of herself and her children.

She wouldn't put up with the judgmental Baptists any longer, even if they were her family. She took great satisfaction in joining the Methodist church, which, anyway, was the denomination her father left when he moved to Union County. She found a small apartment in town on Main Street, from which Roberta and Freddy could walk to school. She furnished this first independent home with a combination of what she had had in storage, salvaged from the divorce, and castoffs from the rest of the family. She had the old double-bed mattress she'd slept on with Fred cut down to fit twin beds. She borrowed a round oak table for the dining room from Aunt Ginny. She bought a porch swing and let Freddy get a dog and Roberta, a rabbit.

More important, however, than her move into the new apartment, she decided it was time to get a job. She needed the money for the children, and she needed the work for her own self-confidence. She had to prove she could do something besides have Fred and her family take care of her.

Considering that she hadn't had a job outside her own house in more than thirteen years, she had to think hard about what she was going to do. Her secretarial skills were gone, even if there had been an opening in town for a secretary, and she wasn't about to be a sales clerk. She was unprepared for the only work at which women could remotely make a living: she had no nurse's training, and, not having been to college, teaching was closed to her. For most other jobs she might have considered, she thought bitterly, she would have needed to be a man.

What was she to do? The solution came to her late in the morning one rainy, windy day toward the end of March. She had spent the hours since Roberta and Freddy had gone to school in no better occupation than entertaining Wesley. She'd tried to do some house cleaning and to run the vacuum cleaner, but Wesley had gotten into so many things while she was doing it, she'd had to give up in frustration. She enjoyed building blocks with Wesley, but she couldn't get a lick of work done.

What she needed, she thought as she leaned back on the couch cushion she'd pulled to the floor behind her, was somewhere she could send him to play for a few hours a day two or three times a week. Though she hadn't known of such a thing when Roberta and Freddy were little, her last year in Delaware she'd noticed that what they called "nursery schools" were springing up everywhere. Union County was a different matter.

It was while she was ruminating over this thought that the answer came to her: she would open a nursery school, herself. There was certainly as much need for a nursery school in Union County, Kentucky, as there was in Wilmington, Delaware. She loved little children who were barely past being babies. She was good at taking care of them and thinking up things for them to do. If she could bring herself to consider caring for children as work, rather than something that kept her from working, this would be just the job for her.

She knew she could arrange to use the church basement at the Methodist church. Aunt Nacky would help her with the rest. Aunt Nacky had been teaching second grade for thirty-five years, and she had a master's degree in education from Columbia University. Her aunt could give her books to read, as well as tell her where to send away for materials and supplies. Advertising would be by word of mouth; in a small town like theirs, everybody would hear about it in twenty-four hours.

And this is what Mary did. Within a month, the nursery school was started up. On Tuesdays and Thursdays, six three-year-olds came to listen to stories, cut out magazines, and dance to Aunt Nacky's records, which they heard on the portable phonograph Mary borrowed from her. On Mondays, Wednesdays, and Fridays nine other four- and five-year-olds came to learn their letters and numbers, sing songs, and draw pictures. The children had milk and cookies for snacks, naps on the church's mats, and Miss Mary to help them with their homesickness and the potty.

It was an exhilarating time for Mary. She had made a job for herself from nothing. She was her own boss, even if she did have to get along with parents who were sometimes difficult. She didn't earn much money at it, but what she earned helped them out considerably. She was able to take Wesley to the nursery with her, and she could be there when the children came home from school. Though there was a boy among the three-year-olds and a girl in the other class she worried about, she enjoyed the children. She liked being called "Miss Mary." She liked their energy, their shyness, and their noise. She loved it when they reached up to put their arms around her neck to hug her.

She was worn out at the end of the day, but she was used to being worn out. She was making something of herself.

Exhilaration over her new job and a feeling of success led to Mary's discontent, however. By the next September, she had become full of enough confidence in herself to become critical of their life in Union County. In spite of her family's love and kindness to her, her revelation that she no longer quite belonged among them, which had come to her the summer before her divorce, had only been strengthened. She couldn't help herself; life with Fred had made her a city woman, with a city woman's ambitions and desires.

Even if she could forget all that, however, it bothered her still more that, having given up the advantages of urban schools, her boys wouldn't even have the same opportunities to achieve in a rural setting what Kas's sons had. What could Freddy, and later Wesley, do if they joined the Future Farmers of America in Union County? Nothing. Being the poor relations (how Mary hated that!) and living in town without a father, neither of the boys would ever be able to raise a calf or prize pig, that was for sure.

As for Roberta, with her there was a different set of problems in small-town life. There was no getting around the fact that Roberta was growing up. A lot of the country girls in her class looked to Mary as though they were twenty years old; one child with whom Roberta had gone home to spend the night resembled a sexy Italian movie star. Another girl in Roberta's eighth-grade class had gotten pregnant and left school to get married at thirteen. Roberta herself wasn't much developed for her age and she was a little behind; she'd been sure she had cancer when she got her first period.

As she always told Roberta, Mary wanted her daughter to be happy. She wanted her to marry a smart man she would love and look up to in the same way Mary had loved and looked up to Fred. If they stayed in Union County, there was a fair chance she'd marry some ignorant person who was a hired hand on somebody else's farm, somebody who'd keep her pregnant all the time and never make her a living. Roberta already had a boyfriend from that kind of family. Her aunts, uncles, and cousins teased her about it, but Mary didn't think teasing would work in her daughter's case. Touchy as she was, Roberta couldn't take teasing like the rest of them. In three or four years, Mary could easily imagine her responding to it by marrying a man who beat his wife, drank, and ran around on her just to show them.

She and the children had been in Union County almost a year; in spite of the life she'd made for herself there, Mary suspected they needed to be somewhere else. What finally precipitated their move to Louisville, however was something utterly improbable, though once again, her aunts had something to do with it.

At the beginning of October Fred wrote to her to say that he was coming to visit the children on the weekend of the fifteenth, arriving on Thursday and leaving on Saturday. Though they had spoken on the phone several times over the past year, it would be the first time Mary had actually set eyes on her former husband since she'd watched him through the window of the train to Jacksonville as he waited on the platform to see them off.

For the first ten days before their father came, Freddy and Wesley were irritable, restless, and excited, and Roberta, morose and absent-minded. As for Mary herself, she was so keyed up with anxiety, newly awakened grief, unwelcome longing, and anger that she hardly knew what to do with herself. She couldn't sleep, and she could barely eat.

She jumped, her heart pounding, when the phone rang the night before his expected arrival.

"Hello?" said Mary, too loudly, nervous that it might be Fred.

"Hello, Mary Virginia?" It wasn't her ex-husband; it was Aunt Nacky, who didn't waste time on nonessentials. "A bunch of us are fixing to take your Grammar and go down to Nashville for the Billy Graham Crusade the day after Fred leaves."

At the mention of Fred's name, Mary drew in her breath; she was embarrassed that her family knew he was coming in the first place. She couldn't believe anybody would dare mention it.

Aunt Nacky went on talking as though she weren't aware of Mary's outrage. "We need you to come along and drive my car. If you do, we can take two cars; it'll make it a whole lot easier with your Grammar coming."

"Tell her it will do her good, Nacky," Mary heard Aunt Ginny speaking over her sister in the background. "We can stop and look in some antique shops in Tennessee."

At the sound of Aunt Ginny's voice Mary flushed. She was pretty certain they'd come up with this trip because they thought she needed it. She never liked sympathy; it made her feel weak and unequal to the person offering it. Right now, when she needed to be strong, she couldn't afford it.

Besides, though she was sure Billy Graham was a man of God—at least, that's what they said—how was she supposed to take a trip right after Fred left? She wouldn't want to see anybody at all, much less be cooped up in a car with a crowd of family for several hours. On top of that, she most certainly wouldn't want to hear some preacher talk about sin or how everything always turns out right for the one who loves the Lord.

If she tried to drive to Nashville and back, she'd probably just run off the road into the first ditch. There was a moment of silence in which Mary didn't say anything.

"You can bring Roberta, too. We're getting two rooms in a hotel down town," Aunt Nacky went on after a while. "It'll only be us women. If a couple of us sleep on pallets on the floor, we'll have plenty of space," Aunt Nacky went on. "I'll pay your way," she said.

There was another silence. "You want Roberta and me to go with you to the Billy Graham Crusade in Nashville, and you intend for me to drive," Mary said at last. She leaned against the wall, adjusted the scarf over her curlers and hitched down her skirt. "What would I do about the nursery school?"

Freddy, who had come into the hall to hear if the phone call had something to do with his father's visit, heard her end of the conversation.

"If you and Roberta are going to hear Billy Graham, I have to go, too," he cried.

Mary saw the tears on her son's face, the nursery school forgotten. "I won't go if Freddy can't," she said. Since the trip was to be all women, she knew they'd never let him, but after his father left, Freddy really would need his mother. She would need to be with her children herself, for that matter, once she put Fred back on the bus for Evansville.

Aunt Nacky wasn't about to give up. "Mary Virginia, Freddy's eight years old. There won't be any other boys or girls his age along. You ought to get away and not worry about your children for a day or two. Freddy'll be fine if you leave him and Wesley at Suzie's. Now, Mary Virginia, think about it. I don't know what we'll do if you don't drive for us."

While Aunt Nacky was saying all this, Freddy was hopping anxiously from one foot to the other. "Mama, take me, too," he insisted. "Don't go without me."

Mary felt trapped. She really couldn't leave Freddy, and she didn't want to go, but she had a sudden attack of guilt when she thought of turning Aunt Nacky and the rest of them down. Suppose they really did need her? They couldn't all squeeze into Aunt Ginny's car, and Nacky would wreck the car for sure if she drove.

It struck her all of a sudden that going to hear Billy Graham would also be the farthest thing from what she would do if she were still with Fred. It might feel good to do something right after he left that Fred would hate so much.

"All right," she said with sudden energy. "I'll drive, but only if I can bring Freddy, and I can figure out what to do about the nursery school."

"Okeydokey," said Aunt Nacky, cheerfully. She had gotten for her niece what she intended with less trouble than she'd imagined. "You go ahead and bring him, and I'll call the parents of your children myself."

It was early Sunday morning when they left from Grammar's house. Mary had gotten the children up and dressed, then dropped off Wesley at Suzie's at 5:00. She had taken Fred to catch the bus at the gas station at 1:00 A.M. the night before. She hadn't slept after he left; the time he was there had been even worse than she expected.

She had burst into tears as soon as he stepped off the bus. The children had leaped all over him. Back at the apartment, they continued to hang on him while he brought out their presents: for Roberta, a three-tiered peasant skirt in dark turquoise paisley: for Freddy and Wesley, big red metal trucks.

Against her better judgment, she had cooked a roast beef and made a coconut pie, both of which he praised in the old way. She let him sleep on the sofa bed in the living room; it was the first night of their lives they'd spent under the same roof in separate beds. She couldn't stand it. He was as good looking and sweet talking as ever. Knowing he was once again divorced, she alternated between thinking about throwing herself on him and wanting to scream at him. Of course, keeping her own counsel, she did neither.

Balancing between these states of mind, between long looks, she had mostly been silent and irritable with him. In spite of what she had previously decided, she had flashed out some ugly words to him the evening he left.

"Now, you've ruined my whole weekend," he'd replied in anger.

"Well, that's too bad," she'd answered, furious. "You've ruined my whole life."

The drive to Nashville was, indeed, exhausting. She'd had her mother and Nacky in the car, as well as Freddy, who cried for his Daddy for three solid hours, and Roberta, who, doped up on Dramamine, refused to speak at all. Mary didn't run off the road, but she did need to have everything Nacky said to her repeated at least twice before she could understand it. Her mother, who held Freddy's head in her lap, petting him and wiping his nose, said nothing. She was going through another silent period.

They settled in the hotel by noon; in one of the rooms, she, Roberta, and Freddy finally had a nap; they slept for several hours while the rest of them went out to see the big city sights.

For Mary, the main event of the Billy Graham crusade as she

experienced it that night had little to do with God. She sat in the hard seats of the huge indoor stadium under bright lights, arching her hurting back and trying to pay attention to the message Billy was delivering. She put her money in the collection plate, barely taking in the thousands upon thousands spread out like a human mountain range around her. Her former husband's face before her eyes, Mary listened as well as she could to a blue-robed, thousand-voice choir battering the audience with the crashing waves of "How Great Thou Art." By the altar call at the end, she was so worn out and ready to be in bed at the hotel, she didn't know what to do. After it was over, she somehow found their car in the distant parking lot. By the time she arrived at the door of the stadium to pick up her mother, Aunt Nacky, and the children, Aunt Ginny had driven on. She drove the four of them back to the hotel.

The others were already there when they'd returned. She had dressed Freddy for bed, made up a pallet on the floor, and put him in it as soon as they'd gotten off the elevator. Roberta went back down to the lobby to do some more of her interminable reading. Mary herself had ripped off her clothes, put on her nightgown, and gone to bed without so much as washing her face or brushing her teeth. She fell asleep immediately, the rest of them shrieking with laughter over her head as they drank orange juice, ate the cake they'd brought, and repeated stories of Pond Fork revivals long past. She couldn't hear their "poor Mary Virginias," nor did she know it much later when her mother climbed into the bed beside her to read her Bible and say her prayers.

Though she had slept soundly for the first night in a long time, she awoke early the next morning before any of the rest of them, even the children. Her stomach was sore, and her mouth was dry. Though she couldn't say why—perhaps it had something to do with Fred's visit— she had awakened knowing that she was going to have to do something about their life. She needed to think, and she needed coffee to do it. Quietly, she stepped over the sleeping children on the floor, dressed, and let herself out, her coat over her arm, to find some coffee at the all night diner at the corner.

Outside, the street lights with their yellow halos put a black shine like rain on the wide road she walked along. She put her anxious thoughts aside; she was simply glad to be out. She noted with pleasure that the sky above the roofs was beginning to turn the deep, luminous purple that skies assume in early city winters as the dawn comes on. She turned up her collar; the air was chillier than she had expected, though it was dry and had the pleasantly bitter, opulent smell of fall. The wind was up; it blew parallel to the ground, stinging Mary's legs and ankles as dry leaves whipped against her skin.

She put her hands in her pockets and walked briskly, her heart rising for no special reason except for the day itself. The imaginary mingled odors of coffee and doughnuts struck her nostrils as she caught sight of the bright lights of the diner toward which she was walking. All she could think of was hot coffee as she hurried toward the little building. She was stamping her feet, now, in the cold.

Then, all at once, out of the blue, the most amazing thing happened. Mary heard a voice talking to her as loud and distinctly as if someone were speaking directly in her ear. It was a strong voice, suggesting common sense and kindness. It didn't occur to her to wonder whether it was male or female, young or old.

"Take your children to the city," it said, distinctly, and that was all.

Mary was astonished. She whipped her head to the left and the right. Her hands still in her pockets, she turned entirely around on the empty sidewalk and stopped stock still. There was no one there.

A kind of sweetness flooded her, and she was filled with euphoria. It was God who had spoken to her, she was certain of it. She knew what to do now, and how to do it. Dazed with happiness, she walked into the restaurant and drank three cups of coffee with dry toast.

By the time she stepped back onto the pavement outside the diner, the sky had turned white; the noise and smells of early morning traffic were beginning to fill the streets.

Back at the hotel, the doors of the two rooms stood open. Bags and the cooler were stacked in the hall. Everybody, including the children, was dressed and waiting for her.

"Good morning," Mary said, hugging herself and smiling "I've been thinking . . ."

"Mary Virginia," Aunt Ginny interrupted.

Aunt Nacky looked at her face. "Hush, Ginny," Aunt Nacky said, "Mary Virginia's trying to tell us something."

"Yes," said Mary. "I've decided. As soon as we can, I'm going to move to Louisville."

There was no pause, no hesitation in their immediate response.

"Mary Virginia," said her mother, Bert, breaking her silence. She walked over from Grammar's chair to give her daughter a hug. "You'll have to be careful and watch your children in that big city."

"I'll drive you up and help you look for an apartment on Wednesday," Aunt Blacky said. "We can arrange about the children's school while we're up there. We'll call cousin Dorothy for help; Dorothy will be thrilled to death!" Dorothy was Mary's mother's and aunts' first cousin on Grammar's side.

"I'll help you pack your dishes," Aunt Ginny went on. Being as tight as she was, she wasn't about to offer money, but other than that, she would do what she could.

"Mary Virginia, you're going to have to get your secretarial skills back," Aunt Nacky went on. "I know you don't have a penny, so you'll just have to let me help you with that. I'll bet they'll take you on at Spencerian Business School in a minute; won't they be surprised to see you back?"

And that is exactly what happened, Mary recalled, as she lay now on her own couch in her own room, waiting for a man who thought she was wonderful to come and take her to supper. Her family had up and moved her without a qualm. She had gone back to school, then found herself a good job as a secretary—not as much fun as before she was married, but good nonetheless. She'd met Charlie through another secretary at work.

The boys were doing well in school. Roberta was about to go off to Hanover College across the river in Indiana in the fall: she had a little money saved from her after-school job and would make more over the summer. She would get a small scholarship; the rest, Mary could pay for herself, with a bit of help from Fred. She was proud of all three children; they were a credit to her.

She'd had a good rest. Mary stood up, pulled down her skirt, and patted her hair. She checked her lipstick in the mirror by the front door. The doorbell rang, and she let Charlie in. He stomped over to the couch and thumped down on it.

"Beautiful as ever, Mary," he said in his pompously theatrical voice. The evening was just beginning.

CHAPTER SEVENTEEN

Richard

You know, Panny, there were some things about both of our lives that made it hard for Richard and me to take the risk of marrying. Richard was very close to his conservative Catholic parents, and they strongly objected to me, a divorced, ten-years-older, Protestant woman with two children. As for myself, as you are only too aware, I had been married before; I wasn't prepared to take that risk again. Even more, however, having seen for years what had happened to my mother when she'd let herself feel the way she'd felt about my father, I knew that being in love in the way she'd been was dangerous for a woman.

Anxieties aside, there was no doubt that I was definitely, wildly in love with Richard. I was in my late thirties and I was like a besotted teenager. I had never felt like this. That Richard was in Milwaukee and I in Atlanta during the academic year preceding a marriage we hadn't yet agreed to only made it worse. In those months apart I was always seeing men in crowds whose shoulders or the shape of the head reminded me of him. With every turn of the light I wondered what he was doing. Constantly, I imagined his long, straight fingers, his mouth, his kindness, and his intelligent attentiveness.

Listen to these three dreams I had of him one night in winter when the moon was full, the winter before we were married, and you'll see what I mean. Perhaps I should apologize for them; they certainly aren't the dreams a liberated woman should be having. There isn't even any plot to them. But Panny, they were wonderful, full of visual and emotional images of such extraordinary strength that, even now, they seem like visions and promises of God.

The first of these dreams, which came to me just as the moon was rising, took place on a vast, high plain somewhere on the steppes of Russia. When the dream began, I was standing all alone in nearly waist-high brownish grass that stretched out in every direction as far as I could see. The sun was shining, but the light was cool and low, as it is in early winter. What I was doing there, I do not know, only that at the start of the dream I was watching the horizon to the east.

As I watched, a rider appeared. At first, this rider was no more than a dark dot in the distance, but as the person came closer and closer, I saw that I was looking at a man. He was on the back of a gleaming chestnut mare who stretched out her neck and tossed her belled mane so gracefully she might have taken lessons in it. Now I could see that the man on the horse was Richard, but Richard splendidly clothed and glowing in a way I'd never actually seen with my naked eyes.

The sight of him filled me with wonder. His head was wound around in a large turban of shiny purple silk, and his soft, dark hair, which was as long as it was in waking life, was curling out around the edges. His beard was also curly like the beard of a Persian warrior on an ancient tiled frieze; it ended at the open neck of his fine, white, full-sleeved linen shirt. His pants, which were also flowing, were luminous purple brocade. They were gathered at the calves in fantastic black felt boots, which curved up at the toes. A wide red sash, also silk, was tied around his waist.

He drew alongside me as I stood in the grass watching. He smiled and looked down at me through black-lashed eyes as green and clear as gemstones. As he jumped off the mare, the bronze bells woven in her mane clanged softly. Richard put his arms around me, and I was filled with sweetness.

I woke up. The moon had risen higher, and I lay there a little in its light, then I slept and dreamed again. This time, I was walking in a scorching sandy desert in an undetermined place in the Near East when I came upon a nomad's long, narrow tent of skins.

With some misgivings, I stooped to enter the door of the tent. When I straightened up, I saw immediately that the whole of the floor and the walls were covered in dazzling Oriental rugs in the most intricate and delicate of designs. As I was admiring them with pleasure, I noticed that there was a low throne carved of ebony at the far end of the tent. On the throne sat a man dressed as Richard had been in the previous dream. As I came closer, I could see that it was in fact Richard, smiling at me. He stood and walked toward me to embrace me, and again I was filled with joy.

The second time, I woke to find myself lying in the moonlight, which streamed through the window opposite the bed. Once more, I fell asleep, and this time I found myself in my dream standing on black sand by a perfectly blue ocean. Above me, birds swooped, calling to one another. At my right hand, mountains arising almost from the edge of the water, rose above me, sharp peaked and snow covered. On my left, waves crashed and foamed against the dark rock out of which the sand was made.

I heard the sound of human feet walking in the sand; a hand was laid on my shoulder. I turned to see Richard, dressed again in the splendid clothing of an Oriental prince. As the breeze whipped his thin white shirt against his arms, Richard nodded and held out a large conch shell to me. I put its shiny peach opening to my ear, and suddenly I found myself listening, not just to the ocean, but to the music of the entire world and everybody in it, singing and soaring with delight. I listened for a moment, full of reverent joy once more as he put his arms around me. Then, for the final time that night, I woke up under the full moon.

Oh, Panny, when I brought Richard to Union County to meet everybody for the first time the summer after we were married, it mattered to me so much that the family like him! Mama was happy with him because she knew he made me happy. Anna Grace and Ben were attached to their stepfather already. It lasted, too; Benjamin was so enchanted with Richard that for the first three years after we got married, Benjamin would hardly let him out of his sight. Richard loved him in return, and Ben knew it. Let me tell you what that son of mine asked me about a year after the wedding.

He and I were having a walk around the block; he was holding my hand and obviously thinking. Benjamin was always a great thinker, even as the five-year-old he was at the time. "Mama?" he said when we got to the steep part of the hill where the houses leave the park by the road.

"Yes, Benjamin?" I replied.

He looked up at me and frowned; he spoke very slowly to make sure I understood what he was asking. "Do you think Daddy Richard would have married you even if you hadn't had Anna Grace and me?" He stopped in the middle of the sidewalk as he waited for my answer.

"Yes, Benjamin," I said. "Yes, I think he would have."

"I thought so," he replied. "That's good."

Of course, I didn't expect you to love Richard as I did, or as Benjamin did, either. I was simply worried that nobody in Sturgis would muster up an even ordinary liking. Our family was famous, after all, for ridiculing its members' potential beloveds. I wasn't about to forget the serious, adult teasing I'd endured over my seventh-grade boyfriend. Nor could I put out of my mind Aunt Hildegard's standard joke, that the only reason everybody accepted her when she married Uncle Quentin was because somebody figured out that she was already actually a distant cousin. It's a good thing I didn't know then what I know now about the way Uncle John Bundy was actually kept from marrying by Grammar as well as his sisters jeering at his various lady friends over the dinner table. Then I would really have worried.

My concerns, however, were not only generic, the ones any family member with any sense would have felt in my position. There were worse things to be feared than that. I couldn't get around the fact that he really was everything I believed our family would find shocking or at least ridiculous. What would you all think about the age difference between us? About his adopted parents, who were Italian and Irish? With undisciplined curly hair and a bushy beard, he was good looking in a way men in Union County weren't supposed to be. He was urban, too, or at least thoroughly suburban. Being from Cincinnati, he didn't have a speck of Kentucky blood in him. He cooked, shopped, and took care of little children like a woman. He was openly affectionate not only with Anna Grace and Ben—I didn't expect problems over that—but he was prone to put an arm around me or kiss me right in front of other people. (Grammar would have curled her lip in disgust!) He was also a Roman Catholic, a member of what I had been taught as a child at Pond Fork Baptist Church was an alien, idol-worshiping religion.

Worst of all, however, he didn't even speak our language. I hadn't realized this before we got married, but he'd clearly demonstrated it already on the Louisville part of our trip.

You recall, Panny, that when Richard and I were married, he still was teaching in Milwaukee. At the end of the school year, I flew up and helped him pack; then we rented a trailer and hauled what he had in his apartment up there back to my house, now our house, in Atlanta.

After spending a week unpacking and trying to assimilate all his stuff into our newly joined household, we were both exhausted. Let me tell you, it is much easier setting up a household starting from scratch than doing what we did. What we needed to do was rest. What we did, instead, was to take Anna Grace and Benjamin to their other grand-mother in Georgia so that we could drive back up to Louisville to see everybody. We arrived the first night, dirty and tired, just in time for dinner with Mama, Fred, Linda, and Liza. (We were so glad to see them; do you remember that Fred and Linda brought Liza to the wed-ding? She could barely walk; she was so cute!)

The next day, we got our aching bones and muscles up early because that's what you're supposed to do in our family if you don't want to be considered lazy and unsociable. We ate and visited with Fred and Linda some more, as well as with some friends of mine and Mama's whom Richard hadn't yet met. By seven o'clock in the evening, the two of us were truly worn to a frazzle.

Mother, Richard, and I were eating supper in her big, comfortable kitchen in the Victorian house on Willow Avenue. The evening air was dry and pleasant with the smell of the garden. The light shining in through the long back windows off the high back porch made soft patches of summer gold where it hit the warm, natural woodwork and the bentwood rocker by the table with the glass lamp on it. Though I wasn't looking at it, the pattern on the wallpaper seemed especially pleasing.

I was slumped over in my cane-bottomed chair at the maple table, staring at the tiny pink roses and green leaves in the milk-glass bowl in the middle of the table. Almost too tired to sit up, I was wondering how Mama got the little bush to grow. Would there be enough light that I could plant one behind our house?

Mama was setting the biscuits on the table and grumbling, as usual, that "they aren't fit to eat" when Richard all of a sudden looked up at her and smiled. He had been spearing a slice of ham with one of Mr. German's nineteenth-century silver forks, on a rose-covered, gold-rimmed Limoges plate my brother Wesley had gotten at an auction when he was eighteen.

"Would you mind if Roberta and I went out to a movie later tonight?" he asked Mama, innocently. It obviously had never occurred to him that he had just spoken words that should never have left his mouth.

I was jolted awake in an instant. I sat up straight and tried to think what to do. Though Richard's family was different, when we visit at Mama's house, we are never, ever supposed to go off all by ourselves any more than we are to sit and read while everyone else is talking. How was I going to fix this mistake?

"No, no . . ." I started to speak. Mama's voice rode over mine.

"Sure," she said, not looking at Richard. "You go on and go to the movies. It's fine with me. Of course"—she was now looking at me as I cringed in my seat—"I told Aunt Dorothy you might be stopping by after supper to see her."

Oblivious to everything, Richard cut himself another bite of ham and forked it up with a chunk of potato salad. I knew very well what Mama was saying, however, and, Panny, it wasn't that, as far as she was concerned, this visit to your elderly first cousin was optional.

"Well, then," I answered Mama hastily, "in that case, then, we'd better just go on down to Aunt Dorothy's. Are you coming with us?"

Richard looked puzzled, but he didn't say anything.

"No," Mama said, shaking her head. "I already told them I wouldn't be coming. But that's all right," she said impatiently. "You two go ahead and go to the movie. You all just do what you want and don't worry about it."

Taking the last biscuit from the basket, Richard sighed with pleasure.

I sighed with fear. Mama had just made her wishes clear in plain Kentucky language that anyone over the age of four ought to be able to understand. Richard was ignoring her.

"OK," he said, pushing back from the table and standing up and stretching. "Thank you for the delicious supper." He smiled. "I'll go get the paper and see what movies are on."

What was wrong with Richard? I'd never seen him act this way. "No, no," I said, horrified. "Richard, I really don't want to see a movie." By now, however, it was too late. Mama's arms were crossed on her chest and her mouth pressed out in a straight line.

Mama didn't say anything.

"Come on," Richard said. "Why not? Your mama says it's OK with her. Let's go; it'll be good for you."

Unwilling to argue with him in front of Mama, I gave up, but I wasn't about to let it drop. Fifteen minutes later, when we went out the door, my heart was still pounding.

"How could you have done what you did just now?" I asked him, angrily.

"Done what?" he answered, defensively. "What did I do?" He sounded genuinely baffled.

"What do you mean?" I replied. "You know very well you said we would go to the movies when Mama made it plain that we were supposed to visit Aunt Dorothy."

"Visit Aunt Dorothy?" he answered, his voice rising. "What does Aunt Dorothy have to do with anything? Your mother told us to go ahead and go to the movies. You heard her yourself."

"Yes," I said, "but you know very well that's not what she meant. She was saying, 'How can you even think of such a thing as going to a movie when what you're supposed to do is get down there and visit your Aunt Dorothy!'"

Richard stopped on the sidewalk with his hand on the car door; he looked at me, astonished. "But she never said any of that," he replied. "Where on earth did you get the idea that that's what she meant?"

"Richard," I answered, not only frustrated but baffled myself. "That is exactly what she said; it was as plain as day."

"Well," he retorted, not at all enlightened. He could see now that he'd made a mistake but not how he'd done it. "If that's what she meant, she should have said so."

"She did, Richard; she said it as clearly as anybody can say anything," I responded.

By now we were sitting in the front seat of the car with the engine running, though we hadn't drawn away from the curb. There was a bad moment of silence between us, made tense by our unaccustomed anger, but even more by the unexpected language barrier that had suddenly risen up like the Berlin Wall between us.

"OK," Richard said at last, defeated by something he couldn't get a handle on. He sighed. "I can't think of how I'm supposed to have known that. Let's go back in."

"She said it as plain as anything," I muttered under my breath, stubbornly. Richard was nice enough to ignore me.

Once in Union County, Richard behaved pretty much as I suspected he would. He talked to you and all the aunts and great-aunts as though it were the most natural thing in the world for a man to talk to women on their own terms. He wanted to discuss recipes, though he kept mentioning olive oil and artichokes and other things nobody in Union County would have anything to do with. He touched me constantly, patting me, putting his arm around me, and calling me Sweetie. He talked openly about his father's family in Sicily, and he told shameless stories about his brother, who ran a funeral home in Cincinnati. He didn't avoid the topic of religion.

Throughout it all, I hardly knew what to think. Though his behavior had been predictable to me, yours hadn't. It was clear that you all regarded him as an oddity, but you liked him and you made him welcome. You all didn't mention his age, or call him a city slicker or an Eyetalian. You didn't even look at each other out of your eyes when he talked about David's funeral home. You might have passed around a few *did you ever in your life?s* or *did you hear what he said?s* after we left to go back to Atlanta, but I doubt it. You couldn't understand what kind of a man he was, but you could see that we suited each other; you were happy for me. I suspect you refrained from gossip.

Panny, during that trip, you and my aunts, my uncles, and my cousins made me happy in Union County in a way I'd never been before. You wanted me there, and Richard too, and you let me know it.

As for the besotted way I saw my husband in those days seventeen years ago, I can report that my vision has been slightly tempered by the everyday realities of sharing a household in which we raised the children.

On the other hand, those three exotic dreams live in me as powerful memories that never go away. When I come across Richard in a place I am not expecting him, when I see him sitting reading in the evening, when we talk about our work or the ordinary adventures of our day as we cook our dinner together, I am often struck by the fact that the man with whom I share the daily chores truly is the man I dreamed of all those years ago. He is still green-eyed, graceful, and attentive, though his hair and beard are gray. To me, he is more beautiful, more mysterious than ever. Believe me, Panny, grace is a wonderful thing.

CHAPTER EIGHTEEN

Willow Avenue

$\mathcal{R}$oberta, Mr. German's here," her mother called from the living room. "Come and say hello before we go."

Roberta pretended she didn't hear. She didn't want to say hello; she had just stretched out on the bed to read some more of what was at the moment her favorite novel, *The Plague*, and she was feeling very existential, alone, and moody.

Before she began to read, she'd been sitting at the salvaged oak library table she used for a desk, writing poetry on her mother's old Underwood. When Roberta felt more down than usual, putting words together to make them beautiful helped her. It made her feel less lost in empty space, suggesting to her that there was more to her life than hurting, missing her father, and screwing up in school.

Her mother couldn't stand hearing the specifics of her unhappiness: the poetry Roberta wrote was the only way she'd figured out to tell her mother her feelings in a form Mary could bear to listen to. This afternoon, Roberta had put the four poems she'd written on the coffee table in the living room so that her mother would find them when she woke up from her nap on the couch.

Right now, Roberta was really tired; she was also feeling sorry for herself. She'd stood on a concrete floor at a counter, working at Grant's from four till eight the evening before, and today from nine till three. She'd been up late for a date last night with a boy she didn't even like. The grown-ups already expected her to heat up supper and baby-sit for her little brothers. The next thing she knew, she said to herself, they would think she ought to mop the floor and clean the bathroom, afterward!

Not that that would satisfy her mother! She'd never work hard enough to suit her mother, especially when she was around the relatives from Union County who had been there for lunch today. Roberta was sure her mother wanted to be able to brag about her daughter because she didn't want them to think she wasn't as successful as her sisters and brothers. Mary talked all the time about how smart, polite, and hardworking her nieces and nephews were; Roberta figured this talk was meant to be an indirect reproach to her.

As Roberta lay on the bed, her book in her lap, her mood darkened as her self-pity deepened. She didn't want to speak to anybody. Why should her mother get to go out and have a good time with some big man with money and leave her by herself to take care of her disgusting little brothers and do all the work? If her mother had just stayed married to her father, Roberta wouldn't have to be in this position.

"Roberta, did you hear me?" her mother called again. "I said, Mr. German's here."

"I'm coming," Roberta answered this time. She emphasized "coming," her voice as close to nasty as she thought she could get away with. She knew her internal grudge against her mother was unfair, but she couldn't seem to stop herself no matter how she tried.

She dragged herself into the living room, looking at the floor. From the corner of her eyes she could see Charlie German sprawled on the sofa, legs apart with his big belly hanging between them. His blue striped tie barely covered the places where the buttonholes pulled around the buttons of his starched, pale yellow shirt. His skin, white and unhealthy from the diabetes he refused to take care of, was as taut over his round face as his shirt was over his stomach.

Mr. German was doing something with his hands and cuffs, pulling quarters from seven-year-old Wesley's ear, at the same time keeping up a barrage of old vaudeville jokes. Wesley, who for some reason, actually liked him, was leaning against his left leg and giggling as he tried to figure out Mr. German's tricks. Freddy, a dignified adolescent of thirteen with a bent toward the law, sat on his hands and watched, embarrassed, from the end of the couch.

255

Roberta glanced with disdain at the childish nature of all this and threw herself on the love seat across from the sofa. "Hello," she mumbled, crossing her arms over her chest, hunching her shoulders, and looking away. Her mother, standing by the fire place, rolled her eyes at the ceiling, shook her head, and frowned a warning to her aggravating daughter.

Mr. German handed the quarter to Wesley to keep, and patted the little boy out of the way. He had been waiting for just this moment.

"Well, well," he said to the slouching girl, grinning with his brownish teeth. He breathed out an "ooph" as he leaned over his stomach to pick up a yellow piece of paper from the table in front of him. "Listen to this!"

"Listen to what?" Roberta, staring out the window over his head, chose not to look at what he had in his hand.

Mr. German didn't give a direct answer. Instead, he cleared his throat, placed his right hand over his heart and began to recite in a sing-song.

"One thousand nights the earth
offers her bed to the sea.
One hundred days the broken eggshell
awaits the sparrow.
One spring the child's grave
expects dandelions and violets,"

he intoned, melodramatically.

"Huh?" Roberta grunted. She was so shocked by what she was hearing that she'd let him get through a whole verse before she could find her voice. "What are you doing with my poem," she shouted at last. "Mama, make him stop!" Her face turned bright red as she leaped off the love seat toward him. "That's private; how dare you read that!"

Freddy and Wesley looked at each other and put their hands over their mouths.

Mr. German twisted around to his right so the yellow paper would be out of reach.

"And I wait" (he read in his dreadful voice),

"not for a love
or life
or a flower.
I wait for the end of waiting."

"That's enough, Charlie," Mary said in the very moment Roberta fell across him, clawing for her poem. She was shaking with humiliation.

Mr. German elbowed her off his chest with distaste. "Here it is," he said, handing it to her with a growl. "How was I supposed to know you can't take a joke?" He turned his head to her mother standing by the mantel and raised his thin gray eyebrows. The look on his face was a combination of crafty innocence, injured pride, and self-satisfaction. "What's gotten into her, anyway, Mary?" he said. "It's a good poem; she should have been flattered that I wanted to read it!"

Roberta rushed out, sobbing, into the room she shared with her mother. She slammed the door behind her. The last thing she heard through the door before she fell asleep face down on the orange chenille bedspread was Mary's raised voice speaking to her brothers in the living room, "Fred, Wesley, you need to go play. Mr. German and I have to talk."

Roberta, her hair still wet where she'd cried on it, woke sometime later to a house that was quiet except for the sound of pots rattling softly in the kitchen. The bedroom door stood open. She was confused; she wasn't certain how long she'd slept, or even whether it was morning or evening.

"Mama, is that you?" she called out toward the kitchen. She noticed she was dressed, and suddenly remembered what had gone on before she slept. Her stomach growled with hunger. "I thought you were going to Mr. German's for supper."

Mary came into the darkening room, wiping her hands on her apron, and sat down on the bed. In a gesture of physical affection that was rare with her older children, she gently put her hand on her daughter's arm. "I changed my mind," she said. "I decided not to go."

"Why, Mama?" Roberta asked. "Because I had a fight with him? You've been looking forward to it for a week." Roberta complained a lot to herself, but a good bit of her resentfulness toward her mother had to do with a painful protectiveness toward the older woman which she didn't want to have to feel.

"I didn't go because he insisted that I had to make you apologize to him for how you acted this afternoon," she answered.

"Me apologize?" her daughter interrupted. She'd forgotten her interest in her mother's welfare from the moment before. "He's the one who ought to apologize! I didn't do anything wrong." Her throat began to close with anger and hurt pride.

"I told him I wouldn't make you do it; he was the one who was ugly," her mother went on. "If anything, he should be apologizing to you."

"What? What did you just say, Mama?" Roberta asked. She couldn't have heard correctly.

"I said, I told him I had no intention of making you apologize; he should apologize himself, not you," Mary said.

Roberta stopped crying and looked at Mary with astonished gratitude. Her mother had taken her part and defended her against an actual man!

"What did he say to that?" Roberta wanted to know when she caught her breath.

Mary pursed her lips, made a face, and laughed. "He said he'd write me out of his will unless you did it."

"He said what?" Roberta cried out.

"I told him he had his nerve suggesting for one minute that I'd ever go out with him because I was interested in his money," Mary went on as though she hadn't been interrupted. "His money! The very idea! I told him to forget about going out with me. I wouldn't go out with him again if he were the last man in the world!"

Roberta sat up on the bed and looked at her mother, waiting for more.

"Now, go wash your face and come into the kitchen so we can eat," her mother only said. "We don't need to say anything else about it." Roberta didn't dare ask any more questions.

Though she absolutely couldn't stand Mr. German herself, afterwards Roberta was sorry for what had happened. As teenagedly self-centered as she was, she was not so selfish that she didn't realize something of what her mother's defense of her had cost. True, Mr. German had insulted her with his crass talk about his will. Still, besides going to Union County for the weekend once a month, Mr. German was all the social life her mother had. Roberta was young, but she understood that Mary had enjoyed herself with him, and that his admiration had been good for Mary.

Roberta had a lot at stake in her mother's happiness. Truly, Roberta wanted her mother to be happy because she loved her mother in a disinterested sort of way. At the same time, there were two other reasons she wanted Mary's happiness that were not so disinterested.

When her mother was unhappy, Mary would become silent and turned in on herself in a way that made Roberta feel invisible. She needed her mother's attention. When she felt her mother couldn't see her, Roberta would get restless and unable to sleep, feeling that she had somehow winked out of existence, that reality had simply closed over the hole in life where she had been.

At the same time, more often than not, when her mother hurt, Roberta hurt; she could never clearly distinguish her mother's misery and memories from her own. Sometimes, indeed, Roberta wondered whether she didn't feel her mother's pain in a more intense form than Mary felt it herself. The loss of the House on the Hill, which Roberta hadn't even seen, the loss of long dead great-aunts, the loss of her mother's childhood in Union County, her obsessive love for her departed husband and her ongoing grief and anger, her hurt pride at being labeled a divorced and therefore dangerous woman, her ambitions for her children, her worries for their safety, her worries about money, her loneliness—all of these kept Roberta in a restless, helpless anguish for her mother that she was convinced she would have to live under the whole of her life.

Now Roberta believed that she had done Mary a terrible injury, as she thought, by running off her mother's one companion.

When it came to the banishment of Mr. German from the household, for a long time Mary stuck to her guns. She didn't go out with him and she didn't talk about him. Though Roberta thought she'd heard her mother speaking with him on the phone once or twice over the summer, Mr. German was still nowhere in sight by the time she went off to her first year at Hanover College at the end of August. Mary hadn't reported any conversations or negotiations with him to her daughter, but, then, Roberta wouldn't have expected it of her.

When Roberta came home for the Christmas vacation, however, Charlie German was back in Mary's life. Roberta knew that she wouldn't be going out with him if he hadn't at least apologized to her mother for the terrible things he'd said. What this conversation had been like, each being who they were, she could hardly imagine. Clearly, however, they had worked out an arrangement where Roberta didn't need to make any apologies of her own.

Practically speaking, the arrangement worked out like this: though Mary went to his house, he ate no meals at hers with the family. He came to her apartment to talk to the boys and give them each Christmas presents—but not Roberta. Her he dismissed as though she did not exist. Not only would he not speak to her, he would not so much as acknowledge her presence in a room with him.

Though she had formerly been as rude to him as she could be, and she didn't even like him, Roberta hardly knew how to deal with such a dismissal. In Mr. German's annihilating presence, therefore, her mouth went dry and her heart raced. Around him, as around her father, she felt herself diminished to nothing. He was another man who didn't want her; that she didn't care for him was irrelevant. In the real world—her world in which her father had left her—men, not women, were the ones who counted.

Her mother didn't seem to notice Mr. German's behavior, or if she did, she must have assumed that, because her daughter didn't like him, it didn't matter to her. In fact, it mattered greatly, but this time, Roberta was not about to make a scene over it. She'd learned her lesson well enough last time. She felt displaced and dislocated, but she reminded herself that she really didn't live at home anymore, anyway.

Things might have continued exactly in this way forever if during the following summer, something nearly catastrophic hadn't taken place: Roberta came home to Louisville at the end of her first year in college to find her mother even more distracted and tired than usual. She seemed to have lost weight, which she couldn't afford, and her hair was a mess. Roberta decided, as far as she was able, not to pay attention to whatever it was that was wrong. Probably, it had something to do with her father. She decided that her own hurting memories were bad enough; she was tired of bearing her mother's grief and anger, besides.

Roberta had been away for nine months. She was feeling adult and independent. She had a summer job that paid well in a doctor's office in St. Matthews. She had recently started going out with a smart boy with a good singing voice from their home church. He had just graduated in chemistry and intended to go off to do graduate work in Iowa in September. She had a good time with him.

Giving shots in the daytime and attending plays, movies, and jazz concerts at night, Roberta did a thorough, callous job of ignoring whatever was going on with her mother until she came home one evening to find Mary waiting for her, draped over the brocade couch in the living room. She didn't stand up when her daughter walked in.

"What are you doing up?" Roberta asked. Feeling trapped, she wiped at her smeared lipstick with the palm of her hand, hoping her mother wouldn't notice.

If she did, she didn't mention it. She had other things on her mind. "I have to tell you something, Roberta," she answered.

"What is it?" Roberta asked, suddenly apprehensive.

Mary went on. "I didn't let you know before, because I didn't want you to worry, but I've had a lump in my breast for a while. I went to the doctor two weeks ago. Today I got the results back from a test he did in the office. He said it probably isn't cancer, but it could be. I'm going into the hospital the day after tomorrow and get it taken out."

"Cancer!" Roberta cried. "You might have cancer? What if you have it?" She flung herself on the couch next to her mother.

"Don't you worry," Mary replied. "You'll have to look after your brothers while I'm in the hospital and I'll need you to help me when I get home, but you'll see. Everything will be all right."

"Yes, but . . ." Roberta had more to ask and to say.

Mary interrupted. "Right now we need to go to bed. I've got a long day ahead of me." She cut off further conversation.

That night and the next Roberta didn't sleep. She cried at work, dropped things, and was irritable toward her boyfriend, who was angered by her touchiness. The ground under her feet, which, ever since they had moved into her grandmother's back room in Union

County, already had the sickening squishiness of a rainy marsh, was turning into no more than muddy water.

The morning after her conversation with her mother, from the bus window on her way to work, she saw a squirrel in the road not far from the corner where they lived. The squirrel, which had been hit by a car, was bleeding from its mouth. Amidst the enormous vehicles around it, it was trying to drag itself to the curb. It could barely move. Throughout the rest of the day and into the night, the image of the mortally wounded squirrel remained inside her like a powerful image from a dream.

The day after that was the surgery. Aunt Suzie and Aunt Kas and the aunts who had brought her grandmother from Union County waited at the hospital with her. Her aunts had alternately looked serious and told funny stories; except for occasional "oh me's" and "oh, Lordy, Lordy's," her grandmother was silent, as Roberta was herself.

When Roberta's mother was wheeled back into her room, her aunts sent her in to see her mother. Roberta stood beside the bed, her mouth dry, and looked at her. She still seemed to be unconscious, and she was bone white. The doctor came out to them after the surgery to say things generally had gone well, but they would have to wait for the test results to know for certain.

No matter what the doctor said, Roberta was sure that Mary must be dying. Roberta was in despair. She gripped the criblike metal rails on the bed to keep from falling. Pity for her mother and fear for herself overwhelmed her.

She turned around when she heard someone enter the room. It was Mr. German, sweating and anxious, eyes bulging in his shiny face and his yellow-gray hair rumpled. Straightway, a rush of gratitude for his presence hit her; whatever their differences before, he loved her mother and he was here with her, now.

She went over to him, extending both her hands. "Oh, Mr. German," she said. "I'm so glad you're here!"

From his height of six feet two, Mr. German looked over her head as though she were not in the room at all.

"Please," she said in desperation. "Please speak to me."

He raised his chin slightly, then turned his back to her. All of a sudden, panic rose inside her like vomit. She didn't know what to do. What would happen to her if her mother died? She certainly wouldn't be able to go back to college. Only her brothers would have so much as a place to live; she wouldn't. Irrationally, it came to her that Mr. German had life and death power over her. He would keep her from getting a job if he could. She'd never be able to earn a living for herself. In a way she had never been yet, she would be absolutely homeless.

From the day she left their house behind in Delaware she had never been able to settle; she had never felt safe. All through high school she worried that they lived one month to the next so close to the bone, financially speaking, that they were in danger of having to move back to the two rickety, entrapping rooms in her grandmother's farmhouse.

If her mother died now, she couldn't live with her father—she just couldn't. In her mind, he had made it clear that he didn't want her when he left six years ago. When she saw him now, he told her jokes about women designed to illustrate how dumb they were. He bossed her around, raising his voice to her and punishing her as though she were ten years old. Besides, her current stepmother couldn't stand her.

She couldn't live in Union County. They loved her, she guessed, but that was the limit of it. She embarrassed her mother around them. She would never be able to be the kind of woman who suited them, and she didn't even want to be. It wasn't their fault, nevertheless, that that was where she had spent the most miserable year of her life; no matter how she thought about it, every visit to Union County since the four of them had moved to Louisville put her back in that mental and emotional place as the child she had been among them.

She, her mother, and her brothers had moved enough times over the past five years that she had no trouble imagining herself taking down the pale curtains in their green living room to pack them away in boxes. Standing in her mother's hospital room by her bed, Charlie German, unspeaking, across from her, she visualized herself wrapping precious dishes and cut-glass bowls in newspapers for storing. She saw herself sort through her mother's drawers and closet, deciding what to keep and what to give away.

What would she do about her mother's things she needed to save for her brothers? Would the boys go to live with Panny, she wondered, or would her father want them? She would be responsible for them, but she wouldn't know what to do for them.

Thinking of it, she sighed to herself and gripped the bars on the bed tighter, and for an instant, her sigh or the pressure of her hands, seemed to bring her mother back to life. At least, her mother opened her eyes and saw her standing there.

"Lean over me," she whispered faintly, not smiling.

Roberta bent over to kiss her; she saw the bandage poking up above the neck of her pink cotton hospital gown. She smelled the scent of alcohol on her mother's skin, and something else she didn't recognize. "Mama, are you all right?" she asked anxiously.

Mary smiled again weakly. "Roberta, you find a nice man to marry, do you hear me? And don't forget to take care of your little brothers," she said, then she sank away from her daughter into whatever place she'd been before.

Her aunts and grandmother were long since gone back to Union County. Roberta's boyfriend came over that night at ten. He was preparing to leave within a few days for the Midwest, where he would do graduate work in chemistry. While she had waited at the hospital to hear about her mother, he'd been at his chemistry lab studying for his qualifying exams. If he were to make it in graduate school—and by extension, the rest of his career—he had no choice but to do well.

Roberta was glad to see him when he came. She liked him; she enjoyed his cynical sense of humor, and his insiders' jokes gave her a sense of belonging. He reminded her of her father, although with her father's jokes, she always somehow felt herself or what she valued to be the butt of them. He was smart, he was interested in a lot of things, and he worked hard. He, with the rest of the academic world, seemed also to Roberta to take scientific, rational male superiority for granted.

Soon, he, too, would be leaving. She couldn't stand it. All of a sudden, she began to cry.

They were on the couch in the living room, and he reached out to put his arms around her. He asked what was the matter.

"I wish I were going with you," she sobbed.

He drew back in surprise, taking his arm away. Though the whole first year of graduate work would be an impossibly difficult time for him, he suggested, slowly, that they might get married in the autumn, after his exams.

This time she was the one surprised. Getting married wasn't what she'd been talking about. Marriage to him hadn't even occurred to her until he suggested it. Still, with her eighteen-year-old girl's logic, she could see, all of a sudden, that marrying him might be the answer to her problems.

Married, she would not be alone in the universe, however her mother's surgery came out. A husband, particularly this rational husband, would not let her take the exhausting pain she lived with seriously; if she didn't take it seriously, surely she wouldn't feel it. He would protect her. If she had to, she could help her brothers. It would be a long time until he became a college professor—he was barely twenty-one, after all—but when he did, he could provide her with the cultured, educated, un-Union County life she wanted to lead, too.

"Oh, yes," she said to him, "let's get married."

He explained that he would be incredibly busy with school; if they did get married, while he was a student, she would have to be the one who took responsibility for the household. Without hesitation, she agreed.

When her mother came home from the hospital the next day, nearly everything was settled. By the next week, when they heard that there was no cancer, everything was arranged.

Her fiancé left for Iowa in the middle of August. Though it made him far more vulnerable with respect to his exams, Roberta wouldn't wait. She went out on a bus on September 7. He was still living in the dorm, but he'd found a small two-room apartment on the second floor of an old wooden building a twenty-minute walk from campus. She moved in immediately.

On the tenth of September, the two of them were married by a Methodist minister in Des Moines. Though both of them seemed tense and anxious, the sun was shining, the sky intensely blue, and the air smelled like dry leaves. The next day he went back to his lab, and Roberta entered her sophomore year in college; the university accepted her credits without any problem. Three weeks later her new husband passed his exams.

At the end of the year, after a friend in the next lab to his died of radiation poisoning, he dropped out of graduate school in chemistry and went to seminary in Dallas to begin training for a new, less radioactive career as a church historian. They lived in a one-room, baby-blue dormitory apartment where they slept on a sofa bed and lived on top of each other. For her junior year, Roberta transferred once again, this time to Southern Methodist University. He continued to be a hard worker. She made friends in the married students' dorm and stubbornly continued her studies.

It was soon after this move that her first cousin Bobby Wynn died in Union County. She learned of it from a letter from her mother:

Dear Roberta,

I'm afraid I have something terrible to tell you. Your cousin Bobby Wynn has been killed in a car wreck. It was so awful. He was just getting ready to go off to college in Florida, you know. (Maybe you didn't.) He was going to study to be an interior decorator. He always did like pretty things even when he was a little boy. I don't think Bob wanted an interior decorator for a son; his boys always had to be so tough and manly.

He was coming back from Pride, and he must have been driving really fast. Apparently, he came around a bend of the road, ran off it, and smashed into a tree. It is so sad.

The funeral was just pitiful. I think Bob's heart has been broken in half. I can't imagine anything worse than losing a child. I'm sorry you couldn't have been there, too. At times like this, you need all the family you can get.

Write to me soon,

Love,
Mama

Not knowing quite what to make of it, Roberta put aside the letter. She received her B.A. two years later and entered seminary herself the following fall to study biblical literature. Protesting to herself her daughter's defection over to what she considered to be the country of the preachers, Mary went to bed for a week.

After another two years in the one-room apartment in Dallas, Roberta and her husband went to England for graduate school at Oxford, where they were for three years. In that place of bright flowers, beautiful golden stone, and ancient towers, they both worked hard and, apart from the inevitable stresses of life in graduate school, enjoyed life in the medieval university city. They lived in a small, shabby, furnished apartment that comprised the top two floors of a tall narrow house in Park Town, across from St. Hugh's College where Roberta was a member her first two years. They made good friends at Linacre College, his college and then, in her final year, her college, as well. They listened to the Beatles, and they punted on the Cherwell. He studied church history in the Bodleian; she studied Hebrew, Syriac, and Aramaic in the Oriental Institute. Most afternoons, they drank lots of tea, though usually not together.

It was the days of mini-skirts, and Roberta, pretending to be good at play, loved them. At the end of her first two years, she wore a black skirt with black fishnet stockings and a low-cut white blouse under her gown to her final examinations. On the last day, she drank champagne and ate strawberries on the grass outside the building the exams had been in. Later, she found out she had done better in them than she had expected.

For Roberta especially, Oxford was a revelation. Compared to her 1960s university and seminary experiences in the States, Oxford was full of women scholars—so many of them, in fact, that they had their own colleges. These women were different from the few female teachers she had had at home. Back there, there weren't many of them, and they had always seemed to keep themselves self-consciously apart from the rest of the hearty, self-confident male faculty. From listening to them talk, she knew they were paid much less than their male counterparts, and they had to endure continual jokes about brainy women and what they really needed from a man.

Even in the daily presence of these strong Oxford women Roberta was never able to work up the confidence that she herself would one day teach what she was learning in the university. Roberta was going back to the States. She would be cut off from paradise, consigned to doing research for her personal edification, alone.

As much as Oxford was to her, for Roberta it was a hard three years. In those days, she was shy and easily demoralized. She was away from her family, though in some ways that felt good because she wasn't always aware of letting them down as she was in the States.

What got her through the last of the three years at Oxford was a new image of God, which came to her out of her discovery of the monastic texts of the early church. She found these texts by accident as she was looking for a Syriac dissertation topic in the Bodleian Library in the form of thirteen ascetical homilies, preserved in a nineteenth-century text and translation, of Philoxenus of Mabbug, a late-fifth-century heretical, Syriac-speaking bishop of what later became the farther reaches of Turkey.

Before her encounter with Philoxenus and his God, the only Christian gods she had known about had been the god of her childhood experiences at Pond Fork Baptist Church, and then the god she was told of in seminary. Belief in either of these gods was impossible for her. As a child, contact with the god of Pond Fork had been excruciating, his love always mixed with threats of abandonment or punishment in a fiery hell for sins and defects she didn't even know she had. As she got older, considering that this was the only real way she had to think about God, she'd unsuccessfully tried to be an atheist. Her attempted atheistic period had lasted throughout high school and later, into college.

In seminary (how she got there was another story) she was told of the god of the liberals. This god was rational, compatible with science, utterly unlike the god of Pond Fork, and blessedly not interested in her personal piety at all. Paradoxically, however, he was equally judgmental and every bit as vengeful as the one she knew from Pond Fork. Interested only in social justice on a large scale, he saved his concern for social activists and those worthy men whom society treated as outcasts. This god, as her classmates were fond of telling her, had nothing but contempt for women who complained about their lot in life, even women like her mother who struggled to raise her children in a world that wouldn't give her, as a woman, a job that paid a living wage.

It was the monastic teachers of the early church, all dead as doornails by the beginning of the sixth century, who introduced her to their new God. From their desert lives of prayer and chosen deprivation and hardship, they spoke of a God who was nothing like these others. Before anything else, their God was generous, compassionate, and willing to make allowances for her beyond her wildest dreams. Their God, moreover, was absolutely not interested in social convention or in anybody, including women, being good in the terms set out for them by society.

Human beings are made for love, she read in these ancient teachers' texts, but for love of God, first. This meant that selves, even if they are female selves, find their center in God, who likes them and wants them; they are not the property of fathers, husbands, brothers, or even mothers.

Of course, Roberta could not afford to assimilate into her bones and sinews much of what she read in those texts at that time; she knew even then that if she did, it would make it impossible for her to function in a larger world that took the inferiority of women for granted. Their words and images, and above all, stories—for this was the way they thought—entered her bloodstream, nevertheless, where they lapped around her spine daily, stiffening it for the work both immediately ahead of her and in the unknown future.

Against her own experience, she believed that what those long dead monastic teachers promised her was true, and she waited for the day she could live out their amazingly radical promises. Her mother had always told her that "blood is thicker than water." Knowing nothing of her grandmother's history and faith, however, and too young to understand the complexity of her mother's, it never crossed her mind that she shared not only a common blood with them, but a common God. Theirs was a God they hadn't met in the churches they'd known, a God who pushed them and made them defiant against the hard flow of the world they lived in as women. In her encounter with this God, Roberta kept to herself. She didn't yet know about her mother or her grandmother. What else could she do? She thought she was alone.

Two weeks before it was time for Roberta and her husband to pack up all their belongings and move once more back to the States, Mary called her daughter in Oxford. The call came in on the pay phone in the downstairs hall of the house in Park Town. An overseas call was so expensive, Mary hardly ever phoned; Roberta was out of breath and anxious by the time she ran down the steps from where she had been translating Syriac in her study under the high eaves on the fourth floor.

"Mama?" she said at once. "Is that you? What is it? What's the matter?"

"Roberta?" Mary answered. "I just had to phone and tell you the news."

"News?" Roberta asked. She shook her long hair away from her ears. Upstairs, she had been working in the sun as it flowed through the bars of the balustrade into her window. In the hall by the front door it was always dark. The contrasting darkness confused her, making her feel as though she couldn't hear. Her mother seemed to be laughing and crying simultaneously.

"It's hard news. Mr. German died. He never would stay on his diabetic diet, you know." Not having seen him for years, Roberta hadn't known.

"He just got sicker and sicker till they put him in the hospital. His doctors argued with him and I argued, too, but he just kept saying if he couldn't eat what he wanted, he didn't have any reason to live."

"It was really sad," she went on. "He was so good to me, and he loved me so much. He thought everything I did was wonderful. I loved him, you know. I miss him something awful."

Roberta had a sudden vision of her mother missing him, and in spite of herself, she was sorry for the man who had not, after all, been very old, and for her mother, too, who had cared for him. Roberta's stomach rumbled painfully.

Mary wasn't finished. "Do you know what he did?" she was laughing now, and probably shaking her head. Roberta was thrown off balance by this sudden change of mood.

"Do you remember that time when he said he wouldn't leave me his money unless you apologized, and how mad I got?" How could Roberta forget? But for that particular event, perhaps she wouldn't have gotten married and ended up in Oxford.

"Well, I told him you weren't going to apologize, and anyway, I wouldn't take his money if we were all starving. I meant it, too. I knew he wouldn't forget what I said. That was fine with me."

"Do you know, he didn't leave me his money. Instead, he left me the interest on his money during my lifetime. It'll be enough that I'll never have to work again."

"Never have to work again?" Roberta sat down on Miss Price's chest, which her landlady had kept full of canned goods "just in case" ever since the end of World War II rationing. Roberta's legs had turned to jelly. Her mother was safe for her old age! It was impossible to take in. But Mary was not finished yet; she was still speaking.

"And do you know what else? He's left me his house—his house on Willow Avenue, all three floors of it! Oh, Roberta, it is the most wonderful house you ever saw, full of the best things like Grammar used to have when I was a child. There are more beautiful old china pieces, Victorian silver oddities, sets of silverware, cut-glass bowls, vases, knick-knacks, lamps, and chandeliers than you can shake a stick at." Even over the phone, Roberta could see the brightness of her mother's eyes as she described this house of hers.

"All of it is so old," Mary continued. "Even Charlie's grandparents' furniture is stored in the attic; it's been there since 1895, when the house was built. And did you know the ceilings are at least twelve feet high? The beds go right up to them. I had an appraiser in so that I could insure everything. He's coming back later after I see better what's here, but he told me the whole place is a museum."

"Oh, Mama," Roberta said faintly, "that's wonderful." She was so overwhelmed by the idea of such a house that she didn't know what to say.

"And he even left me a big insurance policy to have a new bathroom put in, redo the kitchen, and paint and wallpaper everything. I think he knew what was about to happen because he bought new mattresses and Oriental rugs not six months ago. It seemed funny at the time that he kept on insisting that I tell him what I liked.

"Roberta, just think!" she went on. "I have my own house! I never even dreamed of having a house like this. Aren't you glad Charlie wanted me to love his things?

"So, what do you say?" she concluded, without waiting for an answer. "Will you come and look at everything with me?"

Roberta didn't speak for a minute. She was overwhelmed by her mother's sudden, unimagined change in fortune. Even Mary's voice sounded different. Roberta longed to be there, to see and handle everything, but she couldn't do it.

"I'll send you the ticket if you'll come," Mary said beguilingly. There was hope and even unaccustomed laughter in her voice.

There was just too much packing to do so soon before they were to leave England for good, but it was an almost unbearable temptation. "I can't do it, Mama," Roberta replied at last. "There is just too much to do here before we leave."

Mary was more disappointed than her daughter suspected. She argued a little before she gave up. "All right, then." She sighed. "I wish you could be here when they all come up from Union County to help us go through everything, but if you can't, you can't. Well, I love you."

"Me, too," said Roberta, ungracefully.

After they hung up, Roberta continued to sit at her landlady's sturdy chest in the dark hall by the bright blue front door for a long time, thinking the unthinkable and feeling the unfeelable.

After a while, when she got her breath back, she stood up and flung open the door. She squinted her eyes against the bright sun sparkling on the shiny black rail that surrounded the park that lay in the middle of Park Town's circle. The smooth rectangles of stone in the walls of its houses were more golden with the light than ever. With delight, she noticed the bright green of the trees and the summer red of geraniums in the window box across the way.

Her mother had a real house of her own, and for now, at least, it seemed to Roberta that it made up for everything. Out of the blue, her mother was more all right than she'd ever dreamed she could be.

Maybe—just maybe someday—Roberta, too, would inherit a house. Her house, from sources still unknown, could be as many—storied and full of wonders as her mother's. Or it might be a small house, a monk's cell in the desert, a solid hut of rock, a place with two rooms and a window. The shape and size of her house didn't matter. What mattered to her was this: that she would live in it in love, as her ancient teachers promised, as light as words on breath, as free as a story in a kitchen full of family.

CHAPTER NINETEEN

Grace Upon Grace

*F*anny, you know time really is the oddest thing. One morning when Benjamin was six, and he was eating scrambled eggs and toast, he was struck by something as he looked down at his plate. He stopped chewing for a moment while he thought about whatever it was that was on his mind. Finally, he looked back up at me and frowned. A corner of toast still in his hand, he brushed the thick, light brown hair from his forehead, leaving a little bit of grape jelly behind.

"Yes, Benjamin?" I said as the steam rose up from the coffee I was pouring for Richard and me. "Tell me what you're thinking about." Richard, who was perusing the sports page, and Anna Grace, who was reading the funnies, paid no attention.

"Well, Mama," he asked in his slow, questioning voice, "when you were a little girl, did they have cooked food?"

"Benjamin!" I replied, shocked at his question. I set down the coffeepot and stared at him. "Cooked food? Of course they did!" Anna Grace and Richard, still reading at the square table on which our collective breakfast was spread out, paid no attention to this monumental conversation. Benjamin continued to look at me calmly.

"Whatever made you think of that?" I wanted to find out.

He shrugged his shoulders, turned down the corners of his mouth and stuck out his lips. "I don't know," he answered. He picked up his fork and began to eat. He had no more to say on the subject.

After he and Anna Grace went off to school, I couldn't help wondering. How old did my son—and who knew, maybe my daughter, too, even at eleven years old—think I was? How many eons did their mother's life seem to them to span? I tried to recall what I'd thought at their age about Mama and her relationship to time. What I came up with was a clear memory of puzzling over the seemingly impossible: that there had been a world with people, flowers, and houses in it before my mother was ever born. But how could this have been, when, according to the deep logic of my life, it was her very presence in creation that allowed it to exist at all?

Now, when I remember my childhood perception of my mother and I think about these memories of the family which I often believe I carry more in my body than in my head, Benjamin's question appears to be perfectly sensible. If I remember things I never directly participated in; if I know I am who I am; if I work, love, marry, and pray in the ways I do because of things that happened to Mama, you, and Grammar—then what would make me think, Panny, that I do not, unknowing, equally share a single life with all those previous generations whose memories are alive in you—Great-Great-Grandma Nack, her mother, and her mother, too? I can't help wondering where the actual boundaries of our selves are. When I look at it this way, what Benjamin asked me all those years ago makes sense. Perhaps, when I was a child, there really wasn't cooked food yet.

Certainly, my own memories and my feelings connected with those memories have been a mystery to me over the years. Take the matter of loss. The first actual cataclysmic loss in my own life was Mama and Daddy's divorce; it came upon me when I was twelve years old like the death of all love. That year I lived in Union County I felt that I'd been turned out, not just out of the home I'd had but out of any home I might ever have. I was homeless in eternity. But Panny, do you know, at the time of the breaking up of my parents' marriage, what was taking place did not feel new. I experienced what was happening as something repeating itself, as part of a series of events I had already had to survive. Long before we moved from Delaware, the tone and color of my childhood was grief.

I believe now that in my early years, it was your grief and fear I felt, and Mama's, too, which had been passed down to me not only in stories, in conversations, and in warnings about the nature of life, but also in the very makeup of our bodies, which each of us received through the generations from the mothers and grandmothers we may never even have met.

This is why it was not just my own, and not just Mama's, but your fear, grief, and memories that welled up in me indistinguishable from my own that day after my husband left more than twenty years ago. Why else should I, the mother of two, have caught myself walking through the house and moaning, "However will I ever be able to support my three children?" It wasn't simply Mama's plight from twenty-five years before that I was living through. It was also yours, unable to get away from your manic-depressive father who had tricked you into living in the House on the Hill, at the same time you were married to Papa Charles, who loved you but who, terrifyingly, would not provide for you or the children or care for you when you most needed him.

But Panny, if all this is true of my memories of these losses, how much more is it true of my memories of houses! Though I never even laid eyes on the inside of it before I was fifty years old, the House on the Hill has from my earliest years existed in my mind in all its splendor and all its falling-apart shabbiness as the primary house of my life, as the very house I myself was born in. You know already that I can tell you not only the number of the rooms, their exact size and shape, and the precise placement of the windows in the House on the Hill while Mama was growing up in it; I can also tell you all its furniture, where each chair, bed, or table sat in every room in it. I can describe for you how the Murphy bed smelled when it was pulled down in the parlor, how the light fell through the windows of the front room onto the dark, wide-boarded floors summer and winter, how the laundry looked on the table in the dining room, where the lumps were in the mattress in the small unheated room stuck onto the back by the porch, how voices traveled through the walls, what the sound of the clock striking was, and the noise the pages of the newspaper made as they were turned by the comics-hungry children reading on the floor.

I can tell you, too, of Grammar's Beautiful House, the One That Burned, from your first sight of it, not quite built, to the day of the Protracted Meeting when it burned to the ground. I can describe for you Grandpa Sam's room with the rose-covered rug and the chamber pot under the bed, the blue and white tiles around the fireplace, the sound of Aunt Ginny's piano as she played for the beaus, coming up, muffled, through the floorboards. If I had the words for it, I could give you the exact weight in my palm of the little cut-glass punch bowl that sat on the child-sized buffet on the landing of the stairs.

So how can Grammar's Beautiful House, the One That Burned, be gone, Panny? The answer the ancient monks suggest, I suppose, is that it is not, for in the simultaneous, valuing, eternity of God, no house where human lives have been lived is ever really gone.

Four years or so ago (you'd been dead eight years by then) Mama and I were visiting Aunt Blacky in the house in town she'd moved to when the one outside Morganfield got to be too much for her. It had been a long day for me, and, as usual when I go to bed too tired, I woke up in the middle of the night, sleepless.

I was on the couch in the living room, wrapped up in Aunt Blacky's Star of Texas quilt, and I was feeling hot, gritty, and achy from not being able to stretch out. What actually struck me in the darkness when I awakened, however, was not how uncomfortable I was. Rather, it was a question I'd never thought to ask before.

It was late, and neither Mama nor Aunt Blacky was awake so that I could put it to them. I tossed and turned, winding myself up in the tiny colored squares of the quilt, as I attempted to put it from my mind till morning. It was no use. The longer I tried to forget my question, the more it pressed upon me.

At last, I grabbed my bathrobe off the end of the couch and stumbled in the dark into the front bedroom where Mama slept under quilts of her own in Aunt Blacky's tall bed.

"Mama," I whispered, guiltily. "Are you awake?"

"Uh-huh," sleepily Mama whispered back. Since she had been snoring very softly when I walked in the room, no matter what she said, I knew she hadn't been.

"What's the matter, honey?" she asked me, gently. "Can't you sleep?" She reached out her hand and patted the bed.

"No, Mama, I can't," I said, crawling under the covers next to her. I turned over on my back and laid my head with relief on Aunt Blacky's soft, cool feather pillow.

"I've got to know where Grammar's Beautiful House, the One That

Burned, actually was," I said. "Mama, where was it?" What I had awakened realizing was that, however solidly rooted in the actual fields of Union County the House on the Hill was for me, Grammar's old house had no similar solid foundation in my mind. It was absolutely real for me, but it existed in my imagination only in some mythological space between earth and heaven. Yet it had been a solid house, too, as solid as the House on the Hill; it had to have stood in an actual field, as well.

I could feel Mama roll over in the dark to face me. "Why, that house was right where the house was where you always went to visit Grammar, Aunt Nacky, and Aunt Ginny," she said. "How could you possibly not know that?" She went on. "They had another house that burned before Grammar's Beautiful House. It was in that spot, too. Three houses in the very same place."

"Oh," I said, astounded. How could this third house have existed without me even having known of it—or had I? Even more, how could Grammar's Beautiful House, which had seemed to me forever to have existed, like the Garden of Eden, only in some alternate universe, have been right down the road from your farm where I lived that year I'd turned twelve? How could I not have known that Grammar's mythological Beautiful House had been in the only place I'd ever known Grammar's house to be?

Soon, Mama went back to sleep, and I crept back to the couch, more unable to sleep than ever.

Panny, when I try to describe to myself what I felt and thought the first time I saw Mama's new-old house Mr. German left her on Willow Avenue I find I can hardly do it. The images and feelings are so strong and so much on top of each other in my mind that the words simply won't come out right.

I can say that the house was beautiful, of course, in the way of Grammar's Beautiful House, the One That Burned. I suppose the Willow Avenue house looked a bit on the outside like the one of Grammar's: though Mama's didn't have the same wonderful porches, it was white frame and extremely tall, even more than you would expect for a three-storied house. It had green shutters on the windows of the first floor, a splendid double door, also painted green, with cut-glass inserts like prisms, and a low gray stone wall around its yard.

The actual appearance of the house, however, is not what I'm talking about when I say it was like Grammar's House. I mean, its very nature fed and satisfied something in me that had been hungry and hollow for as long as I could remember. The beauty of its rooms, of its enormously high ceilings and rich ornate woodwork, the splendor of the tiled fireplaces and walnut mantels topped with beveled mirrors and flanked by small carved and scrolled pillars; the grace of its pocket doors and cut-glass windows, the wide staircase and the smooth spokes of the banister—home from England, where I had been so long, it was these that filled me up and gave me a kind of rest.

I needed that rest of the soul, too, dreadfully. I had arrived at my mother's house that day in August, overwhelmed with the unhappiness of my personal life, with the loss of my friends in England, and the grief of exchanging a place in Oxford, where I was known and respected, for the position of faculty wife without so much as a library card of my own. It seemed clear to me that, whatever happened in my husband's life, I myself would finish my dissertation and be the kind of submissive housewife I thought my mother had been before her divorce. By my very presence again on American soil and because I was married, I would have no choice but to give up the self I'd come so laboriously to begin to claim. A woman who was married belonged to a man; my belonging to a man would have to determine everything about me.

But Mama's house! She had inherited it from a man, true, but it had come to her not by her giving herself away to him and being obedient, but by refusing to belong to him. Oh Panny, I know you could say that the house would have been hers if she had married him, and of course, you would be right. Still, according to the logic of my own heart, to say this would miss the point. The point was, Mama had become strong; she was willing to endure and make a place for herself and her children in a world that despised her choices. In the end, the beloved house she had lost was given back to her in a wondrous new form. If this was possible for Mama, if I were brave and strong like Mama, might something like this, symbolically speaking, someday be possible for me?

The House on Willow Avenue was simply wonderful. In a place of utter scarcity, for me, all of it was a banquet for soul and body. The Victorian love seat and matching rocker that sat in the living room by the archway into the dining room—do you remember them, Panny? Their rose-carved, curving forms were walnut, and their backs covered in soft blue-green velvet that had been measured out with calipers and tucked into twenty folds or more. To the left of the love seat by the mantel stood a darkly ornate marble-topped table with a shelf below it, and on that shelf and all of a piece with it, lay a carved wooden hound. Do you recall that dog? There was a tiny walnut desk, too, in the opposite corner, with a real roll top and brass-handled drawers up the left-hand side of it. That was where Mama kept the original photographs of the house and its furnishings.

Then, there were the floors! Pale, gleaming oak in every room, including the long front hall, covered with gorgeous Oriental rugs. A cream, diamond-shaped medallion adorned the middle of the deep rose carpet in the living room. Regularly spaced bunches of flowers in dark green, midnight blue, and ivory decorated the maroon rug below the carved walnut oval dining room table and matching chairs in the room beyond it. Small Oriental rugs were everywhere, leading from space to space, and glowing with color as they protected the shining floors from scratches.

In that house there were re-wired Victorian oil lamps everywhere, lamps like the one of painted blue glass that stood on the table by the living room love seat. Everything else in the world was there, too: a foot-high bell jar containing an old-fashioned china-headed doll and dried flowers; opalescent, fluted German bowls decorated with scenes of castles on the Rhine; a silver egg the size and shape of a watermelon with a squirrel and acorns on its top (in the pictures, we could see that it originally stood by the door on a stand to receive calling cards). Glass and china vases, cloisonné boxes, paperweights, small bronze statues of animals, medium-sized statues on pedestals, candlesticks, mirrors—Panny, I could have looked for years at all the things sitting out in plain sight and never come to the end of them, much less come to the end of the dishes, silver, old linens, and other wonders put away behind the doors and in the drawers of the closets, wardrobes, buffets, and dressers.

From the big combined sitting room and bedroom where the house-keeper had once slept on the third floor; through the second floor, with its enormous lady's bedroom divided in the middle by a walnut arch, its small study, and its second pleasant bedroom; down the back stairs to the kitchen and the front stairs to the living room—for me the house was a sign and wonder. Panny, I believe it also was for you, and—who knows?—perhaps it was even for my aunts Kas and Suzie, and my great-aunts Blacky, Nacky, and Ginny who took it all in when the six of you came up from Union County to help Mama see what had come to her.

Mama wrote and told me how all of you sighed and oh'ed as the cupboards were opened and you took out the contents, piece by piece, admiring, handling, turning over, and smoothing out everything with amazed pleasure. You unfolded tablecloths and white bed linens, soft from more washings than anyone would want to count. You balanced the silver in your hands, raised the glass compotes to the light, and laughed out loud. "Just looky here, Mary," you said to Mama a thousand times, and the rest of the aunts, holding beautiful things as though they'd once been lost but now were found, said it too. "Just looky here, Mary, looky here!"

Panny, there is no doubt at all in my mind that that House on Willow Avenue came to us as a pure gift of God's grace. For Mama, I believe it was a consolation and more than a consolation for the loss of the House on the Hill, of Grammar's Beautiful House, and by that time, yes, even of her home with my father. The House on Willow Avenue was a restoration and a redemption. As far as she was concerned, it was her vindication in the eyes of all those, mostly unnamed, men and women, who she believed had expected her to bow down in her troubles and admit her shame and helplessness.

Certainly, Mama seemed to me to change after that. Though she continued to have her fits of melancholy and nostalgia (neither of us will ever really be free of them, I suppose, until we come to the place you are right now, where every tear is truly wiped away), from that time on, her nature began to relax and expand. She started to enjoy her life and not simply to endure it. She began to play bridge and took trips with friends. She had always been generous even when she could hardly afford to be. Now she had beloved things to give away, and it made her happy. She gave me dishes and pieces of furniture she had lovingly restored over the years. She gave things to my brothers, to all of you, and I don't know to whom else as well. It was wonderful.

As for myself, I've told you that from the day I first entered Mama's house, something in me began to be satisfied that had never before been filled. It was Mama's house; and with her memories in my body, it was my house, too. It was a place from which my losses could heal, a place in my imagination, solidly real, that was my home in Delaware as well as the House on the Hill, the loss of both of which it seemed I had felt forever in my bones. The House on Willow Avenue wasn't the desert where I later would live with the ancient monks, but I received it knowingly, nonetheless, as the gift of God. It softened the anger in my heart against the world I lived in at the same time as it stiffened my backbone to begin to think again about claiming as a woman a life of my own.

And Panny, I am certain that the House on Willow Avenue was not simply Mama's house, and by extension mine. It was your house, too. Surely for you also it was a restoration and a vindication, a coming back home to the house in Casey County you'd lived in with Papa Charles when you were first married, a coming back home after your terrible, futile leaving of the House on the Hill. When the dishes sparkled, the rugs shone, the cut-glass windows let in light for your daughter and the granddaughter who was named for you, all that shining, sparkling, and letting in of the light was for you, too, the finding again of what, for three generations, had been lost.

Forgiveness, reconciliation, healing, redemption are funny things, received as gifts of God's grace in ways and places that we never might expect them. Certainly these things seemed to come to all of us through Mama's unexpected inheritance of the House on Willow Avenue. Do they always come in response to love, even the faintest glimmering of love that is hidden or distorted or broken, or does grace come purely without any human longing for it? Or, considering that whatever love we experience is already a gift of grace, does it matter anyway?

And what about this healing of long-term memory? What about your son Bob and his son, your grandson Bobby Wynn?

By the time Mama inherited the House on Willow Avenue, Bobby

Wynn was long since dead. Though Mama wrote to me about him as she did about all my cousins, I hadn't seen Bobby Wynn often in the years before he died. From hints she dropped, I inferred that his adolescence was particularly hard. He continued to be the bane of Uncle Bob's life. Preferring the company of girls, he often got beaten up at school. He was called a sissy. He loved the beautiful things we women of the family loved—antique furniture, dishes, quilts, and flowers.

I wasn't able to come home for the funeral, and I'm not sure I would have if I could. As little as I knew him, I was aware that we were both children who were not able to accept the places that seemed to have been allotted to us by our family or by the world beyond. Though I didn't let myself articulate it, I knew it could be fatal to me to come even closer to Bobby Wynn's death than I already was. I didn't want what was possible for him to become a possibility for me.

As for Uncle Bob and his own wounds, which originated in Papa's mostly successful attempt to steal him from you, his healing was ambiguous. Mama to this day says she's never seen two people so entirely devastated as her brother and Aunt Ida at the funeral parlor before the service. They sat beside each other holding hands on the stiff couch, Uncle Bob, his head back and his eyes closed, repeating over and over, "I just didn't understand. I just didn't understand."

That hot day after the burial in the high cemetery, you all returned to Aunt Ida and Uncle Bob's house. Mama tells me that, as Uncle Bob went up the steps to the backdoor, the flowers that grew around them caught his eye.

"Those were his flowers," Uncle Bob said, starting to cry. "Those were Bobby Wynn's flowers. He loved them so much."

It was only a few years afterward, when he was in town with Aunt Ida, that their house caught fire. In the black and smoking foundations of the house blew the ashes of all Aunt Ida's beautiful early American antiques. The cool dark living room with its polished wood floors and its white shutters was gone. The comfortable kitchen with its trestle table and checked curtains was gone. The visible signs of the favor Papa had bestowed on Bob as he tried his best to steal him from you were gone. Also gone were the visible signs of Bobby Wynn's life and death.

It was several years before Uncle Bob and Aunt Ida rebuilt their house. When the new house was built, it was rough and massive in a pioneer style, quite unlike any other in the family. Uncle Bob arranged the entire inside as a gigantic display case for his new hobby: he had begun collecting Victorian runny-blue semi-porcelain and early American blue-and-white pottery in the One Eye pattern, and he collected voraciously.

The Uncle Bob I knew from that time bore only a passing resemblance to my memory of him as a child. The tough man who wanted to raise mean men was gone. He had become Bobby Wynn. I believe this man would never have turned Mama away at communion. He loved beautiful things, and he openly loved his family.

Uncle Bob developed the heart trouble that eventually killed him, and he could not farm as he had before. Twelve years or so ago, when Mama and I visited you, he would come in at breakfast in his bib overalls, with his creased dark face and his crinkled farmer's neck, to sit with us. He would talk to Mama and ask me, "Well, Berta Marie, how are things with you?"

He would tell us about his garden and especially the flowers he grew there. Though I never saw those flowers with my own eyes, I always imagine him now smiling in the midst of them. The bright colors of July contrast with the dark brown soil and the blue of his overalls—sunflowers and black-eyed susans, orange zinnias and marigolds, cockscombs and red-tinged yellow dahlias.

Once, not long before he died, Mama told me, Uncle Bob drove up to your house early on a summer morning in his dusty red pickup truck. He was dressed in his work clothes, his black hair now gray and the back of his neck dark red and crisscrossed with deep chasms from the sun.

"Come on, Mary, come for a ride," he urged her.

"Okay," Mama said. He had never asked her before.

Uncle Bob took her to the old cemetery on the hill. He parked the truck and they sat in it while he told her about another son's divorce. Tears streamed down his face.

"Mary, I can't stand it," Uncle Bob sobbed. "When we talked about it, I told him I love him right now just as much as I did when he was a baby."

Whatever we want to call it—restoration or vindication—redemption is such a funny thing, Panny. Whatever happened with Uncle Bob, in many ways, at the time, Bobby Wynn's pitiful death hardly touched the patterns of his brothers' and his cousins' lives. I still can't imagine any of my female cousins on a tractor, and I find it hard to believe that any of my male cousins remaining in Union County would ever cook a meal for themselves.

On the other hand, with those two exceptions, the same cousins and their own grown children are doing everything else in the world they want to now. One is even a television actress, as Aunt Nacky should have been. Anna Grace (she calls herself Anna these days) writes music, sings, and makes CDs, and Benjamin is back where Papa Charles started long ago: he is trying to teach school.

Well Panny, I suppose I'm about finished with my storytelling, now. I've said what I have to say, and I've said it right out in the open. It's been hard, too, especially in the beginning. How could it have been otherwise when I was so well trained as a child in our family silence? I should have expected to have headaches, aching muscles, stomachaches, and panic attacks every time I sat down at the computer, though I didn't. I shouldn't have been surprised by the demoralization and shame that would frequently come on me, but I was.

How I had the audacity to write all this forbidden stuff down, I can't be completely sure myself. Paradoxically, in general terms, a lot of it came from the example of my own mother's foolhardiness over the years in going ahead and doing what she thought needed to be done, in spite of what anyone else might think about her. A lot of it came from your own tough example—or was it from the physical memory you passed down to me? Much was from the urging of the ancient teachers who have taught me all along to learn to pray, to push against my own deep reluctance and fears, to seek the truth even when it hurt, and to speak if I wanted to claim my life. "What you have in your heart, you must speak with your mouth," Abba Poemen used to say, and I took him seriously.

There was something else, Panny, I read long ago as a student in one of the greatest of the fourth-century writers I now teach. In the incarnation, Athanasius said, "God became human that we might become divine." Obviously, to make sense of what this theological statement

284

means in the terms Athanasius himself would have used it in his own world is a scholarly job and one I engage in happily. But, Panny, there is another way to hear his words, the way I have heard them repeated often in my own, modern prayer: As the Word became flesh and dwelt among us, so must we, who are mortally silent, also seek to become Word.

Concretely, so to speak, this project really began that weekend in 1984 when I came up to Union County for your funeral. It was late spring, but cold: I recall I wore a navy blue woolen suit, and I remember, too, the sight of the steam condensing during the service on the fancy windows of the new brick version of Pond Fork Baptist Church, as background to the sound of the old peoples' quavering voices singing the hymns you loved. Papa Charles had been gone for two years; Aunt Ginny and Aunt Nacky were both dead, and it was a hard time for us all.

Three things stand out for me when I recall my own state of mind throughout those days afterward, when Mama and I stayed in your run-down, big-roomed, empty house. First, I remember pondering what began to press on me: that because you, whose namesake I am, were dead, it had fallen to me to become the primary Roberta and to keep the memories. In other words, you having passed your medieval tower over to me, I must move into it, accept the tidal river and the solitude, and make it my own.

Second, I remember being struck with horror that the house you'd lived in would be your house no longer. The things you had would be taken out and divided up among those who loved you, and the house, more familiar to me than your own body, would sit empty and alone. Perhaps from this time on, this house in which you lived would contain nothing more than dust motes hanging in the sunlight that crept in under a torn, half-drawn window shade.

Third, I remember understanding for the first time what it really meant for people to die and every memory of them be wiped out without a trace. Except for the way you invisibly would form them, almost certainly you would be no more to your own great-great-grandchildren than Grandma Nack is to my mother—the memory of a shape by the bushes. Soon you would be gone, to live, no doubt forever, in the eternal memory of God, forever in the communion of the saints, but no more here in the world of living people.

That was when I realized how precious my memories of you and Grammar, of my aunts, uncles, and cousins both living and dead, of the stories I'd overheard throughout my life, even of the events I recall of my own painful childhood, are. I began to mull over the memories I carried in my body and my mind, and I realized I must honor them.

Before the funeral, I tried to keep quiet. After I came home, I began to do things differently. I meditated on these stories in my prayer, turning them over and over in my hands to see your faces. I thought about the ways I had myself been formed by them. When Richard and I would share a meal with our friends Cynthia and Allen, I told these stories at the table. As often as not, Allen, who teaches southern culture at my university, would say to me, "Roberta, you owe it to your family to write these stories down."

Five years ago, I began. That I hadn't started three years sooner was connected in some way to my father's death that spring. My grief and anger toward my father had dominated so much of my childhood and adult imagination. Long periods had gone by when I never saw him or wanted even to speak with him. Then, by what still seems to me to have been a miracle, only a little while before you died yourself, Panny, my work gave me the opportunity to visit him regularly, to spend time with him and come to know him in a way I hadn't before. Thanks to the changes in both of us, I learned for certain that he really was a wonderful man. True, he was a fallible human being like the rest of us and no longer the god of my childhood. But Panny, he was still full of flashing intelligence, enthusiasm for life, restless curiosity, joy, and energy, in spite of the emphysema that felled him. I loved him cleanly and without grief in our short time together in a way I'd never been able to in the preceding years, and he loved me and even told me he was proud of me in return. That was such a grace for both of us, such a healing of so much wounded and broken.

My hands simply would not write these words down on the page while he was still alive. He was a private man, much more private than any of you, and for him to have such stories told would have been excruciating. Moreover, he had never meant to hurt me in the ways he had (which is more, I have to admit, than I could always say about my hurting him in return). He would have suffered dreadfully to learn how he had hurt me. I loved him; I didn't want him to suffer at my hands. Once he was dead, however, things felt different. I couldn't hurt him with what I wrote.

What Mama, Aunt Kas, Aunt Suzie, and Aunt Blacky would feel about what I intended to do was another matter, and I didn't know about my brothers, either. In the end, I found I didn't have a choice. These stories were coming to life and pressing so hard inside me that if I were going to be able to sleep nights or think about anything else during the day, I would have to write them down.

I wrote three or four of them in an earlier draft, and in great trepidation I sent them on to Mama. The day I put them in the mail I tried to accept that, given how she always had felt about the public revelation (that is, to one other person) of any of my private, painful emotions, she would have to hate them.

But Panny, amazingly, she didn't. Being a character in a story made her uncomfortable, but she appreciated the fact that I should want to tell that story. She sent what I had written on to Aunt Kas and Aunt Suzie without asking my permission.

"Oh, no," I said, when she told me that. "My aunts will never forgive me!"

Again, their response was not what I expected. "Come on down to Union County," Aunt Suzie said to me on the phone. "We'll tell you a lot more than you know now. We'll take you to Aunt Blacky's and let her tell you even more."

They did, too—too much even to squeeze into these stories.

"I'll bet you never heard that Grammar had a sister who gave birth to an illegitimate baby," Mama said when we all were at Aunt Blacky's not too long after that first phone call. "I think she kept it in the barn till it died."

"How did you happen to hear that, Mary Virginia?" Aunt Blacky asked.

"Mother told me once, a long time ago," Mama answered, smiling.

Panny, Aunt Blacky wasn't about to let you tell Mama something she couldn't top, even if you were dead.

"Actually, there were two babies," Aunt Blacky said, "and they didn't die, either. One of them, a girl, was adopted by a family across the river.

She came right in the kitchen one day and confronted Grandpa Sam when she was twenty years old. I heard Mama tell all about it when I was a child and I wasn't supposed to be listening," Aunt Blacky added.

I looked at her in amazement. "Do you care if I write that down in a book?" I asked. Mama, Aunt Kas, and Aunt Suzie, as well as Aunt Blacky's daughter Kathleen, nodded at me in encouragement.

Aunt Blacky grinned Aunt Nacky's grin and kept on rocking. "Write away," she said. "Tell it all."

Considering everything, what a trip to Union County that was! The first day we were there, Mama and I drove by what should have been your house up the road from the Number Nine Camp, the only one in which I ever stayed with you. Though the family still owns the farm, by that time the house itself had been sold. Panny, the people who bought it had razed it to the ground; not a thing was growing on it other than grass that was greener and silkier than it should have been. They'd remodeled the barn to live in while they built a new house where your garage and the place I helped you pluck chickens were. I could hardly stand it.

The next day on that same trip, Mama and Aunt Suzie took me to the cemetery close to where Aunt Suzie lives to see baby Aunt Caroline's tombstone with the lamb on it. After that, we went to visit the site of the old one-room Templeton School House where all your children were educated up through the eighth grade.

Finally, and best of all, we visited the House on the Hill. It was not the first time I'd laid eyes on that house, of course; Mama had driven me by it often enough in the past. This sight of it was different, however; what I saw I would write about, and what I wrote about as your namesake, I intended to honor.

Of course, the house wasn't at all what I remembered. The white picket fence had long since fallen apart from Papa Charles's neglect when Mama had been a little girl. Obscuring the right side of the house, where your big old pear tree had once stood, there was now only a dilapidated metal shed of a garage full of rusted farm equipment. The yard, which seventy years ago had been bright in spring with Easter flowers, was strewn with duck feathers, chicken poop, and broken plastic toys. The apple orchard, where you hid your colored Easter candy and grass-and-onion-skin-dyed eggs, is no more than a bare yard, and the pond where Mama and my little aunts and uncles skated, pushing kitchen chairs, is gone altogether.

As for the inside of the house (its former inhabitants let us in after some fast talk by my Mama), it is the same and not the same. The two big front rooms are there with their high ceilings, but the hall has been taken out, and a rickety bedroom roughly fills in where the porch was in the back. The dining room is now an awful kitchen, and what was the kitchen is almost a shed. The windows are gone, and the floor out there is only a desolate, cracked concrete. Even in ruins, nevertheless, this house is still the House on the Hill, the house in which you and Mama, and in some significant way I myself, were born.

I know it's a cliche to say that all things change at the very time they stay the same, but it is also true. When Mama moved out of the House on Willow Avenue and into the small condominium she lives in now, Aunt Blacky and Aunt Suzie came up for the day from Union County to help get things in order. It was the end of the school year for me, and having missed most of the moving because of my teaching, I had only arrived. We fetched, hefted, and put away all morning, then had lunch at noon, a lunch unthinkable even from my teenaged years—fancy chicken salad, fancy lettuces with an intricate dressing, and hot croissants.

Afterwards, while the four of us scraped our plates into the garbage disposal and put them into the new dishwasher, I mentioned my childhood memories of Aunt Suzie's biscuits. I asked her if she still made them very often.

"Oh, no," she laughed at me. "I never make biscuits anymore. They're not so good for you, you know. They have too much cholesterol for any of our hearts, and all of us are too fat, anyway."

Astounded, I turned over the meaning of what my Aunt Suzie had just said. Earlier, and inexplicably, she had told me how proud of me my aunts were because of the work I do. For years, I had felt apologetic about my academic life. I avoided talking about it, as though I accepted that it was not a very good substitute for the practice of the real skills of the women of the family.

What could it mean that an aunt doesn't make biscuits anymore because they're not good for you? Had Aunt Suzie by her casual words taken away from me the family power of my womanhood, or had she set me free? Feeling a bit betrayed by the aunts I thought I had myself betrayed, I sat and wondered over the mystery of time passing, and of cooked food.

So, Panny, I bring you as a gift these stories, which are mine, yours, and Mama's, together. In spite of myself, I hope they please you. They please me: slowly built, they have become another house for me, a house of words, another form of the House on the Hill, perhaps, in which I live with you. It is a house, I hope, in which we all may live in this world, in peace and safety.

As for the world to come, two years ago last summer when she was visiting in Atlanta, Mama wanted me to help her organize her funeral service. We two were sitting in the wing-back chairs in my peach-colored living room by the white mantel. She was feeling old, and I didn't like it. She was also clear, however, about what she expected me to do for her.

"Oh, Mama," I said, twisting my hands in my lap, "I can hardly stand to plan your funeral." I could feel my throat tightening with the hateful word.

"Too bad," she answered. "We're doing it, anyway." She picked up a sheaf of papers from her lap. "Look," she said, "I've brought the stuff we need to do it."

I sighed and gave in; sooner or later she'd see to it that I did what she wanted. "OK," I said, "what do we have to do first?"

"Let's pick out the scripture reading," she replied. She took up her black, crumbly Bible she'd set between us on the table. "I can't think of a thing. Do you have any ideas?"

As I was considering three or four obvious possibilities, she burst out suddenly, "Roberta Marie, don't you dare use that one about 'in my father's house there are many mansions.' "

I turned to look at her, astonished. "Mama, why not?" I said. "I would think that you of all people would like a Bible passage about houses!"

"Huh," she retorted. "Maybe so, but don't you know that not a one of us can say what will happen to us when we die? For all I do know, we'll every one of us, end up swinging by our tails in the trees like monkeys!"

I couldn't believe what I was hearing. I had always been aware of her problems with preachers. Still, this was my mother talking, my mother who not only went to church every Sunday, but who, at her age, had just established a quilting circle, was active in the women's society, and recently had run the church bazaar. What she had just said struck me as so funny that all I could do was laugh. I was still laughing later that evening when I fell asleep.

Then, sometime in the night, I had this dream:

Mama and I were lying on our backs, one of us on each side of a long, very narrow, exceedingly shallow wooden boat. Between us, sticking up above our heads and bodies was Mama's maple casket, against which we were so tightly pressed that we could not move.

We were being carried gently by water, though I didn't know what water or where we were going. Not far above our heads I could see beautiful red brick vaulting of the kind that even today still lines the ancient round Byzantine conduits that carry clean water under Istanbul.

As we floated along, the walls of the conduit parted in places to let in sunlight, which shone and sparkled on the dappled water, reflecting up again to shimmer yellow on the brick.

Though I am not aware how I knew it in my dream, I was sure we were moving through these long easy tunnels under a town of great beauty, a graceful, civilized place where many people dwelt in peaceful houses. We wondered about the people who lived in them and we admired what we saw from our recumbent places, all the while speaking of it in quiet voices filled with awe.

For days we floated in our narrow boat, cramped though well content, through the cool and shady tunnels. Then, all at once, the ceiling above us opened and we saw the sky. Our wooden vessel bumped against the brick of the wall. We sat up, rubbed at our eyes, stretched, and looked around with pleasure. An iron ladder in the wall was waiting. We hoisted ourselves upright, and, leaving Mama's coffin behind, we climbed the steps.

We came out at the top of those steps into an enormous garden of wondrous flowers of the summer, spring, and fall—zinnias, asters, and marigolds, roses, peonies, and lilac, sweet peas, nasturtiums, and snow-drops, all blooming at once, regardless of the season. Between the flower beds, fountains threw up water in the air and birds sang.

Beyond the garden lay the houses, houses not like any either of us had lived in before, or you yourself, houses neither old nor new, but tall, made of the same red brick of the passageway our boat had brought us through, splendid and at the same time, wonderfully comfortable. Among all the other houses that were spread out around us, we knew our own at once. By the steps at the back of our house, blue cornflowers bloomed. Its doors and windows were flung open in welcome. The good smells of cooking rolled out of its kitchen, and clean white sheets flapped fragrantly on the line.

Together, Mama and I walked across the flat ground of the garden and houses, through the fresh green grass. In the red brick canals, the soft gray water flowed through its horizontal towers like joy. The boat with its heavy casket was gone. Together, we had come home.